For Reference

Not to be taken from this room

D1417383

# Events That Changed
# the World in the
# Eighteenth Century

edited by
Frank W. Thackeray
&
John E. Findling

THE GREENWOOD PRESS
"EVENTS THAT CHANGED THE WORLD" SERIES

GREENWOOD PRESS
Westport, Connecticut • London

**Library of Congress Cataloging-in-Publication Data**

Events that changed the world in the eighteenth century / edited by
  Frank W. Thackeray and John E. Findling.
      p.    cm.—(The Greenwood Press "Events that changed the
  world" series, ISSN 1078–7860)
    Includes bibliographical references and index.
    ISBN 0–313–29077–6 (alk. paper)
    1. History, Modern—18th century.   2. Revolutions—History—18th
  century.   I. Thackeray, Frank W.   II. Findling, John E.
  III. Series.
  D286.E99   1998
  909.7—dc21        97–21968

British Library Cataloguing in Publication Data is available.

Copyright © 1998 by Frank W. Thackeray and John E. Findling

All rights reserved. No portion of this book may be
reproduced, by any process or technique, without the
express written consent of the publisher.

Library of Congress Catalog Card Number: 97–21968
ISBN: 0–313–29077–6
ISSN: 1078–7860

First published in 1998

Greenwood Press, 88 Post Road West, Westport, CT 06881
An imprint of Greenwood Publishing Group, Inc.

Printed in the United States of America

The paper used in this book complies with the
Permanent Paper Standard issued by the National
Information Standards Organization (Z39.48–1984).

10 9 8 7 6 5 4 3 2 1

# Contents

# Illustrations

# Preface

This volume, which describes and evaluates the global impact of ten of the eighteenth century's most important events, is the third in a multivolume series intended to acquaint readers with the seminal events of modern times. Earlier volumes, published in 1995 and 1996, highlighted events in the twentieth and nineteenth centuries, respectively, and future volumes will cover the most important world events of earlier centuries. There is also an ongoing series of volumes addressing the American experience.

Our collective classroom experience provided the inspiration for this project. Having encountered literally thousands of entry-level college students whose knowledge of the world in which they live is sadly deficient, we determined to write a series of books that would concentrate on the most important events affecting those students (and others as well) in the hope that they would better understand their world and how it came to be. We hope these books will stimulate the reader to delve further into the events covered in each volume and to take a greater interest in history in general.

The current volume is designed to serve two purposes. First, the editors have provided an introduction that presents factual material about each event in a clear, concise, chronological order. Second, each introduction is followed by a longer interpretive essay by a recognized authority exploring the ramifications of the event under consideration. Each chapter concludes with an annotated bibliography of the most important works about the event. The chapters are followed by three appendices that provide additional information useful to the reader. Appendix A is a glossary of names, events, organizations, treaties, and terms mentioned but not fully explained in the introductions and the essays. Appendix B is a timeline of key eighteenth-century events. Appendix C lists the ruling houses and dynasties of the eighteenth century.

The events covered in this volume were selected on the basis of our combined teaching and research activities. Colleagues and contributors made suggestions as well, and for this we thank them. Of course, another pair of editors might have arrived at a somewhat different list than we did; but we believe that we have assembled a group of events that truly changed the eighteenth-century world.

As with all published works, numerous people behind the scenes deserve much of the credit for the final product. Barbara Rader, our editor at Greenwood Publishing Group, has consistently lent her support and encouragement to the project. The staff of the Photographic Division of the Library of Congress provided valuable assistance. Our student research assistant, Bob Marshall, worked diligently to fulfill our every request. Special thanks go to Brigette Colligan, who cheerfully, speedily, and efficiently typed and retyped what appeared to be reams of material. As always, Kirk Klaphaak applied his computer-oriented magic to the manuscript with salutary results. We also wish to thank Indiana University Southeast for supplying us with funds to hire our student research assistant and for paying other costs associated with the project. Heartfelt thanks to Roger and Amy Baylor and Kate O'Connell for opening their hearts and their establishment to us, thereby giving us a congenial, enlightened atmosphere for wide-ranging discussions on every conceivable subject, including our manuscript. Among those who consistently supported and encouraged us are Sam Sloss, Jake Newman, Andy Trout, Sheila Andersen, Kathy Nichols, and Burton Kirkwood. Most important, we thank the authors of the interpretive essays. All were cooperative and presented us with insightful, articulate analysis. Without them, there would be no book.

Finally, we wish to express our appreciation to our spouses, Kathy Thackeray and Carol Findling, and to our children, Alex and Max Thackeray and Jamey Findling, who nurtured our dreams, supported our work, tolerated our idiosyncrasies, and overlooked our idiocies as we grappled with our manuscript. For that we are grateful.

Frank W. Thackeray
John E. Findling

# 1

# Peter the Great Reforms Russia, 1689–1725

## INTRODUCTION

At the start of the seventeenth century, the Russian state found itself in dire straits. During a period known as the Time of Troubles (1598–1613), Russia lacked stable leadership, suffered invasion and defeat at the hands of the Poles, and experienced widespread social chaos. Some sense of order returned only in 1613 with the selection of Michael Romanov as tsar, or ruler. The Romanov dynasty founded at that time ruled Russia until its overthrow in 1917.

Throughout the remainder of the seventeenth century, Russia gradually recovered. However, it remained a semi-Asiatic state far removed from the European mainstream. It looked to the East rather than the West, and it reflected Eastern values and traditions in its style of dress and in its attitudes and practices, such as the seclusion of women. Nevertheless, Western influences managed to seep into Russia. Trade with the West increased, and a number of foreigners, especially Germans and Dutch, resided in the capital, Moscow.

The man who decisively turned Russia westward, Peter the Great, was born in 1672. Tall, strong, and physically imposing, the young Peter displayed boundless energy and insatiable curiosity. He was particularly attracted to military matters, organizing a miniature army of his own

Peter the Great, Russia's dynamic tsar, or emperor, used violence and brutality to reform his backward country. (Reproduced from the Collections of the Library of Congress)

that later evolved into his imperial guard units. From the beginning, Peter insisted that all his associates start at the bottom and work their way to the top, advancing on the basis of merit rather than inherited privilege. Amazingly, he even applied this principle to himself!

Mechanical things fascinated Peter, and his desire to learn more about technology led him into Moscow's small foreign quarter, where he regularly visited with the European technicians and merchants who lived there. Peter not only learned from the foreigners, but also caroused with them. His drunken bouts soon became legendary. At this time Peter also discovered boats. He remained an enthusiastic sailor to the end of his life and is credited with founding the Russian navy.

As tsar, Peter combined a strong interest in the West, especially Western military technology, with an intense dislike of Russia's oriental traditions. In 1697 Peter embarked on an extensive European tour. He insisted on traveling incognito, although he was universally recognized as Russia's ruler. Peter spent much of the trip simply absorbing European life, even spending several days working as a laborer in a Dutch shipyard. Peter cut short his journey to Europe when word reached him in 1698 of a revolt at home by the rambunctious *streltsy*. Returning immediately to Moscow, Peter arrived too late to participate in crushing the revolt. However, he exacted a terrible revenge on the *streltsy*, overseeing their complete destruction. The tsar was utterly ruthless, frequently participating in the gruesome torture and execution of disloyal *streltsy* himself.

One reason for Peter's trip to the West was to drum up support for his military campaign against the Turks. In 1695 Peter had launched a strike against the Turks, who, together with their allies, the Crimean Tartars, dominated the Black Sea and its northern coast. He attacked Azov, a fortress at the mouth of the Don River. Since the Turks could easily supply Azov from the sea, Peter's siege failed and he retreated. However, the tsar was determined to take Azov, and he realized that naval power held the key to success. During the winter, he constructed a flotilla on the Don, and in spring 1696 he resumed his attack on the fortress. Peter's flotilla successfully blockaded Azov, thereby preventing the Turks from reaching the garrison. Within two months, Azov fell to the Russians.

While Peter never ceased in his attempts to expand Russia's borders at the expense of the Turks in the south, the focal point of his reign's military activity was the north, where he challenged Sweden, the dominant Baltic power of his day. After several years of negotiations, Peter joined a coalition with Saxony, Denmark, and Poland directed against Sweden. In 1700 war broke out. It lasted for twenty-one years and was known as the Great Northern War.

Attacking Sweden seemed to make sense because it was a sprawling state without sufficient resources to hold its territory intact and because its new king, Charles XII, was only eighteen years old. Moreover, Peter badly wanted to secure Russia's access to the Baltic in order to facilitate greater contact with the West. However, Charles XII proved to be something of a military genius, and Russia soon found itself in trouble.

At the war's outset, Charles quickly defeated Denmark and then turned on Russia. In late 1700, he routed the Russians at the Battle of Narva. Luckily for Russia, Charles did not follow up his victory, but instead turned against Poland. This respite gave Peter the opportunity to rebuild his shattered army. The reconstructed Russian army then achieved several notable successes against inferior Swedish forces, culminating in the capture of Narva in 1704. One year earlier, Peter had begun the construction of a new capital, to be named St. Petersburg, where the Neva River flows into the Gulf of Finland. Although located in the midst of unhealthy swampland and dangerously close to Russia's enemies, Peter thought the site ideal since it gave Russia a much desired water access to Europe, a "window on the West."

However, the Great Northern War was far from over. Charles XII defeated a Saxon–Polish force and in 1708 invaded Russia. But he became bogged down in the Ukraine, and in the summer of 1709 a large Russian army under the tsar smashed the Swedes at the Battle of Poltava. Charles escaped capture by crossing into Turkey. Ironically, this great Russian triumph was closely followed by a humiliating Russian defeat. In 1710 Turkey, which had remained neutral, declared war on Russia. Peter impetuously led his forces against the Turks and in 1711 found himself surrounded near the Pruth River. Although the Russians capitulated, they were fortunate that the Turks only insisted upon the return of Azov and safe passage for Charles back to Sweden.

The Great Northern War dragged on for a number of years, with the Russians making further gains in the Baltic region. After Charles' death in 1718 and a series of Russian threats to Sweden proper, the war ended in 1721. The Treaty of Nystadt gave Russia the Baltic territories of Livonia, Estonia, Ingria, and Karelia, thereby assuring Russia of its window on the West. In honor of this important victory, Russia proclaimed itself an empire, and the Russian Senate conferred upon Peter the titles of both emperor and "Great."

Peter the Great's domestic policies were as important as his foreign adventures. Determined to make Russia a European power, Peter dismantled the Muscovite state and in its place built a Russia that was European in appearance if not always in substance.

For Peter, military concerns always took precedence. To that end he thoroughly reformed the Russian army, replacing the ragtag Muscovite forces with a professional, trained, and disciplined fighting force. He also created the Russian navy, one that was modern enough and strong enough to defeat the Swedish fleet at Hangö in 1714. Under Peter, Russia also built munitions factories and naval shipyards. Because Russia did not have enough technicians and trained army and navy officers to effect Peter's desired military reforms, he encouraged skilled western Europeans to immigrate.

The modernization of Russia's military forces proved a costly venture, and the Muscovite state was poor and its finances chaotic. Consequently, Peter determined to stimulate the economy and to place the new Russia on a firmer fiscal footing. He encouraged domestic manufacturing, providing labor in the form of state-owned serfs to owners of such enterprises, extending easy government loans, and erecting high tariff barriers to keep out foreign competition. In order to stabilize Russia's finances, Peter reformed the tax structure. To increase revenues, taxes were levied on a bewildering variety of items including boats, beehives, births, beards, and *banias*, or Russian bathhouses. In 1718 a head, or poll, tax replaced the household tax. Henceforth, every male "soul" was taxed. Tax revenues increased dramatically.

In his determination to modernize Russia, Peter insisted that all, including himself, must serve the state. Inherited privilege or rank was ignored, and Peter implemented a type of meritocracy in which ability counted for everything. Many of Peter's closest advisors came from the ranks of the poor and undistinguished; however, because they served the state well they were valued and honored.

In his quest for more servants for his state, Peter insisted that the landowning class fulfill its service obligations. About two-thirds of the nobility were assigned to Russia's military forces, while one-third entered the civil service. Peter also drastically altered Russia's inheritance laws. Only one son was allowed to inherit his father's land; the rest, now landless, were forced to enter and remain in state service in order to survive. One unique feature of Peter's obsession with service was his Table of Ranks, created in 1722. As its name indicates, the Table of Ranks listed in a parallel manner all the ranks of both the military and the civil service. All who entered state service were to start with the lowest rank and work their way up the table, with promotion contingent upon performance.

Peter also reorganized the Russian government. He replaced the old Russian *prikazy*, or central administrative offices, which were notorious for inefficiency and overlapping responsibility, with colleges, then in style in Europe and the forerunner of modern government ministries. In 1711 Peter created the Senate and eventually assigned to it administrative, financial, and judicial duties.

Another major domestic reform destroyed the Russian Orthodox Church's independence and turned it into a pliant tool of the state. This was accomplished in 1721 when Peter replaced the office of patriarch with the Holy Synod, a body of twelve priests supervised by a lay ober-procurator, all appointed by the tsar.

In his drive to westernize Russia, Peter the Great introduced a number of far-reaching cultural reforms. He replaced the old Muscovite calendar, which calculated the years from the supposed beginning of time, with the Julian calendar, which, in turn, remained in effect until superseded by the Gregorian calendar after the 1917 revolutions. He also simplified the Russian, or Cyrillic, alphabet, although he did not adopt the Latin one. He brought newspapers to Russia and speeded up the process of emancipation for Russian noblewomen that had started with his predecessors. Peter concluded that a modern, Western state required an educated elite, and he proceeded accordingly. Not surprisingly, his first schools specialized in subjects that had military value, such as mathematics and navigation. Shortly before his death, he created the Russian Academy of Sciences, which encouraged higher education in Russia.

Peter the Great was so obsessed with westernizing Russia that he even turned his attention to appearances. He insisted that the nobility dress in the Western manner and went so far as to personally shave Muscovites, since he regarded beards as symbolic of Russia's backwardness.

One reform that Peter introduced backfired. Disgusted with the conduct of his son, Alexis, who died in 1718 under torture imposed by Peter, the tsar decreed that henceforth the ruler would have the right to select his successor. This destabilized the normal process by which the eldest son followed his father on the throne. Ironically, in the case of Peter the Great himself, he died in February 1725 without designating his successor.

---

## INTERPRETIVE ESSAY
*Taylor Stults*

At the outbreak of World War II in 1939, the British statesman Winston Churchill spoke of Russia's potential role in that terrible conflict. In a famous phrase, Churchill provided a dramatic image. Russia, he said, "is a riddle, wrapped in a mystery, inside an enigma." To foreign visitors and Western scholars as well as the general public, that nation indeed has been a tantalizing subject to be explored, studied, and interpreted.

Many reasons explain the West's curiosity about Russia and its history. Physical features and climate are one focus. Located halfway around the world from the United States, its remote location seems especially distant. Gigantic in size (it is the largest nation in the world), it includes isolated regions within the Arctic Circle and across the wide expanse of Siberia. Large stretches of forest and many rivers add to its natural beauty and mystery. Russian winters are extreme, and the population must adapt to the seasons that shape their lives. The Russian state links parts of Europe with Asia, blending those regions and cultures in a Eurasian mix.

In addition to physical and geographic factors, the long span of Russian history provides ample drama: tension, crisis, war, and famous leaders. The ebb and flow of migrating peoples, competing for land and resources, fills Russia's history with violence and hardship. Creating a nation-state with a strong centralized government became the goal of many Russian leaders, but only a relative few succeeded in extending control over the entire countryside. One who achieved this goal was Tsar (Emperor) Peter I (1672–1725). His designation as "Peter the Great" signified the power he exerted on his nation. Peter truly appears to be larger than life, both during his years as the Russian ruler and in his later historical reputation. Yet he continues to be controversial, as generations of Russians and scholars describe, debate, and assess his contributions.

There is no doubt that Peter was a significant national leader and reformer. His achievements are noteworthy. He is given credit for modernizing his nation. A widely held view presents Peter as a progressive thinker. An essential consideration, however, is to determine on what basis he is interpreted. Is he to be judged by eighteenth-century standards or those of today? Should he be measured by a democratic yardstick? His role as Russia's ruler forces us to think of him as different from ordinary Russian citizens. But how does he compare to other Russian rulers? Does his personality deserve the attention it often receives?

Despite his larger-than-life reputation, Peter could be rather ordinary, even typical, as measured by the values and expectations of his day. On some subjects he held traditional views, or behaved in such ignorant, boorish, or violent ways that his reputation suffers as a consequence. He had very little formal education, although he did achieve a minimum level of reading and writing. Peter is something of a paradox in history's assessment of him, a fact making his fame and rule even more interesting to later observers and readers. He thus can serve to exemplify the Russian riddle or enigma described by Churchill.

It is impossible to consider Peter the Great without moving quickly into an interpretive mode. Research about Peter and his nation, undertaken by Russian and non-Russian scholars, is extensive. The written record began during his life and continues into our own era. One would not expect specialists to agree, and the field of Russian studies includes spirited controversies about Peter's rule and its impact on his nation. One might ask, "Does Peter deserve the title 'the Great' "? Answers vary according to the questions asked, the resource materials consulted, and the measures used to determine the outcomes of Peter's policies and leadership. History is not cut and dried, as some may believe: fixed and unchanging, not open to debate or alteration. In fact, the process of reviewing and interpreting the past can be controversial, challenging, stimulating, and enriching. History is a lively topic. Historians relish the process of discovery, plus the give-and-take of sharing views with others in the classroom or in their publications.

Most historians believe that Peter deserves to be called "the Great." His powerful leadership and influence altered the shape and direction of his nation. He made his mark on the unfolding of events. That said, it also is true that relatively little of what he did was totally new. Most of his ideas, objectives, and policies continued efforts begun by his predecessors. What is different is the extent and intensity of Peter's efforts and achievements over three decades.

Peter is an excellent example of a historical figure who fulfills two different but complementary roles: the "event-making" and the "eventful" person. This approach, useful in dealing with Peter, can be illustrated through the views of Sidney Hook, whose book *The Hero in History* presents a theory on the assessment of famous historical figures. Some individuals, Hook wrote, were at the right place at the right time to make their impact. (If they didn't create the changes, Hook noted, someone else would have.) An example is Martin Luther. Would the Protestant Reformation have come about in the sixteenth century if Luther had not been present? Most scholars conclude that the Reformation would have occurred nonetheless. The conditions were right for this process. In that sense, Luther was an "eventful" historical figure: important for his contributions and influence, but incidental to causing the fundamental course of events. In the case of Hook's "event-making" persons, strong individuals took charge of their surroundings and consequently shaped history. An example might be Lenin or Hitler, whose impact on their nations and Europe was unique and profound. These two twentieth-century figures would represent examples of Hook's event-making leader. In which category does Peter I fit? Overall, Peter exemplifies the eventful type. He remains a powerful and significant historical figure, nonetheless, leading his nation into the eighteenth century as an important participant in European power politics.

A starting point is the man himself. Poorly educated in a formal sense, but instinctively clever, Peter had little use for the niceties of civilized society. Tall even in his earlier years, reaching an adult height of over six and a half feet, he towered over his friends and associates. As a teenager, he enjoyed carousing with friends and commanding small military units in organized (but imaginary) "combat." Uncouth in dress, rude in manner, and coarse in behavior, the Russian ruler appeared to western Europeans to represent the low level of Russian civilization they either observed or wanted to believe in. His contemporaries and later interpreters often portray the adult Peter as somewhat childlike: a simple person, curious, a practical joker, often motivated by unrealistic or impracticable ideas. His unpredictable demands and high expectations jeopardized the careers of associates who had to implement Peter's orders. Peter was bored by court etiquette and ceremony, and preferred the outdoors or other interests: keenly observing the way things were done (in economic and military life, for example), working with his strong, calloused hands, or relaxing with his close circle of friends. He attended numerous rowdy parties with his favorites, actively planning many of them, and drank heavily throughout his life. His many excesses are well documented.

Suspicious of those he mistrusted, and possessed of a quick anger that could literally prove deadly to foe and friend alike, Peter was subject to moods that could swing erratically. Available evidence suggests that he may have suffered from epilepsy, causing physical problems as well as contributing to his unstable and unpredictable behavior. His early years, when he was little more than a pawn in the struggles of rival families contending for power in Moscow, shaped and fueled Peter's suspicions and fears. This tall and apparently fearless person, the ruler of Russia, refused to sleep alone because he was afraid of the dark. Peter's personal life included ample amounts of stress, tension, and unhappiness. He was forced to marry at an early age to fulfill family and political purposes, but his marriage soon deteriorated. After the birth of Alexis, the heir to the throne, he sent his first wife to a convent for the rest of her life. Several of his children died in infancy or before adolescence. Alexis, his only son to reach maturity, became totally alienated from his father. After many arguments and bitter recriminations, including Peter's belief that his son was guilty of treason against the state, Peter ordered Alexis to be arrested and tortured. While Peter may not have witnessed the torture that led to Alexis' death in 1718, he certainly had no qualms about the elimination of a potential rival.

Meanwhile, Peter had become involved with another woman, Catherine, an illiterate peasant girl. Acquired by one of his generals during a military campaign between Russia and Sweden, Catherine eventually became Peter's mistress. She bore him twelve children, few of whom survived to adulthood. Peter eventually married Catherine, and upon his death in 1725 she briefly succeeded him as ruler of Russia as Empress Catherine I (1725–1727). (The more famous ruler of the same name is Catherine II, or Catherine the Great, who married Peter's grandson and later ruled Russia in her own right from 1762 to 1796.)

Two final examples illustrate Peter's unusual and unstable personality. A reputable historian describes Peter's interest in dentistry and the forcible removal of teeth from hapless members of his palace staff. After Peter's death, several bags of teeth were found under his bed. In another instance, convinced that his wife Catherine was having an affair with a member of the court, Peter had the man arrested, tortured, and killed. The victim's head was placed in a jar of liquid, and Peter demanded that Catherine keep the macabre ''gift'' in her bedroom. She got rid of the gruesome object immediately upon Peter's death.

With a person like Peter leading the nation, it is no wonder that he has become the focus of attention for this period of Russian history. During the years of his adult rule (1695–1725), Peter worked energetically as the Russian tsar: developing the industrial base of the economy; reorganizing the government bureaucracy; expanding Russian territory to the east, west, and south; and reducing the power of real or potential opponents within Russia itself. There seems little doubt that he was a westernizer, willing to borrow knowledge and skills from the West and attempting to adapt them to a Russian environment. Closer examination of these objectives and achievements is needed, however. By the time he came to the throne as a ruler in his own right, in the mid-1690s, Russia already had evolved from a small principality surrounding Moscow into a sizeable and important nation. This growth, beginning in the fourteenth century, was well advanced by the later seventeenth century. Peter's predecessors acquired territory in all directions from Moscow through warfare, diplomacy, and trade relations. Notable in achieving this national growth and unity of the Russian state was Ivan III (1462–1505), known for his achievements as Ivan the Great.

Russia's territorial expansion during Peter's reign moved steadily eastward toward the Pacific coast and the Asian frontier with China. But no major opponents stood in Russia's way east of the Ural Mountains. His campaigns against eastern European states had very mixed results, and Russia did not easily dominate its neighbors. Several of his military efforts either failed to achieve their goals or were victorious only after costly and lengthy campaigns. This is true of his several wars with the Ottoman Empire to the south. In its conflict with Sweden in the Great Northern War, two decades passed before Russia achieved a definitive victory. His diplomatic and military relations with other countries (Denmark, France, Poland, Prussia, and Persia) reveal uneven leadership and mixed success.

Peter's fundamental economic views and policies were remarkably similar to those of his predecessors. Agriculture remained the basis of economic life for the Russian population. Peter is rightly known for his important efforts to expand and modernize Russia's industrial development. The goal was to develop industry useful to his military campaigns, and he imposed a tax system (or raised existing taxes) to provide essential funds for this purpose. These efforts originated under his predecessors, however, and he built on those precedents.

Nor did relations with western Europe begin with Peter, despite his widespread fame as a westernizer. It is true that he was the first Russian monarch to visit the West (France, England, Prussia, Austria, and Holland, among other countries), and he met important European rulers. Economic agreements expanded as a result of these contacts. Peter also took the opportunity to learn more about things that interested him, such as shipbuilding. He personally worked alongside carpenters in Dutch shipyards.

But contacts and expanding economic relations with European nations had existed under Peter's predecessors. Ivan III brought Europeans to Russia, including architects and craftsmen who designed and built several major buildings in Moscow's Kremlin. Ivan IV, who ruled from 1547 to 1584 and was known as Ivan the Terrible, corresponded with Queen Elizabeth I of England and actively recruited Englishmen to live in Russia to assist Russian industry with their knowledge and skills. (As a youth, Peter often visited the Europeans who resided in the foreigners' quarter of Moscow.)

On religious matters, Peter nominally supported the Russian Orthodox Church as a beneficial source of guidance to Russian Christians. He encouraged reforms in the Church: better training for the clergy, elimination of clerical corruption, and greater accuracy of religious writings. But Peter's primary concern was to develop citizens who were faithful (that is, loyal) to the state. He never wished to allow the Christian leadership in Russia to become too independent or to emerge as a potential rival.

The struggle for power and influence between church and state had been an issue for decades. It came to a head during the reign of Peter's father, Tsar Alexis, who ruled Russia from 1645 to 1676. Patriarch Nikon, holding the highest office in the Russian Church, attempted to impose his authority over Alexis' government in the 1660s. If he had been successful, the patriarch and other religious leaders would have been above the political authority of the state. Alexis won the power struggle, Nikon was ousted and banished to a monastery, and the Church's authority was diminished. The Church no longer played such a leading role in Russia.

Like his father, Peter continued these efforts to reduce the power of the clergy. By his death in 1725, the Russian Orthodox Church had been brought under state control as a government department. As an illustration of its loss of independence, Peter appointed an army officer to oversee the new religious affairs department. The position of patriarch as head of the Russian Orthodox Church was abolished, not to be restored until the twentieth century.

The understandable interest in Peter usually focuses on his personality, military campaigns, and leadership as Russian tsar. Comparatively little attention is given to social classes and their legal position during his reign. His well-established reputation as a westernizer and Russian reformer overshadows his actions toward millions of subjects. In truth, however, under Peter the majority of the Russian population was bound in some degree of legal servitude. Serfdom, a term referring to unfree status, had existed in Russia since the tenth century. Legal reforms strengthened the institution of serfdom during the rule of Peter's father, Alexis. Peter took no meaningful steps to reduce serfdom or to alleviate the severe legal restrictions imposed on the masses. In fact, the extent, rigors, and negative effects of serfdom increased during Peter's reign. He personally gave large numbers of serfs to his favorites and supporters as gifts or as payment for their service to the state. When new factories were established as part of his industrial development, thousands of serfs were forced to work as possessions of the state. These unfree persons often lived under harsh and demanding conditions.

Serfs had no legal recourse against mistreatment by private owners or the Russian government. Their only desperate options were to attempt to escape or collectively rebel against their masters. Several famous serf rebellions occurred in the seventeenth century, including one led by Stenka Razin against Peter's father. Razin's movement failed, and he was executed. Similar uprisings took place against Peter and the government, threatening royal authority and the oppressive class system. The most notable rebellion broke out in 1707–1708 under the leadership of Kondrati Bulavin. It failed in the face of Peter's superior military strength. In the twentieth century, Bulavin became a folk hero in the Soviet Union. The communist version of Russian history portrayed Bulavin as a democratic reformer resisting the tyrannical Peter and an unjust political and social system.

In the entire historical record of Peter's lengthy rule of three decades, comparatively few policies or initiatives stand out as uniquely his. Many scholars point to only four important achievements that Peter initiated for his country. One was the creation of a new settlement far to the north that became the Russian capital of St. Petersburg. Peter disliked the historic capital of Moscow, which held bad personal memories and was a potential source of political opposition to his rule. He decided to create a new city, several hundred miles from Moscow, in an area acquired from Sweden. The new border outpost initially served as a fortress to defend Russia against the Swedes. Named after a significant Christian saint who happened also to be the tsar's namesake, St. Petersburg ("Peter's city") became the nation's capital a decade after the first settlement was established there in 1703.

To build a city in the remote northern wilderness adjacent to the Gulf of Finland and the Baltic Sea might have seemed a hopeless dream. Yet St. Petersburg became Russia's famous window on the West, providing greater access to European trade as well as an entry point for importing selected aspects of Western knowledge and technical skills. (In architectural style, for example, St. Petersburg gradually adopted a European look in its public buildings, churches, and elaborate private mansions.) Peter personally supervised portions of the project. Forced to work on construction that required years to finish, many laborers died in the disease-ridden marshes to fulfill Peter's vision. This notable and lovely Russian city rose on the shoulders (and bones) of the victims of the oppressive system that ordered its construction.

His second achievement is the creation of a navy. As Moscow steadily expanded Russia's territory, its borders pressed toward major seas (Azov, Baltic, Black, and Caspian). In turn, this hastened Russia's naval development. Peter's interest in nautical matters, his visits to Dutch shipyards in the 1690s, and the fact that two of Russia's foreign enemies (the Ottoman Empire and Sweden) possessed their own navies encouraged the new venture. Although Russia's military record continued to be dominated by land campaigns with sizeable armies and improved weapons, by Peter's death the Russian Empire stood as a naval power able to compete with its nearest neighbors.

His third achievement concerns the state's relations with the Orthodox Church. As noted previously, Peter sought to make reforms within the Church and to reduce the authority of the ecclesiastic leadership.

His fourth significant achievement was sending Russians to study in Europe. (Some scholars dispute whether this was brand new or had earlier roots. If earlier instances did exist, they were minor compared to Peter's more ambitious policy.) The practice of selecting and sending talented Russians to Europe to learn skills needed in their own country grew out of Peter's own interests and his appreciation of Western technology. Major subjects included navigation, mathematics, metallurgy, mining, shipbuilding, military tactics, weapons manufacture, and organization of factories. The students' task was to absorb knowledge useful to Russia's economy and military, and to utilize that information on their return. Acquiring Western culture had a low priority. However, historical scholarship tends to interpret the results of foreign training as comparatively minor and concludes that the more significant impact came from Europeans living in Russia who were hired to give their service (and knowledge) to the state.

Beyond these four major topics, additional examples of Peter's unusual and unique demands on his people are famous, even if they had limited significance. His insistence on changes in the appearance of the upper classes is well known, requiring them to wear Western attire in place of traditional clothing. His order for the abolition of beards was implemented primarily among the upper strata of society, and stories are told of the tsar personally shaving those who disobeyed his edict. (It was possible to keep one's beard, but only by paying a special tax to the state treasury, providing another source of revenue for Peter's costly projects.) Despite their symbolism representing the modernization of the state and society by replacing traditional ways, such changes meant little in reality.

Those affected by the clothing and beard edicts resented royal interference in their personal lives, and this created bitterness and sullen opposition toward the monarch. The most open and serious resistance came from traditional Orthodox Christians, known as Old Believers, who opposed Peter's religious reforms. They believed beards had great religious significance as well as representing traditional values. Many Old Believers committed suicide rather than change their appearance or beliefs. Others, according to contemporary accounts, quietly saved their shaved beards to be buried with them. Moreover, the great bulk of Russian society (including the millions of rural serfs) were unaffected by the clothing edicts. Requiring these visible but essentially superficial modifications did not readily translate into new habits or changed motivations. Despite the image of an active ruler dramatically and fundamentally altering his people, therefore, the extent and long-term effects of outward changes such as clothing and shaven faces appear far less important than commonly assumed.

A similar assessment can be suggested regarding Peter's modification of the Russian calendar and the Russian alphabet. While noteworthy as interesting evidence of his personal involvement in a wide range of issues, the changes had limited impact on the population at large. A largely illiterate society had no reason to be concerned about eliminating extraneous characters in the written Cyrillic alphabet. He adopted the Julian calendar at the beginning of the eighteenth century; but other European states almost universally jettisoned the error-prone Julian calendar in the eighteenth century, replacing it with the more accurate Gregorian calendar still used today in the Western world.

One might note other examples to make the point, among them Peter's support for the smoking of tobacco or his demands that aristocratic women not only dress in European garb but also be seen at public events rather than kept in seclusion in accordance with traditional values. Such behavior, interesting to be sure, did not substantially alter the fundamental characteristics of society. Examples such as these reflect little more than Peter's activist approach toward many subjects, as he issued a profusion of orders to satisfy his whims, weaken his opponents, or attempt to create new traditions.

His demands were not always well thought out and coherent, or at times even rational. His decree that young noblemen could not marry unless they had mastered mathematics and navigation, for example, understandably created hostility and frustration. Whether such rules helped the state is questionable. Peter made mistakes, sometimes massive ones, and he often had to repair the damage his ideas created. Peter lacked an intellectual vision for his nation, aside from the primary objective of making Russia a military power that could not be defeated by its neighbors. His subservient Russian Senate, in conferring the title "the Great" on Peter in 1722 near the end of his life, did so as a consequence of Russia's final victory over Sweden in the two-decade long Great Northern War. The appellation was not given for trivial reasons. Unfortunately, the later image of Peter too often portrays an invincible and dynamic leader whose actions are interpreted as having similar importance. If Peter is to be known as "the Great," the designation needs to specify meaningful reasons justifying such high commendation.

Did Peter I make long-lasting and significant contributions to his nation? Of course. He made his mark, not only on his own time, but for future decades. He remains a gigantic figure in Russian history whose influence shaped not only certain aspects of his own nation but Russia's place in world affairs.

Of all Peter's efforts in three decades in power, his military reforms are the most significant and enduring. Studies of the Russian military before Peter, and even in the early years after he assumed power, point to the low level of training, the inadequacy of weapons and supply services, questionable battle tactics, and an ineffective conscription system. Armies were relatively small in size, and most troops were discharged after military campaigns. Peter energetically improved each of these categories, so that the Russian military establishment became a dangerous opponent of the Swedes, Turks, Danes, and Poles in the eighteenth century. By his death in 1725, European leaders acknowledged that the Russian military was formidable and often equal to their own. Future Russian leaders built on the excellent military system Peter modernized.

Peter also increased the power of the autocracy, the power of the tsar. As the Russian ruler, he consciously and conscientiously expanded his power as ruling autocrat. No limits existed on his power, and the administration he created did not reduce his authority. His political reforms, including new departments and committees, provided Peter with greater opportunities to impose his will on the nation. His authority was not lessened but rather strengthened by his reformist policies. The theory of Russian political absolutism reached its zenith during his rule.

Eighteenth-century nations, with few exceptions, adopted absolutist principles. Peter's autocratic rule placed him in good company with monarchs of most other nations. The time in which he lived was one when the power of the nation-state greatly increased over its citizens and in conducting foreign and military affairs. Although the concept of nationalism as a political and philosophical theory was not yet well formulated, the concept of the nation-state had become well entrenched in Russia and other countries. Political leadership, in the hands of the monarch, was not always effective, perfect, or fair. Often the contrary was true. But the generally accepted principles of the age interpreted the ruler as the source of law and the provider of order, with the state designated as the agency to implement the ruler's will.

Peter's Russia, both in its concept of leadership and in its territorial size and expanded powers of the state, represented a significant improvement over the Russia of earlier times. He created a political institution and centralization of power that lasted nearly to the end of the twentieth century, both in the imperial era (to 1917 under the tsars) and under the authoritarian communist rule of the Soviet Union.

As noted earlier, Peter initiated few changes or reforms in his nation, with four major exceptions. But Peter's commitment and energy mark him and his age as quite distinctive. Russia by the end of his reign had become more advanced or developed in many categories. Economic development is a prime example.

Social changes were still in their comparative infancy, as was significant maturation of Russia's cultural scene. Nonetheless, early signs had appeared by his death. One scholar speaks of Peter's ideas being sprinkled on the earth to grow with the passage of time. Under his successors in the following decades, more substantial changes took place. The number of foreign nationals who lived and worked in Russia grew, and many Europeans played important roles in Russia's government or cultural leadership. Educational reforms, in their infancy during Peter's time, gradually expanded, and Russia acquired its first university by mid-century.

In conclusion, Peter made a distinctive contribution to his nation. He was an "eventful" man, a leader whose energies responded to conditions as he found them. The impetuous and impatient ruler recognized that without obligatory and forceful measures, Russia would remain bound by tradition, steeped in sloth and inertia. Whether failing or succeeding, Peter provided a solid base for his successors to inherit. As one biographer noted, Peter built a strong framework and foundation. Future leaders completed the construction of the building in its entirety.

So perhaps Russia is not a riddle or a mystery, as Churchill observed in 1939. Study of Russia, especially the important and interesting reign of Peter I, provides deeper understanding of that nation, its people, and its achievements. In such an examination, key persons and eras represent important turning points in the evolution of its history. Without doubt, the era of Peter the Great is one of those crucial periods.

## SELECTED BIBLIOGRAPHY

Anisomov, E. V. *The Reforms of Peter the Great: Progress through Coercion in Russia.* Armonk, NY: M. E. Sharpe, 1993. Recent analysis by a Russian historian, interpreting Peter as a conservative in his effort to strengthen the autocratic system.

Black, Cyril E. "The Reforms of Peter the Great." In *Rewriting Russian History: Soviet Interpretations of Russia's Past*, pp. 242–270. Edited by C. E. Black. New York: Vintage, 1962. Presents and compares the changing communist interpretations of Peter, especially during the Stalin era.

Blackwell, W. L., ed. *Russian Economic Development from Peter the Great to Stalin*. New York: New Viewpoints, 1974. Broad assessment includes economic changes during Peter's reign.

Cracraft, James. *The Church Reform of Peter the Great*. Stanford, CA: Stanford University Press, 1970. Covers Peter's efforts to regulate the Orthodox Church and improve the level of the clergy.

————, ed. *Peter the Great Transforms Russia*. Lexington, MA: D. C. Heath, 1991. Excellent collection of essays assessing Peter's leadership and achievements; very detailed and comprehensive.

de Jonge, Alex. *Fire and Water: A Life of Peter the Great*. New York: Coward, McCann, Geoghegan, 1980. Positive view of Peter's successes in moving Russia away from its old ways, thanks to his insatiable curiosity, dynamic energy, and sweeping authority.

Duffy, Christopher. *Russia's Military Way to the West: Origins and Nature of Russian Military Power, 1700–1800*. London: Routledge and Kegan Paul, 1981. Explores the important influence Peter's military reforms and campaigns had on the rest of the eighteenth century.

Dukes, Paul. *The Making of Russian Absolutism, 1613–1801*. New York: Longman, 1990. Solid presentation includes coverage of Peter as a very significant autocratic leader.

Gasiorowska, Xenia. *The Image of Peter the Great in Russian Fiction*. Madison: University of Wisconsin Press, 1979. Interprets Peter's place in Russian literature, with many examples.

Graham, Stephen. *Peter the Great: A Life of Peter I of Russia*. London: Ernest Benn Ltd., 1950. Older account portrays Peter's national leadership as tyrannical, similar to Stalin's dictatorship.

Grey, Ian. *Peter the Great: Emperor of All Russia*. Philadelphia: Lippincott, 1960. Sympathetic account of Peter and his attempts to make his nation a modern state.

Grunwald, Constantin de. *Peter the Great*. New York: Macmillan, 1956. Emphasizes Peter's dynamic personality and his determination to create a nation equal to Russia's European neighbors.

Kliuchevskii, Vasili. *Peter the Great*. Translated by Liliana Archibald. New York: St. Martin's Press, 1958. One of Russia's most important historians interprets Peter as a restless reformer without a master plan to fulfill.

Massie, Robert K. *Peter the Great*. New York: Alfred A. Knopf, 1980. Very thorough and sympathetic biography, focusing on Peter's dynamic leadership and the creation of a major European power.

Oliva, L. J. *Russia in the Era of Peter the Great*. Englewood Cliffs, NJ: Prentice-Hall, 1969. Comprehensive yet brief and readable account of Peter's rule and significance.

Phillips, E. J. *The Founding of Russia's Navy: Peter the Great and the Azov Fleet, 1688–1714*. Westport, CT: Greenwood Press, 1995. Scholarly account of Peter's development of his new navy in the Baltic Sea and Sea of Azov.

Raeff, M., ed. *Peter the Great: Reformer or Revolutionary?* Boston: D. C. Heath, 1964. Useful collection of scholarly essays, providing various interpretations of Peter.

Riasanovsky, Nicholas V. *The Image of Peter the Great in Russian History and*

*Thought.* New York: Oxford University Press, 1985. Describes and assesses numerous interpretations of Peter from the eighteenth to the twentieth century, although the author's own view is that Peter was an enlightened despot.

Sumner, Basil H. *Peter the Great and the Emergence of Russia.* London: English Universities Press, 1960. Noted British scholar's well-known assessment, often critical of Peter's leadership.

Tompkins, Stuart R. *The Russian Mind: From Peter the Great through the Enlightenment.* Norman: University of Oklahoma Press, 1953. Includes descriptions of social classes and education during Peter's era.

JOHN
Duke of Marlborough.

The Englishman John Churchill, later duke of Marlborough, led the coalition forces that defeated the armies of France's Louis XIV during the War of the Spanish Succession. (Reproduced from the Collections of the Library of Congress)

**2** _____

# The War of the Spanish Succession, 1701–1714

## INTRODUCTION

Warfare dominated much of Europe's history in the seventeenth and eighteenth centuries. The War of the Spanish Succession concluded almost fifty years of ceaseless struggle by France's Louis XIV to enhance his prestige and to increase his influence. Ironically, the war achieved neither; but it was remarkable in the unusual amount of blood shed.

At the start of the eighteenth century, Louis XIV towered over Europe. He had inherited the French throne at the age of four in 1643. By 1661, with the death of Cardinal Mazarin, who had guided France's fortunes during the young monarch's minority, Louis began his personal rule. Louis' France was wealthy, populous, and strong, and he utilized these resources to build a magnificent state that both dazzled and frightened Europe.

Not content to focus on domestic affairs, the Sun King, as the self-important Louis was called, pursued an aggressive foreign policy. In one sense, his belligerence simply continued the seemingly interminable contest between the Habsburg family and the ruling dynasty of France (Louis was the third Bourbon king) for supremacy in Europe. For more than two hundred years these adversaries had dueled repeatedly in such venues as Germany, Italy, and the Low Countries without a clear victor emerging. In another sense, Louis valued foreign adventures as a means to achieve additional glory for himself. In this he was not alone; Europe's eighteenth-century monarchs sometimes appeared to be obsessed with visions of glory, but Louis was by far the most outstanding example of this mind-set. Finally, Louis cited reasons of state for his international behavior. He and his advisors had concluded that France needed to secure a strategic set of frontiers, defined as the Alps in the east and the Rhine River in the northeast. However, achieving this goal would inevitably bring France into conflict with most of Europe, a prospect that failed to dampen Louis' enthusiasm.

The first of the "Wars of Louis XIV," known as the War of Devolution, began in 1667. This struggle included a successful French attack on the Spanish Netherlands, a rich province that comprises the bulk of present-day Belgium. Louis claimed this territory in the name of his wife, Marie-Thérèse, the daughter of Spain's Philip IV. His claim had little validity since Philip had specifically willed all his lands to his son by a second marriage, who ascended the Spanish throne in 1665 as Charles II. Louis' conquests alarmed the Dutch, who formed a Triple Alliance with England and Sweden to mediate peace. The Treaty of Aix-la-Chapelle that ended the war in 1668 gave France only a small slice of the Spanish Netherlands.

Despite his success, Louis loathed the Dutch for thwarting his ambitions and then boasting of it. His hatred intensified when a cartoon showing a moon of Dutch cheese eclipsing Louis' sun was circulated. On a less personal level, Louis knew that Holland would always oppose French control of the Spanish Netherlands and that France could take Belgium only at Holland's expense. Moreover, the Dutch Republic was rich, and Louis always needed money.

Determined to seize the Spanish Netherlands, Louis first bribed England to desert the Triple Alliance, which subsequently collapsed. Then, in 1672, he sent a large French force into Holland that almost overwhelmed his enemies. The Dutch barely survived, thanks to heroic if very painful measures such as opening the dikes and flooding their land, and to the exceptional leadership of William III, Prince of Orange, who never wavered in his opposition to Louis.

After France's initial success, the war bogged down and stalemate ensued. France could not crush the Dutch, and the Dutch could not oust the French. Nevertheless, the rest of Europe viewed Louis with growing apprehension, and William took advantage of this to build a formidable anti-French coalition that included Spain, the Holy Roman Emperor, Denmark, and Brandenburg. The war dragged on for six years, ending only in 1678 with the Treaty of Nijmegen, which gave Louis the large and prosperous Franche-Comté (free county of Burgundy) from Spain as well as several towns in the Spanish Netherlands that he immediately ordered his great military engineer, Sebastian Vauban, to fortify. However, Holland had not been humbled, and William III remained an implacable foe.

Almost immediately after the close of the Dutch War Louis turned eastward, hungrily eyeing the many small German states lying in the Rhine River valley and belonging to the ramshackle Holy Roman Empire. Although part of the Empire, these states were virtually independent; but they were small and weak, and no match for Louis' France. Louis had already been nibbling away at Lorraine and Alsace when his forces seized the important free city of Strasbourg in 1681. Some German states objected to Louis' expansion, but they were too feeble and divided to mount a serious threat; others were bribed into silence. The Habsburg ruler of Austria, Leopold I, who as Holy Roman Emperor could have been expected to oppose Louis, was preoccupied with a Turkish invasion that swept to the gates of Vienna in 1683 before being repulsed.

Eventually, and perhaps inevitably, a coalition formed to block the ambitious French monarch. In 1686 Louis' opponents created the League of Augsburg; by 1689 the League included the Holy Roman Emperor, Spain, Sweden, Savoy, Brandenburg, and several smaller German states including Bavaria, Saxony, and the Palatinate. The League of Augsburg also included Holland and England, the latter now ruled by none other than William III, who had assumed the English throne after that country's Glorious Revolution had deposed Louis' friends, the Stuart family.

The third of Louis' wars, the War of the League of Augsburg, began in 1688. Although France won a number of land battles, it simply faced too many opponents to vanquish them all. At sea the combined English and Dutch navies stalemated the French. Hostilities ended in 1697 with the Peace of Ryswick, which proved to be more of a truce than a definitive settlement. By its terms, Louis recognized William's claim to the English throne and permitted the Dutch to retain a few fortresses in the Spanish Netherlands to serve as a trip wire against French aggression. For his part, William returned French territory in the New World that his English soldiers had seized, and dropped his objections to Louis' annexation of Alsace and Strasbourg.

All this was prelude to the era's major conflict, the War of the Spanish Succession. Although a mere shadow of its former self, Spain was still an important force in Europe, and its empire stretched around the globe. Its monarch, the Habsburg Charles II, was a childless incompetent whose death was expected momentarily from the time he took the throne in 1665.

Anticipating the problems that Charles' death would bring, Louis (who had a claim to the Spanish throne through his wife, Marie-Thérèse, Charles' younger sister) and Leopold I (who also had a claim to the Spanish throne through his wife, Marguerite Thérèse, another of Charles' younger sisters) had long ago decided to partition the Spanish holdings. The terms of partition were continually updated, and other European powers joined in the discussions. Spanish sentiment, which was strongly opposed to any partition, was ignored. Meanwhile, Charles refused to die.

In November 1700 the Spanish king finally drew his last breath. Almost immediately afterwards his will was read, and to the consternation of Europe it stipulated that the entire Spanish inheritance was to pass into the hands of Philip of Anjou, Louis' grandson. Jubilation reigned at Versailles, and the cry went out that "the Pyrenees no longer exist." However, the rest of Europe was not celebrating. Even if the provision in Charles' will that the French and Spanish crowns never be united were followed, the Bourbon family had now gained a decided advantage. And with Louis' well-earned reputation for territorial expansion, few doubted that in practice he would soon combine the resources of Spain and France. Obviously, the balance of power was at risk.

William III took the lead in creating yet another grand coalition to stop Louis. His Grand Alliance of 1701 included England, Holland, the Holy Roman Emperor, Portugal, Savoy, Brandenburg, and several small German states. Only Spain and Bavaria sided with Louis.

Despite the fact that Louis' army would eventually total 250,000 men, an enormous figure for the eighteenth century, victory eluded him. Instead, France suffered costly defeat after costly defeat. Louis' best generals, such as the prince of Condé and Viscount Turenne, were dead, as was his brilliant but ruthless minister of war, the marquis of Louvois; and no one rose to take their places. In contrast, the Grand Alliance featured two brilliant generals: Prince Eugene of Savoy and John Churchill, the duke of Marlborough. Under their leadership, the Alliance routed the French and their allies at Blenheim in Bavaria (1704), and at Ramillies (1706) and Oudenarde (1708) in the Spanish Netherlands. French fortunes plummeted, and civil unrest appeared in France as famine swept the land. Louis was even mocked, albeit secretly, at Versailles.

When Louis balked at the harsh peace terms the Alliance offered, fighting resumed in 1709. The allies won an important engagement at Malplaquet, which was noteworthy for the amount of blood spilled on both sides. While Malplaquet was a victory for the allies, it so drained their resources that they could not advance into France itself. In the following year, the allies suffered major defeats in Spain, and in 1711 peace talks resumed.

By March 1714 the belligerents had signed several agreements collectively known as the Peace of Utrecht. Louis pledged to abandon his long campaign to gain the Spanish Netherlands, and he also dropped his Stuart clients and recognized Anne, who had succeeded William III upon his death in 1702, as queen of Great Britain. (When England and Scotland were united in 1707, the new political unit was named Great Britain.) France also surrendered Newfoundland and Nova Scotia to Great Britain and acknowledged Britain's right to the disputed Hudson Bay territory. However, Louis salvaged his earlier gains in Alsace and Franche-Comté.

While Louis' France was by no means crushed, the Grand Alliance's major partners certainly profited. In addition to a more secure crown and territory in the New World, Great Britain gained Gibraltar and Minorca from Spain. Great Britain also received from Spain the *asiento*, which gave it the right to supply slaves to Spain's American colonies. The Austrian Habsburgs, another of Louis' inveterate enemies, received the Spanish Netherlands, which were now called the Austrian Netherlands. They also claimed Spain's Italian possessions, including Milan, Sicily, and Naples. In addition to thwarting Louis' ambitions, the Dutch received numerous trading privileges and were confirmed in their right to garrison a string of forts, the so-called Dutch Barrier, in the Austrian Netherlands adjacent to the French border. The Grand Alliance's minor partners also benefitted from the peace. The duke of Savoy gained the island of Sardinia from Spain and had his title upgraded to king. Earlier, in 1701, the ruler of Brandenburg took the title king of Prussia as compensation for joining the Grand Alliance.

Spain, which lost the most in the peace settlement, managed to hang on to its New World possessions. Furthermore, Louis' grandson retained the throne as Philip V of Spain; however, the peace agreement stipulated that no single person could ever inherit both the Spanish and French crowns.

Shortly after the end of the War of the Spanish Succession, the now quite elderly Louis died. On his deathbed he is reputed to have counseled his heir to seek peace with his neighbors and to avoid war, regretfully noting that as monarch he "loved war too much."

---

## INTERPRETIVE ESSAY
*Andrew P. Trout*

As the seventeenth century drew to a close, Europe's rulers were seeking a solution to the most important diplomatic question of that era: Who would inherit the Spanish Empire at the death of Charles II, king of Spain since 1665? For one-third of a century his death had seemed imminent. As Charles had no direct heirs, his throne was bound to go to a relative in a foreign ruling family, or dynasty. For territories were considered analogous to landed property, to be inherited and bequeathed in accordance with the fundamental law, or constitution, of the territory. But in England, France, and Spain, at least, rulers were not free to dispose of their states as they pleased, nor could their power compare with a twentieth-century dictator's.

The Spanish inheritance was not simply a Spanish concern. Not only would a foreign dynasty inherit it, but the end result might well affect the European balance of power. Maintaining this balance meant ensuring that no one single family or state acquire territory or armed force sufficient to pose a threat to its neighbors. Many thought that Louis XIV, king of France (1643–1715), had threatened this balance in the 1670s and 1680s.

After the Nine Years' War (War of the League of Augsburg) terminated in the Treaty of Ryswick (1697), Louis was prepared to go out of his way to maintain the peace. Had he persisted in this resolve, the War of the Spanish Succession might not have occurred. Soon after the Ryswick treaty, Louis and William III, king of England and ruler of the United Provinces (Holland), were devising a solution to the Spanish problem. Awarding the entire Spanish Empire to the French house of Bourbon or to the Austrian Habsburgs—Holy Roman Emperors, archdukes of Austria, and kings of Hungary and Bohemia—might have frightened other rulers. No Great Power need apply, in other words. Far better, the diplomats thought, to place on the Spanish throne a member of a second-rate European ruling family. Therefore the two kings, William and Louis, agreed in 1698 that on Charles' death the greater part of his inheritance—Spain, the Spanish Netherlands (Belgium), and Spain's extensive holdings in the New World—would go to Joseph Ferdinand, a young Bavarian prince and great-grandson of the late King Philip IV of Spain (1621–1665). Spanish claims in Italy would be divided between the Bourbons and the Austrian Habsburgs.

Actually, Louis XIV's family had the most convincing claims to the Spanish inheritance; his late wife Marie-Thérèse, daughter of Philip IV, had bequeathed her Spanish claims to her son and her grandchildren. However, rather than risk alarming Europe and igniting a new war, Louis did not press these claims but contented himself with a Bourbon succession in Naples and Sicily.

Disaster struck in 1699 when the Bavarian prince died and no other compromise candidate was available. So in 1700 Louis and William III negotiated a second treaty, awarding Spain, Belgium, and the Americas to Archduke Charles, younger son of the Habsburg emperor Leopold I (1658–1705). Granting these lands to Leopold himself would have upset the balance of power. The treaty reserved Spanish Italy for Louis' son, the dauphin; but since the maritime powers, England and the United Provinces, feared a French presence in the Mediterranean, Louis promised to try to trade Spanish Italy for territories along the French border. The matter remained moot, however, since Charles II would hear of no partition of the Spanish Empire. Moreover, thanks to a series of agreements between Austrian and Spanish Habsburgs, Emperor Leopold thought that he had valid claims to the entire inheritance. He rejected those who advised against war with France and instead staked out the entire Spanish legacy for his family. His fallback position was to settle for Spanish Italy, a passageway from Spain to Austrian territory and therefore of greater strategic value than Spain itself.

Late in 1700 Charles died, but not before signing a troublesome last will and testament. The Spanish were agreed that their empire should remain indivisible. Partition was out of the question. Because France, unlike Austria, had a navy and therefore seemed more capable of protecting the Spanish Empire, Charles named Louis' grandson Philip of Anjou his universal heir; if the Bourbons refused the crown, however, everything would go to Archduke Charles. For their part, Louis and his advisors discussed two options: insistence on the partition treaty of 1700 or acceptance of the will.

From the standpoint of the French state, as distinct from the house of Bourbon, the partition treaty of 1700 was advantageous in offering significant new territories along France's frontiers. But Emperor Leopold opposed that treaty. Speaking for the maritime powers, William III made it plain that he would not fight to defend the treaty; he had signed it to prevent a war, he said, not to start one. So Louis realized that he might stand virtually alone if he tried to impose the partition treaty. He would face the army of Leopold, who was determined to take northern Italy. And it seemed likely that any attempt to bypass Philip of Anjou and place Archduke Charles on the Spanish throne would drag Louis into war against the Spanish people.

Louis chose instead to accept the throne of Spain for his grandson. The argument that probably convinced him came from his foreign minister, Jean-Baptiste Colbert, marquis de Torcy: The Spanish nobility and the populace favored Philip, Torcy reported. Either alternative, the treaty or Charles' will, would lead to war with Austria, Torcy argued, but acceptance of the will need not mean war with other states. Had Louis tried to reassure his neighbors through skillful diplomacy while accepting the crown for his grandson, there is reason to think a big war might have been averted. Instead the French king committed several blunders.

First of all, Charles' will had stipulated that the two crowns, France and Spain, should never be united in the hands of one ruler. It was not in the cards that one person should rule Spain from Versailles, for that would reduce Spain to a viceroyalty of France and might even risk rebellion in Spain. The two crowns on one head would upset the balance of power and alarm European public opinion. So when Louis officially recognized his grandson Philip's place in the succession to the French crown, he was affirming hereditary right in both kingdoms but *not* suggesting that Philip would ever rule both. If Philip ever should come to rule France, he would first have to abdicate in Spain. Why Louis did not make this point clear to the English and everyone else seems incomprehensible. One suggested explanation for his apparent insensitivity to the views of other sovereigns is that he was convinced that the Bourbon inheritance was the only alternative conforming to fundamental law of both the French and Spanish crowns; since he was "in the right," he needed to explain or apologize to no one. If so, it was a high-risk strategy.

At first Louis' acceptance of Charles' will did the French little harm in England, which was experiencing a commercial boom and apparently was content to let sleeping dogs lie. William III in fact said he was "pained" to see the majority in England rejoicing that France had chosen the will over the partition treaty. "As stupid as ever" well summarizes William's view of his English subjects. Many in Parliament expressed disdain for William and the 1700 partition treaty, partly because their king had negotiated it without consulting them. What was more, Charles' will seemed relatively harmless; it was assumed that Philip would eventually become a Spaniard and therefore anti-French. For his part, William worked to manipulate public opinion against the antiwar faction. In the end, however, it was not William's charm but fear and suspicion of Louis XIV that persuaded Parliament to reverse itself in favor of war.

Louis continued to act imprudently. It became clear that he hoped to draw advantage from his ties to Spain, including arrangements for defense and economic cooperation. Meanwhile, the Ryswick treaty and a Dutch-Spanish agreement had permitted the Hollanders to man some fortresses in the Spanish Netherlands as a "barrier" or (more accurately) trip wire against any French invasion of the United Provinces. When no recognition of Philip V as king of Spain was forthcoming from the Dutch,

Louis, with Philip's consent, dispatched troops into the Spanish Netherlands. These surrounded the barrier troops; to obtain release of their forces, the Dutch recognized Philip.

Although William III recognized Philip in April 1701, he did so reluctantly. Louis' obvious determination that the French replace English and Dutch traders in Spanish colonies caused an uproar abroad. Diplomatic notes issued from the maritime powers (England and the United Provinces) insisting that the fate of the Spanish Empire should be decided with the consent of Emperor Leopold and themselves. They demanded that French troops vacate Belgium and that the king of Spain cancel the trade advantages conceded to France. Louis took such demands as a bluff; at this time the military advantage was his. Moreover, Louis feared that if his grandson submitted to demands from outsiders, even from Louis himself, the new king might lose support in Spain and even experience revolt. Rulers could not take for granted their subjects' loyalty and obedience.

When all is said, the French king had managed to make a delicate situation much worse. Louis' aggressiveness in the 1670s and 1680s came back to haunt him. Although the Sun King's territorial goals were limited, William III and many others had swallowed the notion that Louis XIV aspired to "universal monarchy" in Europe. His behavior in 1701, although apparently legal, lent credence abroad to this belief.

That was not all. In the spring of 1701 Emperor Leopold, without a declaration of war, sent Austria's most distinguished commander, Prince Eugene of Savoy, into Spanish Italy to stake his claims. Leopold, in other words, started the War of the Spanish Succession. He also managed to renew his Grand Alliance with the maritime powers: a treaty of September 1701 stipulated that the Austrian Habsburgs would get Spanish Italy and Belgium; Anglo-Dutch trading privileges in the Spanish Empire, threatened by the French, were to be restored. The Grand Alliance pact anticipated a war to prevent union of two Bourbon monarchies allegedly trying to subdue Europe. But the only member of the alliance committed to altering the status quo in the Iberian peninsula was Emperor Leopold. He publicly insisted on the entire Spanish inheritance for his younger son Charles, while admitting privately that there might have to be a partition; but Spanish Italy was nonnegotiable. At the end of the year the Grand Alliance expanded to include the king of Prussia.

Meanwhile, if Louis resigned himself to war, he was optimistic about its outcome, realizing that this time he or his grandson occupied much of the disputed territory. To keep the Spanish Netherlands within the Bourbon camp, he would not have to invade them as he had done in the past. History books are full of examples of kings or ministers who underestimated the difficulty of a military operation they were about to undertake. Louis XIV had done so in 1672 before invading Holland. In the summer of 1914, the outset of World War I, almost no one foresaw that hostilities would lead to disaster, even for several of the "victors." In 1701–1702 neither side realized how difficult, indeed bloody, the war would be.

Louis and his grandson Philip V of Spain were agreed on fundamental issues—more than one can say for the English, Dutch, and Austrians. The Dutch wanted to continue trading with the enemy in wartime; much of what English sailors captured from the Spaniards at the Battle of Vigo Bay (1702) belonged to Dutch merchants. For the English, enemy commerce was something to raid. Moreover, the Dutch suspected their English allies of trying to win undue commercial advantages in the Mediterranean and West Indies. And the Dutch, much concerned about restoring their lost barrier in Belgium, quarreled with the English over control of commerce and ports there. Nor were the allies in perfect agreement about how to wage war. Dutch politicians came to fear that the bold tactics of the duke of Marlborough, the leading English commander and a member of Queen Anne's government, could lose the war in a day.

The war presented Louis with far more serious problems than he apparently had anticipated. In Italy the Bourbon cause eventually failed; Louis was forced to divert troops from there to other fronts in 1706, leaving the Austrians in control of Milan and, eventually, Naples. In Spain, too, the early war years were unpromising, as the French king could only with difficulty prop up his grandson in Madrid. Meanwhile, on the German front, Louis discovered as early as the Battle of Blenheim in 1704 what sort of enemy he was dealing with.

In the seventeenth century the ability to wage war depended heavily on one's financial resources. Early modern European states did not possess the vast wealth available to modern governments. Louis' lengthy wars, from the Dutch War through the War of the Spanish Succession, exhausted ordinary tax revenues and prompted finance ministers to devise special levies and ingenious devices to sustain an ailing treasury. Anything that could not fly away the king would tax, borrow, mortgage, or sell.

As early as 1673 the French crown issued an edict ostensibly organizing workers into guilds, the real object being to persuade those workers to purchase from the government exemptions from that edict. At the opening of the Nine Years' War, the government was selling high offices in the most prestigious of Parisian guilds. For decades the financially strapped government had been selling public offices of all kinds, from powerful judgeships and high financial posts to "offices" of crier, measurer (of grain, salt, charcoal), and much more. Louis' government even absconded with the "mud and lantern" tax earmarked to clean and light the streets of Paris. Now, with the outbreak of war, there would be ample opportunity to create new offices and compel the present holders to buy them up in order to avoid sharing fees with intruders.

The English, too, were forced to borrow, but they had an institution known as the Bank of England to lend money to the government. England's bank, a more solid credit risk than the king of France, is one reason why the island kingdom emerged from the War of the Spanish Succession a Great Power.

During the wars from 1688 through 1714, both governments were experimenting with financial instruments dependent on chance. Beginning in 1694, the state lottery became an established institution in England; lotteries opened in 1697 and 1710, too, and in war and peace these games became an almost annual event in the century and a quarter to follow. As early as 1693—and for a century to come—the French crown was selling annuities guaranteeing a given income for life in return for a stipulated sum of money; these might have proved advantageous for the treasury if only the bureaucrats had bothered to inquire about mortality expectations. By 1700 Louis XIV had opened a lottery to the public; it too would become a semipermanent institution. Nonetheless, his financial plight grew worse as one war year succeeded another. A bad winter and high bread prices, continuing war, and the high cost of government made 1709 probably the most miserable year of the century in pre-1789 France.

The kind of war the duke of Marlborough and Prince Eugene waged came as a rude surprise to the French. Louis underestimated the Anglo-Dutch force arrayed against him on his northeastern frontier. Marlborough captured French fortifications one after another, placing Louis' army on the defensive. Meanwhile France was losing its allies. Conquest removed Cologne from the list, and diplomacy detached the duke of Savoy and the king of Portugal in 1703. The significance of the latter's defection is greater than it may seem, for it coincided with a radical escalation of the maritime powers' war aims. John Methuen, an English diplomat, concluded several treaties between England and Portugal, bringing the latter into the anti-French camp. To insure Portugal against retribution from the Bourbons, however, the maritime powers agreed to place Archduke Charles on the Spanish throne. Ironically, at that time the Austrian Habsburgs wanted no such commitment, for they feared that it would divert Anglo-Dutch energies to Spain, rather than to Italy, which was of paramount interest to the Vienna government. For some Englishmen, a Habsburg Spain seemed to promise more commercial concessions than a Bourbon Spain would ever deliver. What is more certain, though, "no peace without Spain" as a war aim would complicate immeasurably the ultimate achievement of peace. Again, one can see a parallel in World War I, when belligerents on both sides developed an appetite for territorial gains beyond any war aims stated at the inception of the conflict.

Not long after the agreement with Portugal, an Anglo-Dutch force captured the Rock of Gibraltar (1704). Within a couple of years, the Mediterranean Sea, the "Roman lake" of antiquity, was to become an English lake. Never again in this war could a French fleet seriously challenge the English in the Mediterranean.

In that same year, the French experienced a military disaster. After witnessing the fury of an earlier campaign, Dutch civilian commissioners had restrained Marlborough, fearful as they were of his high-risk tactics. In 1704 he broke loose. Planning a thrust at Bavaria, Louis' German ally, he achieved the astonishing goal of moving some 30,000 troops from the Spanish Netherlands to the Danube. There, Marlborough and his Austrian ally Prince Eugene surprised the French. Instead of seizing fortresses, they attacked the Bavarian-French camp at Blenheim. Although the allies lost 20 percent of their 55,000-man force, for the French and Bavarians the result was even more grim: two-thirds of their force of 60,000 were dead, wounded, or missing. For the French this was a crushing defeat; it meant their expulsion from Bavaria and the rest of Germany east of the Rhine River.

After Blenheim the Dutch kept Marlborough on a tight leash for a while, but in 1706, at the Battle of Ramillies in the Spanish Netherlands, he handed the French a second major defeat that, incidentally, diverted French strength from Italy as well. At Ramillies Louis had hoped to win a victory in the field to compensate for the disaster at Blenheim and to lead his enemies to the peace table. Instead, Marlborough's force of 62,000 swept the 60,000 French from the field. And, as one French fortress after another capitulated, Louis' army was forced to vacate the Spanish Netherlands. To sum it up, in one summer Louis and his allies were driven from Italy and the Spanish Netherlands and came close to defeat in Spain, where Archduke Charles was trying to establish himself as King Carlos III.

The Bourbons' military fortunes revived in 1707 when they reoccupied

Belgium, where the people were happy to be rid of the Dutch. But the French learned at the Battle of Oudenarde (1708) that they could not hold Belgium. To meet the French the allies spent less than sixty hours moving fifty miles, an exceptional accomplishment at that time. Moreover, this engagement was no set piece but rather a battle with a fluid front line extending more than two miles. The French lost it, and by December the allies controlled the citadel at Lille, on the French side of the border.

Louis XIV desperately needed peace. The winter of 1708–1709 turned out to be one of the worst of the century. His army had been dwindling, due to desertion and battle casualties. In 1709 Paris was suffering grain shortages and high bread prices, and so was the army. Allied commanders were considering marching to Versailles to dictate peace; in modern terms, what they were demanding was tantamount to unconditional surrender. Normally peace settlements were conditional, arrived at through negotiations in which there might well be winners and losers but each side would very likely concede something in order to end hostilities. In 1709 the allies would concede next to nothing. Number 37 of their forty preliminary articles of peace demanded not only that Philip V vacate the Spanish throne but also that Louis supply money and troops to depose him. Louis explained his plight and the allies' humiliating demands in an appeal to the patriotism of the French people—a rare event indeed in the eighteenth century. The historian John C. Rule wrote recently that that appeal may have "saved" both the Spanish and the French monarchies.

By 1709 the French were willing to pay a price for peace. They might give up gains they had made since the 1648 Peace of Westphalia; they talked of abandoning Philip's claim to Spain if he were guaranteed a kingdom in Italy. Why did the allies not jump at such terms? Did they not realize that their own proposals were unrealistic, indeed senseless? Apparently the allies thought at first that Louis would consent to almost anything they demanded. Although Marlborough and Eugene eventually admitted that the proposed terms were too harsh, some civilian authorities were less realistic. In England they continued to demand "no peace without Spain." Emperor Joseph, who had succeeded his father Leopold in 1705, insisted that his brother Charles would reign in Madrid. Both sides paid dearly for the failure of peace talks, as the Battle of Malplaquet in September 1709 demonstrated.

By July Louis' commander in the northeast sector, Marshal Villars, was telling him he had two choices: accept the peace his enemies offered or give battle, for there was not enough bread to sustain his troops for long.

Louis chose the latter, and the result, Malplaquet, was to become a classic Pyrrhic victory—meaning that although technically the winners, Marlborough and Eugene's forces suffered such losses that they could ill afford one more such victory.

A bird's-eye view of the Spanish Netherlands at that time would have shown lengthy defensive lines—fortifications, entrenchments, and redoubts designed by the French to discourage enemy raids. Facing an allied force of 75,000 at Malplaquet, Villars, with 65,000, decided to dig a long line of entrenchments across the invaders' path; here and there were field fortifications and artillery positions. This, the allies thought, was their chance to break through to Paris and dictate peace. As they struck the French left flank, French infantry withdrew in orderly fashion. Meanwhile, from their entrenchment French soldiers had been firing volleys at around fifty paces. Descriptions of eighteenth-century military tactics may sometimes convey the impression of a stately dance, but Malplaquet was no such engagement; it is said that Europe would see nothing this terrible until the Battle of Borodino in 1812. Dutch forces suffered frightful losses; two battalions were reduced from 1,500 each to less than 50 each. Nonetheless, they moved forward, pierced the French outer works, and planted flags on the palisades; behind a second line of palisades they ran into French infantry. Finally, when it was over, the French gathered their weapons and calmly retreated. The enemy, exhausted, could not pursue them. One estimate pegs allied losses at around 20,500 and French casualties at 12,500; another has the allies losing 15,000, the French 10,000. In either case no eighteenth-century army could endure this kind of war for long.

Forty years earlier Paris, Louis XIV's capital, had begun razing remnants of its old walls and ramparts to replace them with a boulevard, or beltway, around the city. In 1709 the city, safe from foreign troops, would not miss these dilapidated fortifications. The war would continue, but Marlborough would fight no more pitched battles.

A peace conference in the spring of 1710 revealed no progress. The allies still insisted that Louis agree to use military force if necessary to chase his grandson out of Spain. To Louis that was unacceptable, nor would Philip budge from the Spanish throne. What is more, Philip had wide backing from his subjects, who were especially indignant at the attitude of allied forces toward the Catholic Church. By the end of December 1710 it was clear that, with French military aid, Philip controlled almost all of Spain.

By contrast, on the northeastern French frontier events favored the allies as they avoided battle while seizing French fortifications. In August

1711 Marlborough broke through Louis' long defensive line running almost to the coast of Picardy in northern France—a "masterpiece of military engineering," guarded at one end by ten miles of earthworks, at the other by a system of rivers dammed to flood surrounding land. Marlborough regarded this breakthrough as his greatest military achievement. Four months later he was dismissed; a political upset had taken place at home, and this politician-commander was on the losing side.

War weariness was evident on both sides. The human cost of this war was the sort that twentieth-century democracies would tolerate but eighteenth-century monarchies or oligarchies could not. Apart from that, for the Dutch the conflict meant heavy taxes and commercial decline. They were paying a price for tying themselves to England and its promises of towns in the Spanish Netherlands and trade concessions from Spain. England, too, needed peace. In 1709 grain prices were high; Malplaquet symbolized a bloody war that many people hated; forced enlistments and war weariness in general made the Whigs, the ruling party, unpopular. Their opponents, the Tories, were more likely to sue for peace.

Opportunity soon came. In March 1710 some Tories began communicating indirectly with Torcy, the French foreign minister. By August Queen Anne replaced most of her Whig ministers with Tories who were more concerned with colonial empire than with continental Europe. Tories campaigning against needless prolongation of the war won a sizeable majority in the House of Commons in the October 1710 election. They were prepared to discard the most extreme peace demands of the Whigs, including the insistence on a Habsburg succession in Spain. Both sides were prepared for serious peace talks before the unexpected death of Emperor Joseph I (1705–1711) altered the European balance. Now his brother Archduke Charles would become Holy Roman Emperor Charles VI, archduke of Austria, and king of Hungary and Bohemia, and, if allied policy triumphed, king of Spain. The Tories argued that Englishmen had no business fighting to restore the "universal monarchy" of Emperor Charles V (1519–1556).

While negotiations with France proceeded, the English maintained the appearance of unity with their allies by pretending that peace proposals were coming only from the French. By October 1711 a preliminary agreement had been drawn up. The Dutch town of Utrecht was chosen as the site for a peace conference to begin early in 1712. Louis was personally interested in its progress—not only the substantive issues but also the order of seating ambassadors at the table, how many horses each diplomat was allowed, how each was to be addressed.

At Utrecht the atmosphere among the allies was poisonous; the British foreign minister, Viscount Bolingbroke, did not conceal his disdain for the Austrians; he was on better terms with the French, although he noted that they "treat like Pedlars, or, which is worse, like Attorneys." In 1712 the English continued to pretend they were still at war. Secret orders went out to their troops that spring to avoid combat, but their allies learned of them. In any case, by the time of the French victory at the Battle of Denain (July 1712), English forces were gone from the scene.

After fifteen months the Utrecht conference ended as England, Savoy, Portugal, Prussia, and the United Provinces signed peace with France. The treaty is dated April 11/12, 1713. It is alleged, however, that some signatories backdated the agreement so that the signing would not seem to fall on April Fools' Day of the Old Style calendar (still observed in England and British America instead of the Gregorian calendar of 1582). It is not surprising that Emperor Charles VI (the would-be Carlos III) wanted no part of this treaty and intended to fight on. But he eventually gave way, and in 1714 agreed to the peace treaties of Rastatt and Baden.

What emerged from the Utrecht-Rastatt-Baden agreements was a tripartite balance among the Great Powers. France remained a major state. England, strengthened financially by the Bank of England and acquiring Gibraltar, Newfoundland, and Nova Scotia, was a Great Power. (But the license it acquired to sell 4,800 slaves annually in Spanish America reaped no huge profit.) Finally, Austria, having reclaimed Hungary from the Turks by 1699, now had title to Belgium, Naples, and Milan. Emperor Charles VI, persistent if nothing else, delayed recognizing Philip V as king of Spain until 1718.

In significant ways the Utrecht settlement resembled the Grand Alliance's 1701 agreement, which had conceded to the Habsburgs Spanish Italy and Belgium but had not proposed to dethrone Philip as ruler of Spain and the Americas. Partition was the end result after all. Had the principal parties behaved more responsibly from the start, diplomacy might have minimized if not averted war. For a decade Europe wasted its resources only to arrive at a settlement similar to what it might have had in 1701.

## SELECTED BIBLIOGRAPHY

Bérenger, Jean. "An Attempted *Rapprochement* between France and the Emperor: The Secret Treaty for the Partition of the Spanish Succession of 19 January 1668." In *Louis XIV and Europe*, pp. 133–152. Edited by Ragnhild Hatton. Columbus: Ohio State University Press, 1976. A study of an early partition scheme, a treaty never ratified.

Elliott, J. H. *Imperial Spain, 1469–1716*. New York: St. Martin's Press, 1964. A standard work, concluding with the transition from Habsburg to Bourbon rule in Spain.

Frey, Linda, and Marsha Frey, eds. *The Treaties of the War of the Spanish Succession*. Westport, CT: Greenwood Press, 1995. A mine of information prepared by some forty specialists in diplomatic, military, and political history.

Kamen, Henry. *The War of Succession in Spain, 1700–15*. Bloomington: Indiana University Press, 1969. This study of a kingdom at war focuses on the finances of the Spanish monarchy, with comments on the administrative consequences of the war.

Lossky, Andrew. "The General European Crisis of the 1680s." *European Studies Review* 10 (1980): 177–198. A main theme is Louis XIV's confused state of mind in the 1670s and 1680s.

———. *Louis XIV and the French Monarchy*. New Brunswick, NJ: Rutgers University Press, 1994. This important new biography is especially interesting for the legal aspects of the Spanish succession question.

Rowen, Herbert H. "The Peace of Nijmegen: De Witt's Revenge." In *The Peace of Nijmegen, 1676–1678/79: International Congress of the Tricentennial, Nijmegen, 14–16 September 1978*, pp. 275–283. Edited by J. A. H. Bots. Amsterdam: APA–Holland University Press, 1980. An expert on Dutch and French history contends that Louis' Dutch War gained him little and cost him much.

Rule, John C. "King and Minister: Louis XIV and Colbert de Torcy." In *William III and Louis XIV: Essays 1680–1720 by and for Mark A. Thomson*. Edited by Ragnhild Hatton and J. S. Bromley. Liverpool: Liverpool University Press, 1968. An authority on Louis XIV considers Torcy's role as a negotiator and architect of the peace settlement.

Spielman, John P. *Leopold I of Austria*. New Brunswick, NJ: Rutgers University Press, 1977. Good biography of a ruler whose foreign policy concerns stretched from Spain through Hungary.

Symcox, Geoffrey. "Louis XIV and the Outbreak of the Nine Years War." In *Louis XIV and Europe*, pp. 179–212. Edited by Ragnhild Hatton. Columbus: Ohio State University Press, 1976. An excellent summary of French diplomacy in the 1680s.

Thomson, Mark A. "Louis XIV and the Grand Alliance, 1705–10." In *William III and Louis XIV: Essays 1680–1720 by and for Mark A. Thomson*. Edited by Ragnhild Hatton and J. S. Bromley. Liverpool: Liverpool University Press, 1968. Detailed study of diplomatic interaction during the war.

———. "Louis XIV and the Origins of the War of the Spanish Succession." *Transactions of the Royal Historical Society*, 5th series, 4 (1954): 111–134. A leading diplomatic historian views the war aims of various parties.

———. "Parliament and Foreign Policy, 1689–1714." In *William III and Louis XIV: Essays 1680–1720 by and for Mark A. Thomson*. Edited by Ragnhild Hatton and J. S. Bromley. Liverpool: Liverpool University Press, 1968. Examines Parliament's acceptance and then its rejection of the Bourbon succession in Spain.

Trevelyan, G. M. *England under Queen Anne*. 3 vols. London: Longmans, Green, 1930–1934. Readable account of the war from a patriotic English and Protestant perspective, yet highly critical of the allies' "preposterous" peace demands of 1709.

Wolf, John B. *Louis XIV*. New York: W. W. Norton, 1968. A standard biography of Louis XIV, authoritative on the Spanish succession question.

———. *Toward a European Balance of Power, 1620–1715*. Chicago: Rand McNally, 1970. Useful survey of a century of European diplomacy, from the Thirty Years' War to the Peace of Utrecht.

**3** _____

# The First British Empire, 1701–1763

## INTRODUCTION

Beginning in the middle of the fifteenth century, seamen sailing under the flags of Portugal and Spain undertook a series of risky voyages during which they encountered a bewildering variety of lands and peoples. These voyages opened an intense era of European exploration and colonization. Not surprisingly, Portugal and Spain were the first to explore and colonize, building huge empires in a few decades that girdled the globe. Motivated by the lure of gold, dreams of glory, and a determination to spread Christianity, Portuguese and Spanish explorers planted their flags in the New World, Africa, and Asia. However, by the start of the eighteenth century new imperial powers threatened to overtake Spain and Portugal. France and England (rechristened Great Britain in 1707 after the Act of Union linked Scotland with England and Wales) had emerged as the world's most important colonial powers, and for the first two-thirds of the eighteenth century they engaged in a struggle over empire that was so enduring that historians sometimes refer to it as the second Hundred Years' War.

Geographically, the Anglo-French battle for empire took place in three different venues—the North American mainland, the Caribbean islands or West Indies, and India, the Asian subcontinent. In North America,

Port Royal and Kingston Harbor, Jamaica. The first British Empire included holdings in the Caribbean, North America, and India. In the eighteenth century, the valuable sugar island of Jamaica was Great Britain's richest colony. (Reproduced from the Collections of the Library of Congress)

France claimed a huge swath of territory called New France that stretched from the mouth of the St. Lawrence River to the Gulf of Mexico and included the Great Lakes and the Ohio and Mississippi River valleys. England's North American empire comprised the narrow band of land between the Atlantic Ocean and the Appalachian Mountains. In the West Indies both France and Great Britain owned several important islands and a number of lesser ones. French possessions included Martinique, Guadaloupe, and St. Domingue (Haiti); Britain claimed Jamaica and Barbados. French and English penetration of India occurred only gradually and incompletely in the seventeenth century. Late in that century the French East India Company established outposts at Pondicherry and Chandernagor on the subcontinent's southeast and northeast coasts, respectively. The French posts rivaled the earlier trading posts organized by England's East India Company at Madras and Calcutta.

The popular theory of mercantilism provided the intellectual glue that held together the disparate and far-flung English and French empires. According to mercantilist doctrine, a colonial empire provided several major advantages for the mother country. One of the most important was the ability to supply products such as tobacco that the mother country could not produce on its own and would otherwise have to import to its detriment. If the colonies produced gold and/or silver, so much the better, since mercantilists measured the strength of a nation's economy by how much bullion it held. Mercantilists also saw colonies as ideal markets for the mother country's products. By restricting colonial imports to goods produced in the mother country, such as cloth and ironware, mercantilists hoped to stimulate their country's economy or at the least find an outlet for surplus production. To further these ends, the colonies were required to trade exclusively with the mother country. Finally, all the movement of raw materials and finished products inherent in this facet of mercantilism guaranteed a large and prosperous merchant marine that enjoyed a monopoly on the carrying trade between the mother country and the colonies.

The French and British empires in North America differed considerably. While the French holdings dwarfed those of the British, they were sparsely settled. By mid-eighteenth century, barely 50,000 settlers lived in French North America; more than forty times that number lived in the much smaller British colonies. Philadelphia was the world's second largest English-speaking city, trailing only London. Great Britain's surplus population eagerly migrated to North America, while the average Frenchman had no interest whatsoever in going to the New World. Furthermore, New France's economy was less than robust, depending chiefly on a trickle of trade with the native Indians. Britain's North American colonies prospered as agriculture, trade, industry, and commerce burgeoned. The British colonists also had a much larger commitment to independent living than their French counterparts, a fact that would cause the mother country great pain in the near future.

Compared to North America, French and British holdings in the West Indies showed great similarities. Large plantations, often owned by absentee landlords, produced a steady supply of valuable tropical goods such as coffee, indigo, and tobacco that were in great demand in Europe. This was nowhere more evident than in the case of sugar. By the eighteenth century, Europeans were virtually addicted to sugar, and their craving for the sweet product never slackened. Between 1713 and 1792, Great Britain imported £162 million worth of goods—almost entirely sugar—from its West Indian colonies, more than its imports from India and China combined. The sugar island of Jamaica alone exported a yearly average of £600,000 worth of goods. Haiti, the biggest sugar producer, belonged to France. Quite justifiably, these islands in the Caribbean have been referred to as the "jewels of empire."

Sugar is a labor-intensive crop. In order to work the cane fields of the Caribbean and the developing plantations of British North America, the Europeans imported huge numbers of black slaves from Africa. During the eighteenth century, at least 600,000 African slaves were brought to Jamaica alone. Exact figures do not exist, but it is obvious that millions of slaves were brought to the New World during the eighteenth century.

The importation of slaves from Africa gave rise to what is sometimes called "triangular trade." Both France and Britain engaged in triangular trade, but the latter's role was more prominent due in large part to its domination of the slave trade. Triangular trade involved Africa, the colonies of the New World, and Europe. Typically, a ship laden with finished products would sail from Europe to the west coast of Africa. There it would exchange the European goods for slaves. The slaves would be taken to the New World and sold for a very fine profit. The ship would then pick up raw materials—most likely sugar—from the colonial ports and return to Europe, where it would sell its cargo for yet another profit. In this manner huge fortunes were made.

The French and British presence in India was quite different in nature from the colonial holdings of these countries in the West Indies or North America. In India, private companies closely aligned with the state represented the interests of the mother country. England's Queen Elizabeth I chartered the East India Company in 1600. After failing to establish itself in the Spice Islands (present-day Indonesia), the East India Company concentrated on India. France followed the English example only in 1664, when Jean-Baptiste Colbert, King Louis XIV's influential finance minister, established the French East India Company. For decades the British East India Company overshadowed its French counterpart.

The British and French presence in India was confined to a handful of factories, or small coastal trading posts. After all, India was not the wilds of North America. It had an ancient and sophisticated civilization; it was densely populated; and it had impressive political and economic structures. European traders operated their factories only with the permission of India's rulers, and Indian indifference to European goods proved a major impediment to trade. Europe imported great quantities of cheap Indian cotton cloth, but had to pay for it in silver since the Indians desired little or nothing from Europe. Europe's relationship with India began to change after the early eighteenth-century collapse of the Mogul Empire that had held the subcontinent together. During the ensuing turmoil, Joseph Dupleix, the French East India Company's chief administrator in India, brought the company into local politics on the side of first one and then another Indian prince. This strategy paid substantial dividends; when those indebted to Dupleix gained power, they conferred important trading privileges on his company. Dupleix's British rivals were slow to respond, but under the leadership of Robert Clive the British East India Company eventually adopted Dupleix's strategy with stunning results.

The struggle between Britain and France for colonial supremacy occurred during the course of several eighteenth-century wars that included fighting in the colonies as well as much larger military clashes on the European continent. Typically, Great Britain would ally itself with a Continental state and then subsidize that ally generously in order to keep France tied down on the Continent while Britain operated freely in the colonial world. The success of this strategy was noted by William Pitt, British prime minister during the Seven Years' War, who in reference to Britain's alliance with Prussia during that war aptly remarked that he had "won Canada in Germany."

The first of the great eighteenth-century wars that resulted in the establishment of the British Empire was the War of the Spanish Succession. The Treaty of Utrecht (1713) that ended the war gave Great Britain several important French holdings in North America, including Newfoundland and Nova Scotia. The French also surrendered to Britain their claim to the disputed Hudson Bay territory. The British also received the *asiento* from France's ally, Spain, thereby securing entry into Spain's colonial market.

The second of the great wars, the War of the Austrian Succession, ended with the Peace of Aix-la-Chapelle in 1748. Although this treaty contained no territorial changes, the course of the war had convincingly demonstrated Great Britain's superiority on the seas and in most of the colonial world.

The struggle resumed in 1756 with the third and greatest of the eighteenth-century wars, the Seven Years' War, which ended in 1763 with the Peace of Paris. France gave up to Britain all its claims in North America east of the Mississippi River. Canada thus became English. France also surrendered its claims west of the Mississippi to Spain. This spelled the end of France's presence in North America. While France made no other territorial concessions to Great Britain, it was obvious that the British Empire was ascending while the French Empire was declining.

Evidence of this was the British triumph in India. When the Seven Years' War broke out, the British East India Company under Clive moved against the Indian princes who had favored the French. The French proved incapable of supporting their Indian allies effectively because Britain controlled the seas, and at the Battle of Plassey in 1757 Clive crushed France's chief Indian client and placed one of his own Indian allies on the throne of Bengal. With this development, the British East India Company became the virtual ruler of the populous and rich Indian state of Bengal.

Two-thirds of the way through the eighteenth century, Great Britain found itself the world's preeminent colonial power. In achieving this status, Britain had not only superseded the old colonial empires of Spain and Portugal, but also vanquished its major rival, France. However, in a few short years the outbreak of the American Revolution would place the first British Empire at risk.

---

## INTERPRETIVE ESSAY
*Thomas Prasch*

Historians have long pointed to the eighteenth century as the period in which a distinctive Englishness, a definite sense of English national identity, first clearly emerged. After the Glorious Revolution (1688–1689) settled the divisive issues of national religion and the form of government, the eighteenth century was one of relative domestic peace. English artists and writers began to articulate the terms of a distinctive English culture framed by a nationalistic rejection of foreign (especially French) cultural imports, a movement exemplified in, for example, the drawings of William Hogarth, the novels of Henry Fielding, or the English dictionary of Samuel Johnson.

What has been less clearly recognized is the extent to which, however much the eighteenth-century shapers of English national character and culture sought to divorce themselves from the foreignness of Continental models, their new Englishness depended on the silent incorporation of another sort of foreignness: that of empire. At the most general level, it was the profits of empire that provided new wealth and prosperity to Great Britain and made the cultural revolution of the eighteenth century possible. The commercial revolution and, at the end of the century, the advent of industrialism depended on the expanded network of trade between Great Britain and its colonies. Even in the details of the new English culture, the evidence of empire was clear to those who wanted to see it. In the coffeehouses Samuel Johnson frequented, it was empire that filled his cup and pipe. It was empire that put the sugar in the tea the English drank; it was empire that brought the English the tea they put their sugar in.

It is thus not only the struggle, visible in the work of Hogarth and Fielding, to distinguish English national culture from that of the French or Italians that we should notice when we seek to understand the emergence of English identity in the eighteenth century. It is also what Hogarth and Fielding chose not to see: that Englishness depended on the labor of African slaves transported from trading posts on the West African coast to the plantations of the Caribbean and the American South; that Englishness counted on the producers and merchants of China and India, who supplied the East India Company with cloth, spices, and tea; that Englishness incorporated those who left the island's shores to settle first Ireland, reducing much of the population to landless renters, and then North America, pushing the indigenous peoples of the continent westward as they created space for themselves.

Not all of this was the work of a single century. Indeed, the origins of the British Empire can be traced to the Elizabethan era, when the English first began competing with Spain and Portugal in the spheres of exploration and conquest. The basic contours and structures of the first British Empire were already established at the outset of the eighteenth century.

The subjugation of Ireland was completed in the seventeenth century in the wake of a series of failed rebellions by Irish Roman Catholics. Land confiscated from rebels was turned over to Scottish and English settlers as plantations by James I at the beginning of the century. Oliver Cromwell's savage wars in Ireland in the 1640s led to further confiscations, leaving only a quarter of Irish lands in the hands of Roman Catholics. Finally, Irish support for the overthrown James II in 1689–1691 resulted in a series of punitive parliamentary acts that severely limited the political power and land rights of the Catholic majority.

In North America, the settlement of the eastern seaboard of what is now the United States was also largely completed by the end of the seventeenth century. Through the course of the century, settlers recruited by companies seeking profits in commercial agriculture (as in the case of the Virginia Company, founded in 1609) or a place in which to exercise religious freedom (as with the New England colonists, who received a royal charter in 1628 and began emigrating in the 1630s) or benefitting from proprietary grants by the king to favored courtiers (the basis for colonial foundations from Maryland in 1632 to Pennsylvania in 1681) flocked to the New World. Furthermore, the establishment of a plantation economy based on slave labor in the southern colonies and the integration of New England into the "triangular trade" that transported slave labor across the Atlantic was fully established before the end of the seventeenth century. The status of slavery was enshrined in colonial legal codes, and the provision of African slaves was ceded to a chartered monopoly (the Company of Royal Adventurers from 1663 to 1670; the Royal African Company after 1672). The seizure of New York in 1664, a byproduct of the Anglo-Dutch wars of the seventeenth century, completed the seaboard settlement; only Georgia (founded in 1732 as a penal colony and a buffer between English possessions and Spanish-controlled Florida) and Florida (not acquired until the decisive British victory in the Seven Years' War and the Peace of Paris of 1763) remained to be added.

English settlement in the West Indies proceeded at a pace roughly comparable to that of the North American colonies, and to a large extent it followed the model established there of proprietary royal grants. The first settlements, beginning in the 1620s, focused on Barbados and the Leeward Islands. It was in the course of Cromwell's wars that the Spanish were driven out of Jamaica in 1655, with British settlement of the island secured over the next decade. African slaves were first introduced almost at the outset of colonization—some sixty slaves were brought to St. Christopher in 1626, and a decade later Barbados law institutionalized slavery—but it was only in mid-century, as the availability of native labor in the West Indies declined, that African slaves became the dominant form of labor. As in the American South, the Royal African Company had an official monopoly on slave provision, although in practice the monopoly was far from complete. Only in the wake of the Seven Years' War, with the addition to British holdings in the Leeward chain, did the territorial outlines set in the seventeenth century change.

In Africa the English presence amounted to a series of trading posts to facilitate the slave trade along the West African coast. Other European slave traders—Dutch, Portuguese, and French, especially—manned similar posts along the same coast. Where such posts did not exist, shipboard trading for slaves still occurred. From an African point of view, the slave trade created a much wider geographical nexus, extending both inland and further south. But from a European point of view, penetration into the interior was limited and permanent settlement was minimal. During the eighteenth century, the English firmly established their primacy in the Atlantic slave trade, largely supplanting the Portuguese and Dutch as the major suppliers of slaves to markets throughout the New World. This did not, however, significantly alter the structure of their organization in Africa; the number of trading settlements increased, but their relationship to African polities changed little. Nor did minor territorial changes, such as the acquisition of trading posts from France in 1763, significantly change the general picture.

In Asia and the Indian subcontinent, the basic geographic locus of English claims had already been established in the seventeenth century. The East India Company, founded in 1600, was granted a monopoly on English trade with Asia; to make good on that monopoly, however, it had to deal with both competition from other European powers and the established states of Asia. Restricted by the Chinese to limited trading in the port of Canton, and frozen out by Dutch advances from Indonesia, officials of the East India Company focused on India (as, for similar reasons, did the French Compagnie des Indies Orientales).

As in China, the East India Company established factories or trading posts at key points on the Indian subcontinent: first in Surat on the northwest coast (1612); then Madras, on the east coast (1638); then Bombay, part of Charles II's wife's dowry (1661); and, in response to growing trade opportunities in Bengal, Calcutta (1690). Already after 1660, the company had begun to recruit and arm Indians, called sepoys, to provide military defense of its trading posts. In part because of the opportunities presented after the collapse of the Mogul Empire and in part in response to intensifying competition from the French, the character of British involvement in India would change dramatically over the course of the eighteenth century. Its geographical focus, however, would not: the cities that provided the center for British trade in India in the seventeenth century would become the linchpins of its expanding territorial control during the next century.

In terms of the geography of empire, it is really only in two areas that the eighteenth century marked any significant shift over the earlier period of empire-building: in the Mediterranean and in Canada. In the Mediterranean, Gibraltar (1704) and Minorca (1708) were critical acquisitions for strategic purposes, although minor as colonial holdings. The two military positions gave Britain unprecedented control of access from the Mediterranean to the Atlantic, a control it would make good use of in the wars of the eighteenth century.

Among England's claims in the Americas, only its control over Canada was, by the end of the seventeenth century, less than secure. The Hudson's Bay Company was granted a chartered monopoly for trade in the territories in 1670; New England fishermen also exploited the waters off Newfoundland. By then, however, the French already had substantial and long-standing claims in the area, with settlements in Quebec and Nova Scotia and extensive trading routes into the interior. These claims were anchored by trade alliances with Native Americans and broader claims to the whole trans-Mississippi region. It was only with the Peace of Utrecht in 1713 that England gained a firm foothold in Canada, and only in the wake of the Seven Years' War in 1763 that French competition was eliminated.

Not only was the empire's geographical focus set by the end of the seventeenth century, but the structure of imperial relations was by then firmly established. Basic to that structure was the vision of empire as a commercial machine designed to enrich the mother country. The doctrine of mercantilism, which envisioned colonies as economic extensions of the mother country, supplying raw materials and markets for Great Britain exclusively, was legislatively enshrined in the Navigation Acts. The acts of 1660 and 1663—which mandated that only English ships carry goods to or from the colonies and that imports to the colonies had to be shipped through England—were supplemented by later legislation. Thus, insofar as the formation of the British Empire contributed to the creation of a worldwide commercial system, the mercantilist legislation that governed imperial trade sought to ensure that Great Britain would remain at the center of the new global marketplace.

Mercantilism had its political side in the relationship of the monarchy to the various elements of empire. Thus the colonies themselves, whether originating with joint-stock companies or proprietorial grants, owed their existence to royal charters. When chartered companies failed, the king took their place; thus, when the Virginia Company folded in 1624, Virginia became a royal colony. The companies that carried out much of the trade among colonies and between the colonies and the mother country owed their existence to royal grants of monopoly over territories (as in the East India Company or the Hudson's Bay Company) or particular forms of trade (as with the Royal African Company). Just as the commerce of empire centered on England, so the politics of empire centered on the English monarchy.

The shifting political balance in England itself over the course of the seventeenth century had an enormous impact on the actual mechanics of imperial rule. The struggles for power between Parliament and king that resulted first in the Civil War and Interregnum (1640–1660) and then in the Glorious Revolution concluded with a settlement that increased the relative power of Parliament, a resolution that contributed to the discontent that would eventually spawn the American Revolution. In particular, the interlocking sovereignty of king and Parliament that was a product of the Glorious Revolution undercut the autonomy of colonial legislatures. Whereas before 1689 colonial political bodies operated in relationship to the king or his representative, the royally appointed governor, they now found themselves in a new subsidiary relationship to a consolidated English state that included both king and Parliament.

During the eighteenth century, as the English state sought to consolidate its hold on the colonies and colonial trade, colonial legislatures found themselves relegated to the political sidelines by the new power combination of king and Parliament. Significantly, before the final move toward war and independence, North American colonists hearkened back to earlier political arrangements when they addressed their grievances against parliamentary actions to the king. But if open conflict between colonial and English legislatures developed fully only in the eighteenth century, the roots of that conflict lay in the preceding decades: in the political settlement of 1688–1689.

If the basic geographical outline and general structure of the first British Empire were products of previous centuries, it is nevertheless only in the eighteenth century that the empire reached its zenith. The obvious question, then, is: What changed in the eighteenth century? The answer is twofold. First, and most significantly, there was a dramatic shift in scale. The commercial network of empire, the Atlantic slave trade, and the movement of settlers from Great Britain to the colonies all began before the eighteenth century, but the sheer volume of all these transactions boomed after 1700. So did government expenditure in support of empire, especially in the course of war. Second, and partly in response to this growth, there was a process of consolidation, primarily but not exclusively the by-product of the series of European wars with imperial dimensions from the War of the Spanish Succession to the Seven Years' War. In response to the threat to empire these wars posed, Britain consolidated its power over its empire. Consolidation not only changed the dynamics of empire but sowed the seeds for its destruction.

The dramatic shift in the scale of imperial enterprise can be measured in levels of consumption of almost any commodity produced in the colonies. Sugar provides the classic example. In *Sugar and Slavery*, Richard Sheridan estimates that English imports of sugar from its West Indies colonies amounted to less than 28,000 tons in 1700, but over 112,000 tons by 1775; 75 percent of that amount was for home consumption. The steadily increasing demand for sugar drove the West Indies colonies increasingly toward monoculture, or single-crop agriculture.

The same forces fueled the rising demand for African slaves. Several other factors also contributed to the increased level of the British slave trade, most notably the *asiento*, a provision of the 1713 Treaty of Utrecht that gave Great Britain the right to supply slaves to Spanish territories. More generally, England's growing dominance of the seas made it the most reliable trader and allowed it to provide the best terms of credit.

Calculating the actual scale of the slave trade has proven difficult, but Philip Curtin's estimate in *The Atlantic Slave Trade* that some 9.5 million African slaves survived the famously difficult middle passage has been generally accepted; some estimates, however, suggest almost twice that number. In a trade that stretched over four centuries, almost half that total arrived in the eighteenth century. Richard Sheridan estimates that British ships brought a million and a half slaves to the West Indies, and as many more to the North American colonies and non-English territories, between 1627 and 1775; 82 percent of that total were shipped after 1700.

The consequence of this massive influx of slave labor is clearest in the population ratios of the slave colonies, especially the West Indies. According to John McCusker and Russell Menard in *The Economy of British America*, slaves constituted only a quarter of the population in the West Indies in 1650, 78 percent by 1700, and 91 percent by 1770. Nowhere in the American colonies did such figures prevail, but in the lower South (where the production of export crops was a major factor, as in the West Indies) slaves rose from 18 percent of the population in 1700 to 45 percent by 1770, and in the upper South the slave population tripled after 1700 to reach 39 percent by 1770.

These figures must be framed against a generally rapid growth in population throughout the colonies. The North American colonies, Mc-Cusker and Menard also show, grew from around 260,000 settlers in 1700 to over 2.1 million in 1770. Even in the Canadian provinces that had been acquired in 1713, the English population around mid-century totalled 2 million, as against only 70,000 French settlers. A growing population contributed in turn to an expanding trade. Over the same period, the rate at which the value of exports from the colonies increased was roughly twice the rate of population increase. Meanwhile, the collapse of the Mogul dynasty in India, especially after the death of Aurangzeb in 1707, opened up economic and political opportunities for both native and English traders. For the Indian trade over the course of the century, Phyllis Deane and W. A. Cole in *British Economic Growth* have shown that the value of imports from India rose from £775,000 in 1700–1701 to £5,785,000 by 1797–1798; exports to India increased from £114,000 to £1,640,000 over the same period.

Ever since the British scholar Eric Williams first proposed a direct link between British imperialism and the advent of industrialism in *Capitalism and Slavery*, the issue of the connection between imperial trade and Britain's early lead in the Industrial Revolution has been hotly debated. While the direct ties argued by Williams have largely been discredited, the massive growth of imperial trade made several clear contributions to English industrial development. The empire fostered the extensive trade networks and growth of sea power that created markets for industrial production. Wealth derived from the empire contributed in broad ways to English economic growth and advanced the development of financial and credit mechanisms that would be key to industrialism. And the empire, and the trade networks that survived the empire's fall, provided a resource base for English industrialism; for example, textiles led the way in early industrialization, and the textile industries in turn depended on the importation of cotton.

Such dynamic growth in trade in all parts of the British Empire fundamentally altered its nature, as well as the relationship between the British center and the imperial periphery. Nothing shows this more clearly than the shifting focus of attention of the wars of the eighteenth century. During the War of the Spanish Succession, colonies figured little in the conflict until the terms of the peace treaty were made. The War of the Austrian Succession was fought out in Canada, the Caribbean, and India as well as on the European continent, but the peace treaty largely restored the colonial status quo. The Seven Years' War began in the colonies with conflict between the British and French on the American frontier; battles in the colonies raged from Canada and the American frontier to the Caribbean, from the trading posts of West Africa to the factories of India; and the peace settlement significantly altered the colonial balance of power. Finally, what began in 1776 as a rebellion of English colonials rapidly expanded into a worldwide conflict, with France and Spain challenging Great Britain in all the arenas of empire. The treaty that established American independence in 1783 was thus signed not in Philadelphia or London, but in Paris.

Through the course of these wars, and more generally in response to the changing scale of empire, Great Britain worked to consolidate its position in territorial, commercial, and political terms. This process of consolidation, while it operated from the same set of assumptions that had been present from the empire's founding (especially those embodied in the doctrine of mercantilism), changed the empire's actual operation dramatically. The consequences of the policy of consolidation are nowhere more apparent than in India and the North American colonies.

In India, the impact of imperial wars and political instability on the perceived need to protect the East India Company's commercial relations and territorial outposts led to an increasingly direct British rule over a growing portion of Indian territory. The instability also unleashed the greed of company officials, especially in the wake of Robert Clive's military victories in Bengal (1757–1760). From the time the British began to recruit sepoys in 1660 to the beginning of the Seven Years' War, both British and French companies had tended toward an ever deeper direct involvement in the Indian political scene, moving from trade agreements to formal alliances with native rulers to the placement of native surrogates in positions of power. The fragmentation of political authority in India in the eighteenth century, the consequence of the collapse of Mogul rule, widened the opportunities for such manipulation.

Joseph Dupleix, the governor of the French company, in many ways perfected the mechanisms of European intervention in Indian politics, backing a palace coup in the Carnatic region of the south of India in 1749. Clive, supporting a rival claimant, was largely outmaneuvered by Dupleix until 1752, when he seized and held the French fort of Arcot, turning Dupleix's tactics against him. The situation in the south was only completely resolved as a result of outside forces: the French recalled Dupleix in 1754 and sacrificed his gains (and most French power in India) at the peace table in 1763.

Clive, meanwhile, took the lessons he had learned north to Bengal. In 1756 Siraj, newly enthroned as nawab, attacked East India Company settlements in Calcutta. Clive defeated Siraj in 1757 and then made a military alliance with him. However, for a price, Clive backed one of Siraj's generals, Mir Jafar, in a palace coup, and provided Jafar with the military backing that kept him in power until Clive left for England in 1760. Mir Jafar returned the favor by extending gifts and concessions to company officials, and most critically by lifting all customs duties on even private trade by company representatives.

Five years of political anarchy and levels of company looting and mismanagement that scandalized even the British led to Clive's return in 1765, and his return effectively constituted the beginning of direct British rule. Clive took over revenue collection powers from the government but left judicial power in Indian hands; Warren Hastings, his successor, completed the takeover process in 1772 by reorganizing the judiciary. Meanwhile, back in London, questions about company conduct led Parliament to pass a Regulating Act (1774) that gave Parliament limited supervisory authority over the company; the act was strengthened significantly in 1784. These moves anticipated the British state's complete displacement of the East India Company early in the nineteenth century. The consolidation of Britain's trading position had inevitably led it from merely commercial involvement with autonomous Indian merchants and governments to territorial occupation and direct rule.

The attempt by the British government to consolidate its transatlantic position led to the destruction of the first British Empire with the revolt of the North American colonies. Ironically, it was largely the direct consequences of the greatest British imperial success, its victory in the Seven Years' War, that would aggravate long-standing tensions to produce the American Revolution. The Peace of Paris (1763) would confirm the territorial integrity of the American colonies, especially with the withdrawal of French claims to the frontier and the ceding of Canada to the British. But the huge debts created by the war effort, and the British Parliament's conviction that the colonies should materially assist in recouping war costs, dovetailed with longer-term British efforts to legislate away the loopholes in the Navigation Acts to bring colonial holdings in line with mercantilist theory.

However, mercantilism was always more a theoretical ideal than a reality. Nowhere was this more true than in the transatlantic trade, where the impossibility of enforcing the Navigation Acts effectively resulted in extensive unofficial trading, smuggling, and piracy. British victories at sea in the wars of the eighteenth century, however, and consequent British naval supremacy significantly curtailed unofficial channels of trade. British attempts to regularize customs collection and increase the tax burden on colonial subjects in the 1760s rapidly led to open conflict, especially after the passage of the Stamp Act in 1765. And when full-scale war broke out a decade later, the other European powers, still smarting from their defeat in 1763, quickly entered the fray.

The Treaty of Paris in 1783 conventionally marks the end of the first British Empire. Most obviously, the North American colonies were lost. Much of the rest of the empire seemed to be in disarray. Ireland had picked up from the American colonials anti-tax and self-rule rhetoric and tactics of mobilization, and the British government, unwilling to compound its problems, had appeased the Irish with the removal of trade restrictions and expanded legislative autonomy. The East India Company by 1780 was on the brink of bankruptcy, and parliamentary action was required to regulate its governance of Indian territories acquired in the wake of Clive. Opponents of the East India Company forced impeachment proceedings against Hastings, calling public attention to the abuses of company power. The French meanwhile had been supporting Indian attacks on Madras and Bombay, contributing to the instability of the British position on the subcontinent. The tensions between French and English settlers in Canada had not been resolved by the attempted compromise proclamation of 1763, nor the revision of the Quebec Act (1774).

The ideological assumptions that supported empire were under assault as well. Adam Smith's *Wealth of Nations*, coincidentally published in 1776, fundamentally undermined the economic logic of mercantilism, arguing instead for free trade as the basis of relations among states and between states and their colonies. Edmund Burke's political philosophy was shaped by grappling with empire; he had been born in Ireland, and his parliamentary speeches addressed grievances of American colonists, the treatment of slaves in the West Indies, and company abuses in India. His conception of the distinctive character of civil societies in North America and India shaped his opposition to government imperial policies. Burke's most noted opponent in the debates about political society, the radical Thomas Paine, was also shaped by imperial experience, crafting his vision of the rights of free peoples during his tenure in the American colonies. Paine's *Common Sense* (1776) provided polemic justification for the American rebels' cause. And by the 1780s the antislavery movement, spearheaded by the evangelical William Wilberforce, had begun to make significant inroads in Great Britain.

If the first British Empire died in 1783, however, it was a curiously incomplete death. England retained control over its possessions in the West Indies, India, and Canada. In the decades immediately following the Treaty of Paris, England was able to consolidate its power in India, through a combination of legislative controls on the East India Company and expanded direct rule in India, and in Canada, through the Canada Act (1791), which reworked the governmental structure. Further, even Britain's losses were not absolute. If its political power over the North American colonies had been lost, soon after the American Revolution trade returned to prerevolutionary levels.

The first British Empire also left deep and lasting legacies that no mere political reversal could easily erase. This is most evident in the huge population shifts that were connected with the creation of the empire: the massive resettlement of Europeans, especially British, in North America; the vast diaspora from Africa, bringing black slaves not just to British possessions in the West Indies and North America but to Spanish and Portuguese holdings in the Caribbean and South America, and creating in the process a transatlantic black subculture; and the establishment of European settler elites in strategic positions in India and, to a much lesser extent, on the West African coast. Even England itself was affected by these shifts, for it is in the eighteenth century that the first stable communities of racial minorities appeared in English port cities, and above all else in London.

The world trade network developed to support the British Empire in the eighteenth century also survived its collapse. West Africa, for example, was now firmly locked into the global marketplace, its political structures and economy permanently transformed by the demands of the slave trade. Interactions with European traders brought new merchant elites in Africa unprecedented power, and new states organized to supply the slave trade replaced earlier political orders along the coast. With the end of the slave trade, Africans would find other goods—ivory, rubber, or minerals—to keep their place in the international market. In India, where trade with Europe already had a long history, the eighteenth century marked the transformation of those trade relationships to the disadvantage of first the native merchants and, by the end of the century, the native producers. The terms of the Indian trade were increasingly dictated by the needs of Great Britain. And in North America, as noted above, trade relations between the colonists and Great Britain were quickly resumed after independence; by the end of the century, Britain was once again the major trade partner of the newly independent state.

These legacies of the first empire provided the foundations upon which Britain's second empire, already begun in the late eighteenth century with the first Australian settlement (1788) and the reorganization of relations with Canada and India, would be built. The new empire would be different in significant ways: founded on free trade, and actively working to end the slave trade; changed in its geographic focus to center on India, with major new centers of development in the Pacific and Africa; less focused on settler colonies. But the roots of the empire's resurgence, the colonies and trade networks retained by Britain after 1783, can be found in the remnants of the first empire.

## SELECTED BIBLIOGRAPHY

Bayley, C. A. *New Cambridge History of India*. Cambridge: Cambridge University Press, 1988. Bayley's work is perhaps the standard history of India. It is useful both for relations between Great Britain and the nations of India and for the internal history of the Indian subcontinent.

———, ed. *Atlas of the British Empire*. London: Toucan, 1989. The atlas provides a useful overall picture, with abundant maps, of the British Empire and the relations between mother country and colonies.

Bose, Sugata, ed. *South Asia and World Capitalism*. Delhi: Oxford University Press, 1990. The contributors to this volume explore various dimensions of India's integration into a world capitalist system. The volume is particularly useful for understanding the economic ramifications of British rule in India.

Bowen, H. V. *Revenue and Reform: The Indian Problem in British Politics, 1757–1773*. Cambridge: Cambridge University Press, 1991. Bowen focuses on the issue of British imperial power in India at a critical period both in India and in Great Britain. His study centers on the tension between the East India Company's economic aims and advocates of humanitarian reform.

Colley, Linda. *Britons: Forging the Nation, 1707–1837*. New Haven: Yale University Press, 1992. Colley's already classic study seeks to map out the making of British national identity in the eighteenth century. She attaches great importance to British colonial encounters and politics in the formation of national character.

Curtin, Philip. *The Atlantic Slave Trade: A Census*. Madison: University of Wisconsin Press, 1969. Although somewhat dated, Curtin's book remains perhaps the most ambitious and thorough attempt to provide exact figures for the extent of the transatlantic slave trade.

Curtin, Philip, Steven Feierman, Leonard Thompson, and Jan Vansina. *African History*. Boston: Little, Brown, 1978. A useful survey of African history, this volume also provides general background, organized by region, on the impact of British imperial ambitions and the slave trade on Africa.

Deane, Phyllis, and W. A. Cole. *British Economic Growth, 1688–1955*. Cambridge: Cambridge University Press, 1962. Deane and Cole remain the standard source for statistical analysis of British economic growth since the Glorious Revolution.

Dresher, Seymour. *Capitalism and Antislavery: British Mobilization in Comparative Perspective*. Oxford: Oxford University Press, 1986. Dresher makes a convincing argument about the dynamic relationship between the development of an antislavery movement in Britain and the shifting terms of industrial capitalism in the late eighteenth century. As background to that argument, he also illuminates the conditions that allowed the development of slave systems in the British Americas.

Engerman, Stanley L., and Robert E. Gallman, eds. *The Cambridge Economic History of the United States*. Cambridge: Cambridge University Press, 1996. The volume is useful for understanding both the economic integration of the American colonies into the British imperial system and the economics of American slavery.

Fryer, Peter. *Black People in the British Empire: An Introduction*. London: Pluto Press, 1988. Attempting to overturn conventional portraits of the British Empire that focus on white power figures and the movement of white peoples, Fryer's study focuses on the central place of blacks (understood in the British sense, as including peoples of the Indian subcontinent and most Asians) in the imperial picture.

Gilroy, Paul. *The Black Atlantic: Modernity and Double Consciousness*. Cambridge, MA: Harvard University Press, 1993. Interested in incorporating the black experience into the conventional understanding of "Englishness," Gilroy argues that an accidental by-product of the transatlantic slave trade was a unified transcontinental black cultural experience.

Graham, Gerald S. *A Concise History of the British Empire*. London: Thames and Hudson, 1970. A useful general outline and narrative history of the British Empire, with solid treatment of the eighteenth century.

Marshall, P. J., ed. *Cambridge Illustrated History of the British Empire*. Cambridge: Cambridge University Press, 1996. A useful and lavishly illustrated general history of the British Empire, this volume includes a sketch of the origins of empire and the eighteenth-century background.

McCusker, John J., and Russell R. Menard. *The Economy of British America, 1607–1789*. Chapel Hill: University of North Carolina Press, 1985. A convenient source for understanding the economic relations that underpinned political developments between Britain, the American colonies, and the Caribbean islands.

Newman, Gerald. *The Rise of English Nationalism: A Cultural History, 1740–1830*. New York: St. Martin's Press, 1987. Surveying literature and art of the period, Newman sees the latter half of the eighteenth century as central to the creation of an English national character, developed through a set of contrasts between England and continental Europe.

Osae, T. S., S. N. Nwabara, and A. T. O. Odunsi. *A Short History of West Africa: A.D. 1000 to the Present*. Rev. ed. New York: Hill and Wang, 1973. A handy survey of West African history, reliable both in its account of the slave trade's impact on West African society and political systems and for its early history of British imperial claims along the West African coast.

Pocock, J. G. A., ed., with Gordon J. Schochet and Lois G. Schwoerer. *The Varieties of British Political Thought, 1500–1800*. Cambridge: Cambridge University Press, 1993. The currents of empire figure significantly in the shaping of British political thought in the eighteenth century, and the contributors to this volume recognize the interplay between political philosophy and the growth of empire.

Ranelagh, John O'Beirne. *A Short History of Ireland*. 2nd ed. Cambridge: Cambridge University Press, 1994. A reasonably objective survey in which Ranelagh sketches the phases of British colonialism in Ireland during the eighteenth century.

Reitan, Earl A. *Politics, War, and Empire: The Rise of Britain to a World Power, 1688–1792*. Arlington Heights, IL: Harland Davidson, 1994. Reitan's book is a useful survey of Britain's development as a major power in the eighteenth century, with ample attention to issues relating to empire.

Said, Edward. *Culture and Imperialism*. New York: Alfred A. Knopf, 1993. Although some of his specific arguments are problematic, Said nevertheless makes an important contribution by insisting that we see how imperialism shaped domestic culture in the European powers.

Sheridan, Richard B. *Sugar and Slavery: An Economic History of the British West Indies, 1623–1775*. 2nd ed. Kingston, Jamaica: Canoe Press, 1994. Sheridan's detailed economic history of the British possessions in the West Indies focuses on the interplay in the Caribbean between the development of slavery and the plantation system, the transition to cash-crop monoculture, and the integration of the West Indies into the transatlantic trade.

Spear, Percival. *India: A Modern History*. Rev. ed. Ann Arbor: University of Michigan Press, 1972. Spear's central emphasis is on the interaction between India and the West, which makes his account of the integration of India into the British Empire in this period especially useful.

Visram, Rozina. *Ayahs, Lascars, and Princes: The Story of Indians in Britain, 1700–1947*. London: Pluto Press, 1986. Visram's study of this largely neglected subject turns on the central thesis that peoples of the Indian subcontinent have long had a place in Britain.

Willcox, William B., and Walter L. Arnstein. *The Age of Aristocracy: 1688 to 1830*. 6th ed. New York: D. C. Heath, 1988. Perhaps the most standard survey of English history, Willcox and Arnstein's volume provides a basic outline both of the shaping of British Empire in the period and the consequences for British domestic politics.

Williams, Eric. *Capitalism and Slavery*. Chapel Hill: University of North Carolina Press, 1944. Williams' much-contested work on the connections between capitalism and slavery remains a useful starting point for understanding the centrality of slave-based economies to the emergence of Britain as a major power.

# 4

# The War of the Austrian Succession and the Seven Years' War, 1740–1763

## INTRODUCTION

Almost incessant warfare involving virtually all the European nations characterized the first two-thirds of the eighteenth century. The fitful peace that followed the conclusion of the War of the Spanish Succession ended in 1740 when general fighting not only engulfed the Continent but also spread to such distant locales as North America and India. The conflict unfolded in two stages: the first, usually known as the War of the Austrian Succession, lasted until 1748; the second, called the Seven Years' War (known in America as the French and Indian War), raged between 1756 (1754 in America) and 1763.

Well before the War of the Austrian Succession began, tensions ran high among the European states. In some instances the source of tension lay beyond the Continent. For instance, Great Britain, France, and Spain struggled with an intense colonial and commercial rivalry that centered on the New World. French expansion in North America alarmed the English. If France were to link its colonial possessions in Canada with its colonial possessions on the Gulf of Mexico, England's colonies on the Atlantic seaboard would be hemmed in and possibly threatened.

The question of commercial relations with the large Spanish Empire proved even more important. Spain continued to practice a form of rigid

During the North American phase of the Seven Years' War (French and Indian War), the British general Edward Braddock was defeated and killed in battle near present-day Pittsburgh. (Reproduced from the Collections of the Library of Congress)

mercantilism that barred non-Spanish ships from its colonies. Of all the European states, only France enjoyed access to the lucrative Spanish colonial market, but even its entrée was strictly limited. However, since Spanish colonial demand far outpaced the supply of legally imported goods, smuggling flourished. Great Britain was the chief beneficiary of this, and many Englishmen grew prosperous on this illegitimate trade. On those occasions when Spanish authorities apprehended English smugglers, they treated them harshly, thereby infuriating the British public. Demands for war (and the opening of the Spanish colonies to trade with England) were heard with greater frequency, and the British prime minister, the peaceable Robert Walpole, squelched them with difficulty. When an English smuggler, Captain Robert Jenkins, testified before Parliament that the Spanish had cut off his ear as punishment, Walpole yielded to the war party, and the so-called War of Jenkins' Ear pitting Great Britain against Spain began in 1739. Unwilling to see England gain the advantage in the New World, France's aged and equally peaceable chief minister, Cardinal André Fleury, reluctantly led his country into war against Great Britain.

European tensions on the eve of the war centered chiefly on the fate of the Austrian throne. Charles VI, the Habsburg ruler of Austria, who also served as Holy Roman Emperor and thereby was the most influential figure in the German-speaking world, was nearing death. As Charles had no male heirs, he had spent the last years of his life collecting signatures from European monarchs pledging themselves to allow Charles' domains to pass peacefully to his oldest daughter, Maria Theresa. This agreement was known as the Pragmatic Sanction. Among its signatories were King Frederick William of Brandenburg-Prussia and France's Bourbon king, Louis XV, who signed even though the Bourbons had traditionally competed with the Habsburgs for supremacy on the Continent. However, when Charles died in 1740, European rulers ignored the Pragmatic Sanction and nibbled away at Maria Theresa's inheritance. Spain tried to recover some of its former possessions in Italy, and, with the help of Louis XV, the Bavarian ruler Charles Albert had himself elected Holy Roman Emperor, the first non-Habsburg to be elected Emperor since the fifteenth century. Most ominously, Frederick William had died, and his brilliant but unscrupulous son, Frederick II, sought to enlarge Prussia's boundaries. With only a scintilla of legal justification but an abundance of audacity, Frederick invaded the prosperous Habsburg province of Silesia in December 1740.

The young and inexperienced Maria Theresa staggered under these blows, but she managed to recover. She rallied the crucial Hungarian nobility to her side when she appealed to their sense of chivalry and promised to honor their customary privileges. She also received subsidies from Great Britain, but no troops. Although this support allowed her to hold her empire together, it was not enough to oust Prussia from Silesia.

Meanwhile, the war party in France gained strength, excited by the prospect of striking at the Habsburg enemy. Specifically, France wanted the Austrian Netherlands (present-day Belgium). Although Fleury desired peace, he was overwhelmed, and France entered the fray. Great Britain, fearing French domination of the Continent, consequently intervened.

With France and Great Britain now at war, fighting moved beyond Europe. In Canada, the British defeated France and captured Louisbourg, the key fortress dominating the St. Lawrence River; in the Caribbean the British drove Spanish and French naval forces from the scene; in India, the French captured the important English trading post at Madras.

In Europe most of the fighting took place in the Austrian Netherlands, where the French eventually defeated a combined British, Austrian, and Dutch force. Austrian efforts to expel Prussia from Silesia failed, as did a French attempt to raise rebellion against Britain in Scotland. By 1748 general exhaustion prevailed, and an inconclusive peace was concluded at Aix-la-Chapelle that reinstated the status quo ante bellum with an important exception that allowed Frederick II to retain Silesia, an outcome that infuriated Austria.

The Treaty of Aix-la-Chapelle proved to be nothing more than a truce during which the belligerents rebuilt their strength in anticipation of renewed fighting. During the truce, the most important event was the Diplomatic Revolution of 1756. Austria, led by its foreign minister, Prince Wenzel Kaunitz, had begun to rethink its strategic position. The rise of Prussia presented a serious challenge to the Habsburgs, especially in the German-speaking world. Clearly Austria wanted to weaken Prussia, starting with the recovery of Silesia. To accomplish this, Kaunitz worked to draw France to his side despite the long-standing rivalry between Habsburg and Bourbon. Luckily for Kaunitz, the French also disliked Frederick's expansionistic ambitions and agreed to a Franco-Austrian alliance directed against Prussia. Kaunitz also lined up Russia, which was anxious for war against Prussia, as well as Sweden, Spain, and Saxony. Great Britain, in order to maintain a balance of power on the Continent and to protect its king's holdings in the German state of Hanover, switched alliances as well, abandoning Austria and allying itself with Prussia.

Frederick, acutely aware of how the balance had shifted against him, launched a preemptive strike against Saxony in August 1756, thereby igniting the costly and destructive Seven Years' War. Although the war was basically a continuation of the War of the Austrian Succession, it clearly reflected the changes brought about by the Diplomatic Revolution. Prussia, allied with Great Britain, which supplied money but not men, now stood against a formidable combination of Austria, Russia, France, and Sweden.

Against overwhelming odds, the Prussian army, led by Frederick himself, fought well. Its victories in late 1756 at the Battles of Rossbach and Leuthen significantly strengthened Frederick's position. Nevertheless, the combination of forces against Prussia was too great. In 1757 Frederick was defeated at the Battle of Hochkirch, and Sweden invaded from the north; in August 1759 the Russians smashed his army at the Battle of Kunersdorf. At times both Austrian and Russian forces occupied Berlin.

Although Frederick earned the appellation ''the Great'' for his tenacity and apparent military prowess during the Seven Years' War, ultimate defeat seemed inevitable. Nevertheless, fortune smiled on Frederick. The French, preoccupied elsewhere, reduced their commitment to Austria and limited their role in the fighting. The Austrians and Russians failed to coordinate their movements and, perhaps more important, grew increasingly suspicious of each other. Then, in 1762, Frederick's implacable enemy, Empress Elizabeth of Russia, died. She was succeeded by Peter III, an unstable, irrational character who idolized Frederick. Peter soon withdrew Russia from the war, and Prussia was saved. Austria, totally exhausted, could not defeat Prussia alone, and peace negotiations opened. By the terms of the 1763 Treaty of Hubertusburg, Prussia retained Silesia, whose seizure by Frederick in 1740 had proven to be the cause of much bloodshed.

Like the War of the Austrian Succession, the Seven Years' War was a global one. In fact, Great Britain and France had resumed hostilities in North America as early as 1754. This French and Indian War began when a contingent of English colonists under George Washington entered the disputed Ohio River valley and was defeated by a French force stationed at Fort Duquesne (the site of present-day Pittsburgh). The following year at the same locale, the French and their Indian allies defeated a much larger force of British regulars under General Edward Braddock. Shortly thereafter, the French pushed the English from the Great Lakes region.

Despite these initial French victories, Great Britain ultimately prevailed. Not only did Britain have a preponderance of resources and a superior navy, but in 1757 William Pitt began to direct the British war effort. A tireless and determined supporter of Britain's colonial expansion, Pitt poured Britain's resources into the global struggle against France while devoting only enough money and attention to European events to keep France tied down. His program paid huge dividends for Britain. In 1758 British forces captured both Fort Duquesne and Louisbourg. In the following year they took Quebec, and Canada fell to Great Britain. The British also enjoyed success against the French in the Caribbean, taking Guadeloupe, Grenada, and Martinique.

Great Britain and France also clashed in India. Under the leadership of the energetic Joseph François Dupleix, the French East India Company had made important gains in India by extending French support to native princes in their interminable struggles with each other in return for both territorial and trading concessions. Robert Clive, a clerk who rose to direct the British East India Company, successfully copied this technique.

Operating through these two companies, Great Britain and France jostled each other for position in India. Dupleix's recall to France in 1754 immeasurably aided the British, and when the Seven Years' War broke out Clive moved vigorously against the French. He and his Indian allies defeated France's most important Indian ally at the Battle of Plassey in 1757 and later seized the main French trading post at Pondicherry, thereby giving the British East India Company control over much of southern India.

In 1763 the Peace of Paris brought the Seven Years' War to a close. By the terms of the treaty, France relinquished its position in India. France also surrendered its North American claims in Canada and east of the Mississippi River to Great Britain. French claims west of the Mississippi as well as the settlement at New Orleans went to Spain, which had surrendered its claims to Florida to Great Britain. France also ceded Grenada, St. Vincent, and Tobago to Britain.

---

## INTERPRETIVE ESSAY
### Franz A. J. Szabo

Though the mid-eighteenth century conflicts traditionally called the War of the Austrian Succession and the Seven Years' War did not unfold on the same military scale as the great struggles against French hegemony that bracket the eighteenth century, they were nevertheless costly, bitter, and bloody. Certainly they give lie to the stereotypical image of that century's "civilized" and "limited" warfare. In most history texts, the monumental struggles against Louis XIV and Napoleon Bonaparte overshadow these conflicts, but they were no less consequential for Western civilization. Indeed, by introducing a number of permanent shifts in the geopolitical dimensions of European, and for that matter global politics, they may have been even more so.

The names assigned these wars, however, are very misleading. Rather than two relatively coherent conflicts, they were a series of overlapping clashes fought in many different areas with shifting emphases as well as fluctuating priorities. Often they were driven by short-term, ad hoc responses to perceived problems. That North Americans would refer to them as King George's War and the French and Indian War respectively, or that in Germany they are known as the three Silesian Wars reflects this reality. Alliances of convenience repeatedly came under strain as interests seldom coincided and regional priorities differed markedly. Though most participants strove to establish or participate in some sort of international "system" to cement their security interests and to give cohesion to broader ambitions, these seldom survived the ever-changing fortunes of war and the shifting sands of diplomacy. Domestic factional strife, financial strains, and the sometimes surprising battlefield verdicts further unsettled policy. There was no common start and no common end to either conflict, and many belligerents were never even at war with the bitterest enemies of their allies.

The mid-century wars grew out of and eventually transformed an international system that had emerged in response to Louis XIV's aggressions in the late seventeenth century and early eighteenth century. That pattern of international relations featured a relatively clear-cut balance of power centered on the long-standing Habsburg-Bourbon rivalry. However, what had begun as a French fear of encirclement by the Habsburgs in the sixteenth century had evolved into a widespread fear of French ambitions by the beginning of the eighteenth. Europe's maritime powers, Britain and Holland, supported Habsburg resistance to French expansionism. France attempted to destabilize the Habsburg monarchy's rear by alliance with Sweden, a forward Polish policy, and surreptitious aid to the Ottoman Empire. The Habsburgs, for their part, attempted to neutralize this French "eastern bloc" by supporting the ambitions of a rising Russia. The notion that this constellation embodied a "natural order" was widespread, and many political theorists waxed eloquent about the system's capacity to guarantee peace among the European powers.

What is therefore noteworthy in the quarter century following the death of Louis XIV in 1715 is how fluid this supposed natural order turned out to be. Implacable enemies became allies, and even alliances cemented by family ties turned into enmities. Spain's ambitions following the division of its empire as a result of the War of the Spanish Succession provided for great instability. Spain's Iberian and colonial possessions had passed to the Bourbons, while most of its Continental possessions in Italy and the Low Countries had passed to the Austrian Habsburgs. Spanish determination to recover some ground on the Italian peninsula roiled the waters. Austrian and Russian victories that eroded France's eastern bloc, along with Britain's growing commercial appetite, added further instability. For the most part, however, conflicts in this era concerned what might be called peripheral adjustments to an international system whose tone was permeated by a reasonable recognition of limits on the part of most leading statesmen, and whose objectives were largely the stabilization and refinement of an imperfect but satisfactory equilibrium.

To this fluid but largely predictable pattern of international relations came a meteor whose impact destroyed all hitherto existing calculations. This was the notorious "Rape of Silesia." The young and ambitious new king of Prussia and elector of Brandenburg, Frederick II, in defiance of his country's international commitments, attacked what he perceived to be a vulnerable Habsburg heiress, Archduchess, Queen, and, later, Empress Maria Theresa, to despoil her of some of her richest lands. Neither vaguely legitimate claims to some Silesian duchies nor revenge for a putative mishandling of his father by a Habsburg emperor motivated Frederick. He characterized the dynastic claims manufactured by his zealous court archivist as "the work of an excellent charlatan," and he even briefly indulged in the illusion that an amicable relationship was possible after the rape. With almost brutal frankness, Frederick confessed that he was driven by a desire for the limelight and for historical immortality. If modern historians can characterize the reckless policy of Wilhelmine Germany at the beginning of the twentieth century as a grasp for world power, Frederick's was a very similar all-or-nothing grasp for Great Power status. He undertook this gamble for no reason other than that he thought he could get away with it.

Frederick II is perhaps the central figure of the mid-century wars; he is certainly the animating force behind the wars. Prussophile, German nationalist, and Nazi historians have stampeded to dub Frederick "the Great," and Western historiography has largely fallen in line. But for all his comparatively modest accomplishments as an "enlightened despot," his undoubted military and administrative talents, or, for that matter, his glamorous reputation as a prodigious if self-serving author, he only had the makings of a noteworthy, but not outstanding, monarch. As one of his more critical biographers has pointed out, without the conquest and successful retention of Silesia, Frederick II would hardly have been "Frederick the Great." The centerpiece of Frederick II's historical immortality remains the felony he himself had earmarked for this purpose.

It is therefore all the more important to point out how uncertain this conquest was, and how fortuitously Frederick escaped with his booty intact. The politically decisive battle of Mollwitz in April 1741, which confirmed Frederick's possession of Silesia for the time being, was not a convincing military victory. Rather, it substantiated Frederick's perception that Austrian potential was not inconsiderable and would be brought to bear on him alone if the conflict were not broadened. Thus, while desperately trying to avoid involvement in a protracted war himself, he realized that an extended international conflict would distract and drain Habsburg energies. In this he was fortunate indeed, for Mollwitz strengthened the political position of France's most notorious military hawk, Marshal Charles de Belle-Isle. Desiring the complete destruction of France's "hereditary enemy," Belle-Isle urged that France abandon the policy of moderation that had prevailed since the close of the War of the Spanish Succession. The Alliance of Nymphenburg and its attendant treaties, which brought together the predatory claims of a French-sponsored anti-Habsburg coalition (Spain, Bavaria, Saxony, and Prussia), aimed at nothing less than the destruction of Austria and France's uncontested domination over the German world. Dismemberment of the Habsburg monarchy thus became the key objective of the subsequent military campaigns.

It is perhaps symptomatic of both the stability and fluidity of the international system in operation since 1715 that British policies initially remained ambivalent. They became more clear-cut only with a change of domestic administration and a growing perception of France's desire for hegemony. This return to the patterns of the War of the Spanish Succession, as well as Frederick II's ready perfidy with any and all allies, soon led to startling Habsburg military victories and a collapse of the French initiative in Germany. A reassessment of French policies, which ensued in 1743, however, reaffirmed France's hegemonic ambitions. The second family compact with the Bourbons of Spain in October 1743 now gave the conflict a colonial dimension otherwise still very secondary in everyone's consideration. From France's formal declarations of war on Britain and Austria, through its campaign to conquer the Austrian Netherlands, the intensification of the naval conflict on the high seas, and the plans to invade England and foment Jacobite rebellion in Scotland, the targeted objective for France decisively shifted from destruction of Austria to destruction of Britain.

In the face of these onslaughts, Britain experienced some distressing months, especially during 1745. The victories it did achieve on the high seas, but especially the capture of Louisbourg in Canada by a colonial militia, therefore assumed all the more importance. Although the capture of Louisbourg was of limited significance in the grand strategic scheme of things, it was psychologically critical, not only as a boost to morale but also as the beginning of the systematic penetration of global trade issues and colonial priorities into a broader spectrum of British political opinion. As British fortunes began to recover with successes in Italy and the defeat of the Jacobites, the tables began to turn. Now many confident British elites were ready to embark on their own forward policy designed to humble France, and the war could well have dragged on for several more years had the more bellicose voices on all sides been heard. What ultimately silenced them and placed limitations on the ambitions of all combatants were fiscal realities.

If there is one dimension of the mid-century wars that historians have tended to examine in greater detail in recent years, it is their financial impact on the combatants. Despite the apparently modest scale of the military operations in comparison to wars at the beginning and end of the eighteenth century, the relative costs of these conflicts reached unprecedented heights. In the Seven Years' War, statesmen were disconcerted to discover that within only a few months military expenditures escalated to as much as three times prewar estimates. In the War of the Austrian Succession, only the Habsburg monarchy had begun with critical shortfalls due to numerous existing loans that ate up ordinary revenues and almost doubled the national debt. But during the war itself, almost all the participants brought themselves to the verge of economic paralysis. By 1747 French overseas trade was so crippled and revenue streams so reduced that the minister of finance could forecast only the gloomiest scenarios if peace were not reestablished immediately. Even Britain, which had acted as a Continental paymaster, feared that unacceptable increases both in taxes and in the national debt might bring on national bankruptcy. Such concerns certainly acted as powerful incentives to bring the conflict to an end.

The Peace of Aix-la-Chapelle, which ended the War of the Austrian Succession, therefore, was essentially a peace of exhaustion. By basically restoring the status quo, it solved few of Europe's international problems. Frederick II, who had maneuvered in and out of the war with a mixture of deft duplicity and sheer luck, had thereby managed to retain Silesia. Otherwise the peace left few participants satisfied, and no participants feeling secure. Indeed, certain antagonisms were clearly aggravated, though the question of which alliance combinations would best serve the future interests of each of the powers was still left open. The subsequent Diplomatic Revolution, rather than being a simple turning from one firm European alliance system to another, was, in fact, not really so revolutionary. In many ways it was a return to the kind of flexible policy of the 1715–1740 period, though this time freedom of action was more constrained by greater implacability in Anglo-French rivalry and by a clear shift of Habsburg priorities to the Prussian threat.

Also new was North America's capacity to shape events in Europe. Traditionally, European wars had had a ripple effect on the Americas; now an American conflict decisively accelerated prospects of a European war. As both French and English statesmen brought into clearer focus the significance of world trade, the importance of North American developments became increasingly apparent. Dynamic population growth among the English colonists also added an unstable element. A surging population meant a surging market for the mother country's products and a corresponding enhancement of that market's importance. At the same time, the commercial prosperity of the Americas only whetted the colonists' appetite for more, and land hunger made them cast a greedy eye on the territories of the vastly outnumbered though militarily better organized New France, and of the technologically less advanced and inconveniently situated indigenous peoples. Driven by an ambitious agenda, but militarily too weak to affect it themselves; reckless in its implementation, but lacking proper coordination to carry it through, the British colonies increasingly drew the mother country into the American vortex.

This had momentous consequences, not only for North America, but also for Europe. Developing an ever sharper focus on global trade issues, and increasingly drawn into first covert, then overt war with France by the actions of its self-willed but demanding colonists, Britain sought to cover its Continental flank as best it could. Optimally, it would have preferred peace and neutrality among the other European powers—to keep both Austrian and Russian friendship, but also to secure Prussian neutrality. It had long been the Achilles' heel of British foreign policy never to see clearly enough how other powers perceived their own self-interest, and this time there was certainly an inadequate sense of how adversely a neutrality agreement with Prussia would affect Austria and Russia. As for Frederick II, though he certainly had an ongoing expansionist agenda and was prepared to seize opportunities as they arose, fear of Austrian revenge dominated his immediate policy. Unable to conceive of an Austro-French rapprochement, and persuaded that Russia was Britain's obedient puppet, he was confident that an agreement with Britain would effectively isolate Austria and scotch its desire for revenge. The result was the famous Convention of Westminster, which quickly achieved the opposite of what both Britain and Prussia desired.

Austria, already soured by Britain's almost callous indifference to the Habsburgs' primary concern with Silesia in the previous war, abandoned the long-standing British option. Russia, far more independent of British subsidies than Prussia assumed and far more hostile to Prussia than Britain had understood, ceased to act as British surrogate and mercenary. France, angered at Prussian duplicity and afraid of isolation in its already blazing colonial war with England, saw that a compromise with Austria was necessary. The result was a series of defensive treaties that foreshadowed the alliance of the three great Continental powers against Prussia. Realizing his fatal diplomatic error, Frederick II sought to rescue the situation with a military option. Looming encirclement, he calculated, could be avoided with a lightning strike against the linchpin of the alliance, the Habsburg monarchy. Consequently, he began a preventive war with a quick assault on the German principality of Saxony, through which he planned an invasion of the Habsburg province of Bohemia.

The capture of Saxony was a tremendous asset to Prussia, both strategically and materially. Saxon troops were dragooned into the Prussian army, and the occupied principality was mercilessly exploited throughout the subsequent war. Strategically, the occupation of Saxony also rounded out the core of territories from which Frederick could operate and provided a platform for a quick strike toward Prague. But at the same time, the conquest of Saxony and the ensuing invasion of the Habsburg monarchy cemented rather than dissolved the grand alliance so patiently assembled by the Austrian foreign minister, Count Wenzel Anton Kaunitz. The planned lightning-strike military operation also soon went awry. The Battle of Lobositz in October 1756 was a clear sign for the Prussian king that things were not unfolding as they should (fearing disaster, Frederick, not for the first, nor for the last time, prematurely fled the battlefield only to have his subordinates snatch victory from the jaws of defeat). The costly victory at Prague in April 1757 was a further warning, and the subsequent defeat at the Battle of Kolin in June ended Frederick's gamble. He was forced to retreat from Bohemia, and the prospects of delivering a knockout blow to his Habsburg enemies dimmed considerably. The initiative seemed to pass decisively to the Allied coalition, as Austrian, Russian, and French forces began to close in on Prussia. However, the coalition's hopes of themselves delivering a knockout blow to Frederick were also dealt a crippling setback with disastrous defeats in November 1757 for the French at Rossbach and in December for the Austrians at Leuthen. This was undoubtedly very bad news for the allies, but it was also bad, and perhaps even worse, news for Frederick. Now he faced the one thing he wanted to avoid at all costs, a protracted war.

Frederick's survival depended on his ability to take unexpected initiatives and to keep his enemies off balance. The scope and effectiveness of these initiatives shrank every year. In 1758 he could still attempt to strike across his borders (as he did with an invasion of Moravia), though in that year he was forced to conclude that retreat rather than battle was the better part of valor. From 1759 onward, he could only remain within the confines of his Brandenburg-Saxon-Silesian redoubt and react to allied initiatives. In this monumental struggle, Frederick was fortunate to be king as well as principal military commander, for he was able to take risks of a kind allied generals, responsible to higher monarchical authority, could not dream of, and that, indeed, he himself would hardly permit his own subordinates. The benefit of interior lines also made it easier for him to react quickly to specific threats, gave him shorter supply lines, and allowed him to operate at less cost than his enemies. His strategy of sucking occupied Saxony dry of its resources and debasing his own coinage, when combined with very large British subsidies, made him more than competitive in what might be called the critical war of fiscal attrition. Finally, Frederick benefitted from the military talent of his field commanders, including his brother, Prince Henry, and his brother-in-law, Duke Ferdinand of Brunswick, whose British mercenary corps effectively protected Prussia's western rear throughout the war.

The allied war effort, in turn, was hampered by two critical problems. The first was the natural strains to which an alliance, whose partners frequently had mutually exclusive objectives and different regional priorities, was subjected. As a result, the coordination of allied operations was always only tentative at best. The second, which has received much less attention from historians, was the problem of finding safe winter quarters between campaign seasons. Forage and supply were such critical dimensions of eighteenth-century warfare that allied armies often had to retreat to home bases even after victories had been won in the field. This gave Frederick the repeated breathing spaces that were critical to his survival. Yet for all that, the grip of the vise was inexorable, and Frederick's prospects darkened from year to year. He might well speak of a "Miracle of the House of Brandenburg" when the allies did not effectively follow up the devastating Austro-Russian victory over the Prussians at the Battle of Kunersdorf in August 1759, but he would need to be the beneficiary of repeated miracles to avoid eventual defeat through attrition. Indeed, such "miraculously" fortuitous qualities were not lacking in the Battles of Liegnitz and Torgau in 1760, which seemed to postpone the inevitable for another year; but by the end of 1761 even Frederick had to concede that the war was lost.

However, yet another "miracle" saved Frederick and dramatically altered the course of European history. The death of the Russian empress Elizabeth and the accession of the deranged, infantile, and sadistic Prussophile tsar Peter III, who considered expansion of his small German principality of Holstein-Gottorp to be more important than the Baltic interests of his Russian Empire, and who switched sides long enough to make Austrian victory through attrition impossible, provided the decisive event of the Continental war–a miracle so unlikely that Joseph Goebbels would later use it to inspire Hitler to carry on a hopelessly lost war in 1945. Frederick merely had to hold out and avoid any major battle, while the Austrians had to trap and defeat him. The Austrians, on the verge of bankruptcy and already having had to make drastic army cutbacks in 1760 and 1761, might still have had the personnel but hardly the material resources to do so. At the Peace of Hubertusburg in February 1763, the Habsburg monarchy was compelled to bow to the verdict: Prussia retained Silesia and survived as a European Great Power.

The Anglo-French war, which had not begun propitiously for Britain in 1755–1756, turned into one of its most spectacular triumphs by 1760. The resolute policies of the Pitt-Newcastle ministry brought dramatic victories both on the high seas and in colonial areas. The almost fanatical dedication of William Pitt the Elder was certainly an important animating force, but the essence of Britain's victory lay in the clarity of its priorities. The decision to focus purposefully on the conflict's colonial dimension proved inspired. It not only resulted in significant territorial gains, but also reaped important financial windfalls from virtually complete control of the three great pillars of transatlantic prosperity: the high-demand consumer products of the Caribbean islands, the incredibly rich fisheries of the Grand Banks of Newfoundland and the Gulf of St. Lawrence, and the notorious slave trade from African coastal outposts. Nevertheless, the monumental fiscal exertion that would have been required to achieve complete victory of the kind that Pitt and his supporters desired was beyond even a victorious Britain, and it, too, had to settle for a compromise peace. France's retreat from India and its loss of Canada were significant reverses, but these were essentially losses of potential which injured French prestige more than French power. At the Peace of Paris, France's retention of its Caribbean islands and its share of the North Atlantic fisheries and the African slave trade permitted it to preserve all the essentials of a global economic infrastructure. That proved more than an adequate platform from which to scheme revenge against Britain in the following generation.

Thus the great mid-century wars of the eighteenth century did not seem to bring the kind of decisive verdicts that the defeats of Louis XIV and Napoleon had in 1715 and 1815, respectively. Yet the impact of these wars cannot be underestimated. To begin with, they confirmed and accelerated the eastward shift of Europe's diplomatic framework. Spain and Holland, long in decline, clearly sank to secondary status, while the rise of Russia and the emergence of Prussia as great European powers were now uncontested facts. The Habsburg monarchy, too, fundamentally refocused its political world view from the Holy Roman Empire's concerns with its western frontier to the monarchy's central and east European core; that is, its Austrian, Bohemian, and Hungarian lands. The new European international system with its familiar five Great Powers survived well into the twentieth century, and some of the lessons learned in these wars survived along with it. For instance, in the Seven Years' War allied propaganda had argued that if Prussia were successful it would be seen as a vindication of Prussian militarism, and would force other countries to undertake similar "reforms." This growing militarization of society, to which the French Revolution's *levées en masse* added only a quantitative dimension, obviously so scarred European societies that only the virtual destruction of Europe in 1945 was able to bring a sobering reassessment of the virtues of such policies.

The economic dimensions were even more far-reaching. The quantum leap in global perspectives that these wars engendered not only heralded the Age of Imperialism, but also anticipated the day when hegemonic global powers understood that the most effective instruments of control were economic rather than territorial. Above all, however, it was the fiscal havoc wrought by these wars that had the most momentous consequences. Most immediately, the costs of these wars were instrumental in plunging France into a downward spiral of debt which was the primary cause of the French Revolution. For Britain, two very consequential results can be cited. On the negative side of the ledger, attempts to recover some of its costs by taxing its American colonists—who had demanded military intervention in the first place—led to rebellion and the eventual establishment of the United States of America. More positively, the financial infrastructure developed to finance the wars, particularly the effective tapping of public credit, laid the groundwork for the Industrial Revolution's capital market. On the European continent, numerous states, but above all the Habsburg monarchy, drew the lesson that the key to Great Power status lay in broad economic development and social emancipation, which animated the political agenda of Continental "enlightened absolutism" for the next three decades. Nor, finally, can one underestimate the importance of the fiscal dimension for cultural developments. In contrast to the lavish scale of patronage and expenditure in the baroque period, postwar fiscal restraint made the neoclassical ideal of "noble simplicity and quiet grandeur" not only more attractive, but also more affordable. The growing embourgeoisement of noble artistic patronage, and to some extent even the triumph of bourgeois culture in the late eighteenth century, can thus be attributed to these events.

Concluding in a more speculative vein, one could perhaps muse about the foundation laid for the global ascent of the British Empire and that of the English language, which accompanied it. Wary twentieth-century eyes might cast a suspicious glance back to the British expulsion of the Acadians from Nova Scotia in 1755 as the first great exercise in "ethnic cleansing." On an even larger scale, one might well wonder if the defeat of the French in North America, which burst the dam impeding the English colonists' westward drive, was not the defining moment in unleashing the full fury of Manifest Destiny on the indigenous peoples of North America. Whatever the merit—and pleasure—of such conjectural musings, it is clear that the apparently modest "cabinet wars" of the mid-eighteenth century were anything but modest in their import.

## SELECTED BIBLIOGRAPHY

Anderson, M. S. *The War of the Austrian Succession, 1740–1748.* New York: Longman, 1995. This eminently readable recent account is part of the Longman Modern Wars in Perspective series.

Black, Jeremy. *The Rise of the European Powers, 1679–1793.* New York: E. Arnold, 1990. An excellent English-language survey of eighteenth-century international relations with a good bibliography of older English-language works.

Brewer, John. *The Sinews of Power: War, Money, and the English State, 1688–1783.* New York: Alfred A. Knopf, 1989. One of the important new books addressing the problem of war finance and the impact of the war's fiscal dimension on the belligerents.

Browning, Reed. *The War of the Austrian Succession.* New York: St. Martin's Press, 1993. A recent comprehensive survey of the War of the Austrian Succession with an extensive bibliography of works in all major Western languages.

Cobban, Alfred, ed. *The Eighteenth Century: Europe in the Age of Enlightenment.* New York: McGraw-Hill, 1969. An older, lavishly illustrated survey of the principal features of eighteenth-century societies, with a good chapter on military developments.

Dann, Uriel. *Hanover and Great Britain, 1740–1760: Diplomacy and Survival.* New York: Leicester University Press, 1991. A brief but insightful account of the critical Hanoverian dimension of British foreign policy during the mid-century wars.

Dickson, P. G. M. *Finance and Government under Maria Theresa, 1740–1780.* 2 vols. New York: Oxford University Press, 1987. A magisterial survey that clarifies the complexities of Habsburg war finance.

Dorn, Walter L. *Competition for Empire, 1740–1763.* New York: Harper and Row, 1940. Though now somewhat dated, this lively and engaging volume from the Harper Rise of Modern Europe series is still the only comprehensive English introduction to the mid-century wars.

Duffy, Christopher. *The Army of Frederick the Great.* Newton Abbot: David and Charles, 1974.

———. *The Army of Maria Theresa: The Armed Forces of Imperial Austria, 1740–1780.* Vancouver: David and Charles, 1977.

———. *The Military Experience in the Age of Reason.* New York: Routledge and Kegan Paul, 1987.

———. *The Military Life of Frederick the Great.* New York Atheneum, 1986.

———. *Russia's Military Way to the West.* Boston: Routledge and Kegan Paul, 1981.

———. *The Wild Goose and the Eagle: A Life of Marshal von Browne, 1705–1757.* London: Chatto and Windus, 1964. These six volumes by the dean of eighteenth-century military historians give balanced accounts of the various military dimensions of the mid-century wars from the Austrian, Russian, and Prussian perspective.

McKay, Derek, and H. M. Scott. *The Rise of the Great Powers, 1648–1815.* New York: Longman, 1983. A useful analysis of European diplomatic relations from the Peace of Westphalia to the Congress of Vienna.

Middleton, R. *The Bells of Victory: The Pitt-Newcastle Ministry and the Conduct of the Seven Years' War.* Cambridge: Cambridge University Press, 1985. The most important modern account of the successful British prosecution of the Seven Years' War.

Riley, James C. *The Seven Years' War and the Old Regime in France: The Economic and Financial Toll.* Princeton, NJ: Princeton University Press, 1981. A careful and detailed analysis of the impact of the Seven Years' War on the French economy.

Schweizer, Karl W. *Frederick the Great, William Pitt, and Lord Bute: The Anglo-Prussian Alliance, 1756–1763.* New York: Garland, 1991. A recent survey of the Anglo-Prussian alliance during the Seven Years' War that contains important new insights.

Showalter, Dennis E. *The Wars of Frederick the Great.* New York: Longman, 1996. This important new assessment of Frederick II's military strategy is another volume in the Longman Modern Wars in Perspective series.

Szabo, Franz A. J. *Kaunitz and Enlightened Absolutism, 1753–1780.* New York: Cambridge University Press, 1994. The only major English-language study of the Austrian foreign minister, this work concentrates on domestic policy, but attempts to show the impact of the Seven Years' War on the Habsburg monarchy.

# 5

# The Enlightenment, c. 1750

## INTRODUCTION

Strictly speaking, the Enlightenment was a development rather than an event. It was a new way of looking at the world that emphasized reason and natural law at the expense of revealed truth and tradition, and it held out the promise of almost unlimited progress for mankind. The influence of the Enlightenment proved so great that the eighteenth century became known as the Age of Reason.

Many of the Enlightenment's antecedents can be found in the seventeenth century's Scientific Revolution. In particular, the discoveries of the English mathematician Isaac Newton laid the foundation for the Enlightenment. Newton's 1687 masterpiece, *Mathematical Principles of Natural Philosophy*, seemed to provide a plausible explanation for the operation of the physical universe. Relying on careful scientific observation and the use of human reason as opposed to divine intervention, Newton's research was universally acclaimed. By the time of his death in 1727, a growing number of Europeans aspired to become the Newtons of statecraft, economics, and justice, to name just a few disciplines.

Seventeenth-century philosophers also paved the way for the Enlightenment. By the middle of the century, the Englishman Francis Bacon and the Frenchman René Descartes had successfully attacked the underpin-

The nimble-witted Frenchman François-Marie Arouet, best known as Voltaire, was a driving force in the Enlightenment, an intellectual movement that extolled the virtues of reason. (Reproduced from the Collections of the Library of Congress)

nings of traditional intellectual inquiry. They argued that truth is knowable, but that it is not revealed. Rather, it must be discovered through painstaking observation and experimentation to which human reason must be applied. The implications were startling. If man could discover the truth, or how the laws of nature worked, then this knowledge could be used to create an ever better world.

Perhaps the most influential successor to Bacon and Descartes was the Englishman John Locke, whose late seventeenth-century writings enjoyed considerable popularity. Locke's commonsensical approach to problems struck a responsive chord. His *Essay Concerning Human Understanding* rejected the concept of innate ideas, or ideas held by all at birth, arguing instead that man's mind at birth resembled a blank sheet of paper. According to Locke, what man came to believe reflected his life experience, or the environment in which he lived. A poor environment led to the degradation of humanity; however, an enriched environment could lead to the improvement of the human race. Locke's ideas clearly suggested that policies designed to better the environment could and should be implemented; betterment of the human condition was clearly within man's grasp.

Locke was convinced that the betterment of the human condition depended upon the preservation of man's natural rights. In his *Two Treatises of Government*, published in 1690, Locke declared that men are "by nature free, equal, and independent," and that each man possesses certain natural rights, including life, liberty, and property. The question was how best to protect these rights so that man could achieve his full potential. Locke maintained that man, in order to protect his status and to enhance his rights, voluntarily enters into a contract with his fellow men to establish a government to fulfill this purpose. Thus government is not of divine origin; rather, it is created by mortal men to do their bidding. If it fails in this purpose—if, for example, it tramples upon the rights it was created to protect—then those who made it have the right to destroy it and create a new government in its place. Locke's ideas had a profound effect on the Age of Reason.

The Enlightenment, with its emphasis on the scientific collection of data, the discovery of natural laws, the employment of reason, and the conviction that progress for mankind was not only possible but probable, fired the imagination of most literate eighteenth-century Europeans. Its strongest supporters were called *philosophes*. Although not philosophers in the strictest sense, the *philosophes* employed the methodology of the Enlightenment to deal not only with philosophical questions but also with practical matters. Many of the *philosophes* were accomplished publicists, and they spread the views of the Enlightenment with—paradoxically—an almost religious-like fervor.

Probably the figure most closely identified with the Enlightenment is Voltaire. Born into a prosperous but nonnoble Parisian family in 1694, Voltaire began life as François-Marie Arouet. Witty and irreverent, he soon ran afoul of the authorities and was confined in the Bastille, a fortress-like prison in the heart of Paris. Upon gaining his release, he adopted the pen name Voltaire. After another brush with the law, he settled in England for several years, where he familiarized himself with Newton, Locke, and Shakespeare. Returning to France an unabashed Anglophile, Voltaire wrote his *Philosophical Letters on the English*, in which he heaped praise on the English for their relatively free society and their sense of religious toleration.

In fact, the need for toleration became a recurring theme in Voltaire's writings. Pouring out a steady stream of essays, letters, plays, commentaries, and histories, Voltaire employed a clever, sarcastic, satirical style to make his point. Writing with exceptional clarity, Voltaire lambasted the intolerant behavior of his contemporaries, especially organized religion. He despised the Roman Catholic Church, regarding it as a bastion of bigotry and superstition. In authoring the famous phrase *écrasez l'infâme* (crush the cursed thing), Voltaire called for an end to bigotry and superstition and implied that organized religion should be destroyed as well.

While Voltaire hated the Church, he was no atheist. Like many *philosophes*, he was a Deist. Deism likened God to a watchmaker and the universe to a complex timepiece. The watchmaker—or God—had created this unique timepiece—the universe—set it in motion, and walked away to pursue other interests. Deists ridiculed such ideas as miracles, supernatural revelation, divine intervention, and the power of prayer.

Still, Voltaire the rationalist saw a clear social value in religion. Unlike some of his contemporaries, Voltaire did not hold the human race in high regard. Like his onetime friend, Frederick the Great of Prussia, Voltaire thought that most men were stupid, greedy, and intemperate, and that religion served to keep the unruly masses from exploding.

In his most famous novel, *Candide*, Voltaire pointed out the imperfections in the world and mercilessly ridiculed those optimists who believed that the world as it then existed was the best of all possible worlds. *Candide* thus served to excite the growing number of Europeans who wanted fundamental changes in their society.

One *philosophe* who sought change was Montesquieu, a French nobleman born in 1689. Baron Montesquieu turned his considerable energies and his faith in the methodology of the Enlightenment to political questions. In his 1748 classic, *On the Spirit of the Laws*, Montesquieu concluded that no single type of government was superior. Rather, he argued that each country should have the type of government appropriate to its size, history, climate, traditions, and work force.

Like Voltaire, Montesquieu admired Great Britain, especially its constitution. He concluded that the British system of government worked so well because it rested on a separation of powers and a system of checks and balances. The separation of powers clearly divided governmental functions into three spheres—executive, legislative, and judicial. Furthermore, a system of checks and balances guaranteed that each of these spheres was independent of the others and supreme in its own realm. Consequently, the power to govern was diffused and the sanctity of individual liberty enhanced.

The career of Jean Jacques Rousseau presents a paradox. Not only was the neurotic Rousseau almost totally alienated from his fellow man, but much of what he wrote denied the primacy of reason and extolled the virtues of emotion. In this context, Rousseau should be seen as the father of nineteenth-century Romanticism, an intellectual movement that in many ways was the antithesis of the Enlightenment. However, in 1762 Rousseau wrote *The Social Contract*, one of the Age of Reason's major works. In *The Social Contract* Rousseau postulated a theory of modern democracy or, depending upon one's view, modern totalitarianism. Rousseau argued that "each of us puts his person and all his power in common under the supreme direction of the general will." Individual self-interests must be subordinated to the will of the community or the general will. In theory at least, *everyone* participates in the formulation of the general will and, once formulated, *everyone* must adhere to it. Thus the general will, as an expression of the people, is absolute, and all must conform to it.

While many *philosophes* focused on purely philosophical questions and others concentrated on political matters, yet another group of *philosophes*, called the Physiocrats, dealt with economic matters. Applying the methodology of the Enlightenment (which, of course, was based on the methodology of modern science), the Physiocrats sought through observation and experimentation to discover the natural laws of economics. Early Physiocrats such as the marquis of Mirabeau and the court physician François Quesnay asserted that all wealth derived from the land, and attacked mercantilism, the prevailing economic form of the time, which called for significant state regulation of economic life. The Physiocrats advocated that the state take a hands-off approach to the economy and encouraged a spirit of laissez-faire, or letting individuals do as they pleased in economic matters.

The most famous and effective advocate of laissez-faire economics was Adam Smith, a Scottish professor who published *An Inquiry into the Nature and Causes of the Wealth of Nations* in 1776. Smith synthesized the work of the Physiocrats. Emphasizing the primacy of natural law, he condemned mercantilism and urged that government's role in the economy be reduced to that of a passive bystander providing for national defense, ensuring domestic tranquility, and undertaking a limited number of public works that individuals would not attempt. Smith maintained that the economy, left free of regulation, would operate according to the laws of economics, the most important of which is the law of supply and demand. According to Smith and others, whenever individuals were able to pursue their economic self-interest, the end result would be the greatest good for the greatest number.

The great vehicle used to spread the ideas of the Enlightenment was the *Encyclopédie*, edited by Denis Diderot, the Age of Reason's most important publicist. The first volume of the *Encyclopédie* appeared in 1751 and the last in 1772. It included seventeen volumes of text and eleven volumes of illustrations. The *Encyclopédie* featured articles by all the masters of the Enlightenment, including Diderot and his chief assistant, Jean Le Rond d'Alembert, a major figure of the Enlightenment himself. Its purpose was to persuade rather than to inform. Diderot and his collaborators wanted both to expose the shortcomings of a society based on tradition and irrationality, and to introduce the reading public to the virtues of rational thought and the scientific method. Despite the opposition of both the Church and the state, the *Encyclopédie*, and the Enlightenment itself, succeeded with consequences that continue to be felt today.

---

## INTERPRETIVE ESSAY
### *Linda E. Mitchell*

The Enlightenment was not a single historical event, and it had a variety of impacts on the intellectual communities of Europe and America throughout the eighteenth century and into the nineteenth. The Enlightenment was also not a single unified system of concepts propounded by a coherent body of intellectuals; it included thinkers as diverse as Voltaire, Montesquieu, Jean Jacques Rousseau, Edward Gibbon, Immanuel Kant, and David Hume. All of these writers could be considered members of the Enlightenment community. They all agreed that the important intellectual issues of their world revolved around the place of reason in the intellectual scheme; the role of human progress in the development of civilization; the centrality of the human individual in the world scheme; and the definition of nature and its relation to God. However, they disagreed fundamentally on the focus, images, and motivations of the community itself and the ideas that seem to have defined it. Some of the most influential thinkers, such as Rousseau and Johann Gottfried von Herder, can be considered in many ways proponents of "anti-Enlightenment" perspectives. In addition, the political revolutions in English America and in France, which made claims to following a program of Enlightenment philosophy in championing the individual and in proclaiming their systems more rational than those that preceded them, were in fact antithetical to mainstream Enlightenment ideas that the philosopher should never be politically involved and that monarchy was an essential component of any political system in order to maintain public order. Thus, it is very difficult to discuss the impact of this "event" in a way that suggests that the impact was universally the same. The best way to approach it is to discuss a number of broad themes—reason, individualism, and progress—that were typically found in Enlightenment writing, to discuss the influence of those themes on the political, social, economic, and intellectual developments of the age, and to outline the internal conflicts within the Enlightenment community with respect to these themes.

The first broad theme is the Enlightenment emphasis on the superiority of reason over emotion. The origins of this idea lie in the seventeenth century rather than the eighteenth, in particular with the thinkers of the Scientific Revolution. Francis Bacon, Thomas Hobbes, John Locke, René Descartes, and above all, Isaac Newton all contributed to the Enlightenment idea that reason can overcome human fallibility and that humanity can progress (itself a theme that will be discussed further below) and be perfected through rational inquiry and rational activity. The Enlightenment also embodied a rejection of this idea of the superiority of reason in the work of Rousseau, who emphasized instead the emotional, and who considered the rationalist arguments to be the product of a decadent civilization. In this, as in so many ways, Rousseau represents a turning away from Enlightenment rationalism toward the dominant cultural phenomenon of the next century, Romanticism.

Although the Enlightenment consideration of reason as superior to emotion tended to dominate intellectual discourse, even those who agreed with this proposition disagreed on the meaning of the term. Some thinkers, especially those of the early French Enlightenment, continued to associate reason with the philosophy of rationalism developed by Descartes. Others, especially English intellectuals, associated reason with Baconian methods of scientific inquiry. Newton's synthesis of Baconian and Cartesian methods influenced the later years of the Enlightenment, in particular the years after Voltaire's and Jean Le Rond d'Alembert's championing of Newtonian physics, and prompted yet another change in the meaning of the term. Reason, for the so-called High Enlightenment and the years that followed, came to mean not just the superiority of the mind over the body (the Cartesian definition), or the superiority of experimentation over hypothesizing (the Baconian definition), but the superiority of science and the so-called scientific method over humanistic or impressionistic courses of study.

As an accompaniment to this valuation of science, the "language" of mathematics, first championed by Hobbes as the only rational form of discourse, and then appropriated by such thinkers and scientists as Gottfried Wilhelm Leibniz and Newton to use as the new language of physics, became the supreme symbol of rationality. Through mathematics humans could come to understand, in completely objective fashion, the "secrets" of the universe. This emphasis on mathematics not only advanced the development of new and different forms of calculus, analytic geometry, and other advanced mathematical systems, it also reinforced the perception that human language was somehow imperfect, and that a truly rational system would be expressed mathematically. It also suggested that humans would, in the end, be able to understand fully the nature of the universe through the language of mathematics. This, in turn, placed an even greater emphasis on the practice and study of the natural sciences, especially physics, as an intellectual pursuit superior to the study of the humanities. Such an emphasis had a significant influence on future centuries. For example, the nineteenth-century political philosopher Karl Marx called his theoretical system "scientific" socialism, thus implying that it was objective and rational, in comparison with the idealists who had preceded him.

The emphasis on reason and "objectivity" was seen not only within the scientific community. Indeed, the Enlightenment's intellectual world was quite small, and "humanist" philosophers and "natural" philosophers not only coexisted but also worked to blur the traditional distinctions between science and the humanities. Thus, political thinkers as diverse as Montesquieu (a monarchist) and Thomas Jefferson (a republican) proclaimed that a rational system of law and government was attainable, and that such a system would be representative of Locke's idea of "the consent of the governed."

The emphasis on reason also prompted philosophers outside the natural sciences, among them David Hume, to reject any approach to understanding the physical world and the world of human actions that rested on the "false science of metaphysics." Thus, Hume's highly influential essay against belief in miracles undermined the individual's adherence to the "revealed" truth of the Bible and to the possibility that God could transcend natural law. Hume's limitations on God's actions were supremely rational, and based on similar ideas presented by John Locke. If God is perfect, then God could create only a rational system of natural laws. God, therefore, cannot arbitrarily alter those laws in an irrational (and therefore imperfect) way to make miracles possible. Thus, even though Hume does not deny the existence of God (very few Enlightenment figures did so), he does call into question the possibility of a specifically Judeo-Christian God who is active in the world and can affect the day-to-day events of the world.

Hume was not alone in limiting the Supreme Being to working within a rational scheme and within a world of reason. While most Enlightenment thinkers, from Newton to Voltaire and beyond, acknowledged the existence of a Supreme Being, most also rejected organized religion as both irrational and man-made, and proposed instead a system usually known as deism in which God is the creator of the world but not a part of the world and therefore not active in it. In the United States after 1778, the postrevolutionary emphasis on the need for absolute religious toleration and the separation of organized religions and the political structure was a product of this emphasis on rational belief in God. While most Enlightenment *philosophes* (those who actively participated in the Enlightenment, helping to publicize and popularize it throughout the Western world) were not adherents of any particular organized religion, they tended to oppose them all on the principle that the dominance of one organization over others was irrational and therefore distasteful. Thus, there would be no rational need either to align a state with a particular religious perspective or to exalt one particular faith over the others.

Some *philosophes*, among them even Rousseau, rejected traditional religion as being empty superstition, but advocated the creation of a "civic" religion by the monarch or political leader as necessary for the maintenance of a civilized and moral society. The rejection, based on reason, of organized religion led other *philosophes*, particularly those who followed the philosophy of Baruch Spinoza, to a radical concept of pantheism, the idea that nature itself is divine and that God and nature are one. While very much in the minority—and while, indeed, occasionally persecuted for their beliefs—the radical pantheists were nonetheless significant to the Enlightenment in that such beliefs could be voiced and discussed relatively openly within the broadly based context of toleration which the rational religion of deism provided.

The emphasis on reason also had a significant effect on the development of social theories, as well as in the development of theories of gender. Although the *philosophes* claimed to be subjecting all conclusions of past intellectuals to the "light" of rational discourse, they nonetheless accepted without question many basic tenets of the past, particularly those of the classical Greek philosophers, Plato and Aristotle, in their studies of human behavior and human dynamics. The *philosophes* accepted without question the concept that the male was the more perfect biological form and that the female, if not "deformed," as Aristotle would have it, was at least a lesser form. Enlightenment thinkers ascribed reason in its highest form to human males and questioned whether females were indeed capable of rational thought. The chasm between mind and body that had developed in classical Greek culture widened in the Enlightenment to a virtual rejection of the female's ability to go beyond her physical nature and to attain reason. The legal systems that developed out of such emphases on reason embedded this conviction that only men could be truly rational into the very fiber of their laws. This development ultimately relegated women to the same category as children, the insane, and the mentally deficient: all submembers of humanity who are incapable of true rational thought, all of whom should be bounded by the institution of adult male dominance.

This situation prompted protests by both female and male authors—although the protesters were more typically female—all of whom used Enlightenment theory against male claims to superiority. For example, Abigail Adams' famous letter to her husband, John, in which she urged him to "remember the ladies," presented her protest against the continued oppression of women within the family in the same terms that John and his fellow members of the Continental Congress used to protest the oppression of the American colonists by the English monarchy and Parliament. In the later years of the eighteenth century, in part in response to the French Revolution, Mary Wollstonecraft, Germaine de Staël, and Olympe de Gouges all wrote in defense of the rights of women, in particular their rights as citizens and their rights to receive both equal employment and an education equal to that enjoyed by men.

The assumed incapacity of women to attain reason was linked to the belief that women were "feeling" creatures rather than "rational" ones; that women were defined by their biology in ways that men were not. Even if women might potentially be able to achieve rationality, as some *philosophes* suggested, they nonetheless were physically incapable of that achievement because they were "swamped" by their sensory perceptions and therefore could not concentrate on one idea at a time, the process of reflection thought necessary for attaining reason.

These ideas are illustrated quite clearly in one of the most important documents of the Enlightenment, Diderot and d'Alembert's *Encyclopédie*. In this vast compendium of knowledge and Enlightenment opinion, the articles on "Man" consider the most enlightened form the *honnête homme*, or honorable man, defined as the bourgeois (as opposed to the aristocratic) ideal: hardworking, responsible, and willing to accept his obligations to public life and the state, no matter the consequences. The *honnête femme*, on the other hand, is defined as a mother who is chaste and virtuous, and who nurtures and cares for her husband and children selflessly and submissively. This description is the foundation for the nineteenth-century notion of the wife/mother as the "angel" of the house; it led, in the eighteenth century, to a distinction between morality, which was seen as a domestic virtue, and reason, which was a public virtue divorced from morality, thus justifying doctrines of political and social expediency as rationally good even when they were morally questionable.

Some modern-day historians have seen in these debates about the nature of women the virtual invention of "gender" as a social definition divorced from the biological nature of "sex." What is ironic about the rejection of the female's ability to reason is that the environment of the Enlightenment *philosophes*, particularly those in France, was significantly dependent on women. Women acted as hostesses to meetings of *philosophes* which were referred to as "salons"; they patronized writers, artists, and musicians who would have been indigent without the financial assistance of their female patrons; and they supported the program of the Enlightenment even while being spurned as actors in that program. For example, the creators of the *Encyclopédie*, including d'Alembert, the marquis de Condorcet, and the baron de Turgot, all frequented the salon of Mademoiselle de Lespinasse even though their intellectual work denied women a place in the "Republic of Letters." In England the rejection of female participation was much more overt: the Enlightenment thinkers of that country popularized the exclusively male gentleman's club and the equally exclusive coffeehouse as the appropriate venues for intellectual discourse. Rousseau himself championed these all-male institutions as "defeminizing" the intellectual milieu and advocated their development in France.

The focus on reason also led Enlightenment thinkers to reject the influence of the historical past on the present day and to propose a kind of "end" of history. In many ways, the preeminent intellectual work of the Enlightenment was Edward Gibbon's *Decline and Fall of the Roman Empire*, which encapsulated many Enlightenment ideas. Gibbon proclaimed the "end" of history in the "modern" age of the eighteenth century, which had finally emerged from the darkness of the past into the light of modernity. He rejected the culture of Christianity and praised the classical past on the basis that Greek and Roman philosophy, politics, and law all represent the development of rational systems which were hopelessly lost during the Middle Ages (another idea coined during the Enlightenment). Gibbon defended the creation of "masculine" systems based on classical models and rejected the "feminization" of culture which had infected the rationalism of Rome through the adoption of Christianity. The rejection of the past led some *philosophes* to claim that they could create a "new world order" which was purely rational and which was uninfluenced by the emotionalism and decadence of Europe's historical past.

Finally, reason was conceived of as a universal ideal, one which would be shared by all cultures when they reached the level of civilization enjoyed by Europe in the eighteenth century. This claim to universality was possibly one of the most influential, as well as one of the most diabolical, intellectual claims made by the *philosophes*. It presupposed that the rationalism of the *philosophes* was not influenced by cultural attitudes, historical trends, or human fallibility. It was enshrined as an all-encompassing system, one that had universal application: rational laws could be devised that would pertain to all cultures. The *philosophes'* belief in the validity of their system led to their conclusion that European culture and its emphasis on scientific inquiry along Western models was the goal to be attained by all other cultures. This belief in the universality of western European rational systems, then, justified the imperialism of the later eighteenth century and also justified attempts to wipe out cultural pluralism (i.e., the maintenance of minority ethnic cultures in areas dominated by one particular culture) within Europe itself, for example in Great Britain with respect to Ireland and Wales.

This concept of the universality of reason had detractors even within Enlightenment thought. Herder, in particular, proposed a model of cultural relativism which claimed that each cultural system is rational for its particular "climate": its geography and physical boundaries. More-over, all cultures contain a "spirit" of the nation which is specific and appropriate to each. Thus, what is good for England is not necessarily best for France; what is rational in Germany might not be rational in Russia. This view, formed at the end of the Enlightenment, led to the nationalism of the nineteenth century: one of the most influential ideologies of the modern age.

A second broad theme is the Enlightenment emphasis on the importance of the individual in creating a rational system. The *philosophes* did not believe that communal action could bring about a rational culture; indeed, the origin of theories of crowd psychosis could be found in Enlightenment glorification of the individual over the collective. Although this idea of the individual had been evident in earlier intellectual movements, such as Renaissance humanism, the Enlightenment concept of the individual was much more powerfully influential. It contained Locke's idea of the need for consent in the development of a "civil" government, and thereby influenced the creation of revolutionary documents such as the American Declaration of Independence and the French Declaration of the Rights of Man and of the Citizen. It contained the Newtonian idea of the power of the individual intellect mastering the intricacies of the universe through the study of physics and mathematics, thereby influencing the development of the most significant nineteenth-century theories of history, those of Hegel and Nietzsche. In addition, rejection of the centrality of the individual, such as that expressed by Karl Marx and by Rousseau's concept of the general will, was couched in Enlightenment terms.

The power of the individual in Enlightenment thought also significantly influenced ideas about society and gender distinctions in the eighteenth century. The concept of the equality of man was thoroughly intertwined with the concept of individual authority. Together they produced the possibility of an egalitarian state in theory, but in practice most Enlightenment *philosophes* did not see all individuals as inherently equal or endowed with the "inalienable" right to pursue "happiness." For the *philosophes*, such rights were extended only to those individuals who embodied the capacity for reason; and for most of the Enlightenment thinkers this meant adult males of the middle classes and above. The very claims that empowered these males, mandated their education, and exalted their position as individuals marginalized the working class, the poor, and all women. Only members of the so-called radical Enlightenment supposed that Locke's concept of inalienable rights related to all of humanity. This radical fringe, condemned by most monarchist *philo-*

*sophes* as "republicans," was eventually to influence the ideologues of two of the most important political events of the eighteenth century: the American and French Revolutions.

The difficulty that moderate *philosophes* experienced with assigning rationality to all humans can be seen particularly in the problematic relationship that Enlightenment thinkers had with female monarchs such as Catherine the Great of Russia and Christina of Sweden, both of whom embraced Enlightenment ideas. The *philosophes* with whom they corresponded paid them the highest compliment they could think of: they proclaimed them men, and thus capable of attaining reason and of acting in the world as free individuals.

The third broad theme of the Enlightenment is the idea of human progress from a state of barbarism to a state of rational civilization. Unlike philosophers of the ancient world, who theorized that their contemporary state was a state of decline from a presumed "golden" age, and unlike the theologians of the Middle Ages, who believed that humanity was being punished by having to live in the world and to mourn its fall from a state of perfection in the Garden of Eden, the *philosophes* of the Enlightenment believed that their age was one that could transcend previous ages and that humanity could, in fact, progress toward a more perfect state of being. Intimately connected with the supremacy of reason and the value of scientific discourse, this concept of human progress has had far-reaching implications since its late seventeenth- and early eighteenth-century origins. First, the concept of progress was a supremely optimistic view of humanity. Second, the Enlightenment thinkers created specific criteria for what they determined to be progressive: anything that could be termed rational or scientific, or that conformed to the "laws" of nature and of science. A significant corollary to this idea of progress was the idea of harnessing or controlling nature, which was perceived as being in need of human control. Thus, the beginnings of industrialization in England and in America were hailed as progressive, rational, and logical. The possible effects of industrialization—pollution, unemployment, exploitation, destruction of natural resources, and so on—were considered inconsequential to the more important goal of progress. The economic theories of Adam Smith, who proposed a capitalist, free-market economy as the only rational system, led to the idea that competition (or what Smith referred to as "the war of all against all") in the marketplace brought progress. This idea in turn led to other views of competition as progress: Thomas Malthus' idea of the competition for resources, which results in the appropriate and rational impoverishing of the working class in order to promote a progressive economy; Charles

Darwin's idea of the evolution of species being dependent on competition among members for scarce resources in which the strongest survive; and ultimately Marx's idea that the struggle between classes results in revolutionary upheavals by which civilization progresses from a state of master-slave relationships to a state of egalitarian freedom.

Another issue influenced by Enlightenment concepts of human progress was that of penal punishment and the care of the insane. The incarceration of criminals and the insane in institutions was seen as a rational act, and one which was progressive, even while certain kinds of punishment, such as the use of torture, were perceived as inhumane and regressive. Humanity was seen as limited in its ability to progress unless inherently unstable elements of the population were placed under strict regulation and control. This idea led to the penal colony and the insane asylum, institutions that separated the "uncivilized" from the civilized. To some extent, both of these institutions were also seen as prescriptive or corrective. Both moral depravity and insanity began to be considered as diseases: criminal behavior could be construed as a social disease, while insanity was considered a "mental illness." Thus, penal colonies and insane asylums not only served to separate the uncivilized from the civilized, but were also seen as beneficial and instructive. The inmate of either institution could, in theory, be "rehabilitated" and could return to civilized life as a healthy and responsible member of society.

The conviction that humanity is progressing along rational lines also led to the establishment of strictly patriarchal conceptions of marriage and family that became embedded in the revisions of national law that "enlightened" despots, such as Frederick the Great of Prussia, promulgated in their kingdoms. Frederick's revision of law was hailed as an embodiment of Enlightenment ideals. In the section on the "family-state," Frederick outlines the family structure that will prevail in Prussia: "Hence it follows, judging by the sole light of reason, that the husband is master of his own household, and head of his family. And as the wife enters into it of her own accord, she is in some measure subject to his power."

The wife is seen not as an individual, but as the husband's "assistant" in the family. Such changes in the law, based on Enlightenment principles, can be seen at their strictest in the law code promulgated by Napoleon, which designates men as the only political and legal "persons" in the empire and which substantially limits the rights of women, some of which, such as inheritance of land, they had previously enjoyed during the so-called Dark Ages.

The belief in the ability of rational men to construct rational structures, ones governed by immutable and universal laws, led to changes not only in legal codes and in government, but also in the fine arts, literature, and music. The rejection of the baroque as an artistic style that emphasized the artificial and the decorative elements in art and music, and the adoption of neoclassicism as a "natural" and "rational" style constituted a significant step in the development of Enlightenment ideals. The eighteenth century witnessed the development of strict laws of musical composition, as well as of artistic style, which emphasized proportion, balance, and simplicity, in contrast to the florid and exuberantly complex decorative style of the baroque. It was also the era in which the modern novel was developed, a literary genre bounded by strict rules even though novelists tended to chafe against the restrictions of the form. Poetry and drama were also made to conform to "rational" strictures; the poetry and drama of the ancient world, in particular of Greece in the fifth century B.C., became the literary model, just as fifth-century architectural styles became the model for the designers of châteaux and manor houses in Europe and of public buildings and universities in America.

The Enlightenment was above all an intellectual movement. Despite its popularity among the learned community, the precepts of the movement did not always translate smoothly into practical political activity. In many ways, the political and social tensions of postrevolutionary Europe illustrate the problems inherent in applying Enlightenment ideology to actual events. The French Revolution was claimed by its proponents to be a direct outgrowth of the Enlightenment: it was a movement that based its principles on Lockean and Rousseauian models of the social contract; it proclaimed the rights of the individual; it rejected the authority of the established Church. Even its mode of execution—the guillotine—was considered to be rational, humane, and a product of advanced technology (as well as being efficient). The supporters of the French Revolution were initially empowered by its success. Authors, such as Mary Wollstonecraft, who defended the actions of the French revolutionaries could justify further political radicalism (such as Wollstonecraft's defense of the rights of women) as being the rational outcome of the Enlightenment program.

The critics of the French Revolution were at first disadvantaged by the success of the first French republic; however, the overthrow of the liberal government and its replacement with the so-called Reign of Terror brought about a reversal in their fortunes. Now the critics could claim that the revolution was, in fact, an anti-Enlightenment event. Proponents of the more moderate Enlightenment program who supported monarchy, even the political regime known as enlightened despotism, and a limited franchise of landowning and merchant elites could disavow the political radicals who claimed to share their vision of a rational and ordered world. The radicals themselves disagreed about the course of the revolution: it was difficult to justify as rational and logical the slaughter of thousands in the Terror and the pan-European conquests of Napoleon. While both sides of the debate over the French Revolution could claim Enlightenment antecedents for their ideas, neither side could claim that its position was entirely consistent with mainstream Enlightenment ideology. In the end, political leaders at the Congress of Vienna decided on pragmatic solutions to their political conflicts; dedication to philosophical ideals was not conducive to success in practical politics, although those solutions were couched in the language of reason and moderation.

Ultimately, the impact of the Enlightenment on the eighteenth century can be seen best in the resistance of some important intellectuals to its most significant elements, the emphasis on reason and rationality, the championing of the individual over the collective, and the optimistic belief in human progress as coming about through scientific and technological advancement. In the late eighteenth and early nineteenth century, the resistance to Enlightenment precepts coalesced in Romanticism, a countermovement that deliberately and consciously rejected anything that smacked of "enlightened" rationality. The Romantics championed emotion over reason, rejected the idea of universal and immutable laws, and embraced the vision of the uncultivated natural world as better representing the glory of God than did human civilization and advanced science and technology. Beginning with Rousseau and Herder, and continuing with the developers of German Romanticism such as Johann Wolfgang von Goethe and Johann Christoph Friedrich von Schiller and the early nineteenth-century English poets Lord Byron, Percy Bysshe Shelley, and John Keats, some intellectuals turned their backs on the complacency of Enlightenment optimism and returned to the exploration of those elements of human endeavor and the natural world that the Enlightenment had rejected: the glories of Gothic architecture, the emotional impact of medieval romantic literature, and the pristine beauty of the preindustrial countryside. This retreat from rationalism did not occur spontaneously. Rather, it developed directly out of the same seventeenth-century sources the Enlightenment had used: Descartes, Locke, Newton, and so on. The difference was that the Romantics appropriated elements of these systems of thought that the *philosophes* had rejected, especially those elements that championed mystical experience and oneness with nature, and that downplayed the centrality of the human mind in human progress. Just as the Enlightenment could not divorce itself entirely from the philosophies, ideas, and contexts that had preceded it, so too did Romanticism incorporate and appropriate what it found relevant from its predecessors.

## SELECTED BIBLIOGRAPHY

Anderson, M. S. *Europe in the Eighteenth Century, 1713–1783*. 3rd ed. London: Longman, 1987. The chapter on the Enlightenment provides a useful introduction to the topic, and the bibliography is excellent.

Behrens, Laurence, and Leonard J. Rosen. "Part III: Hobbes and the Social Contract" and "Part IV: Condorcet and the Progress of Civilization." In *Theme and Variations: The Impact of Great Ideas*. Glenview, IL: Scott, Foresman, 1988. A useful introduction to two important ideas of the Enlightenment. The authors introduce a series of primary sources, dating from the seventeenth to the twentieth century which outline the development of particular ideas across different disciplines and over time.

Berlin, Isaiah. "Herder and the Enlightenment." In *Aspects of the Eighteenth Century*, pp. 47–105. Edited by Earl R. Wasserman. Baltimore: Johns Hopkins University Press, 1965. An important article on one of the most controversial iconoclasts of the eighteenth century. Herder is seen both as a figure of the Enlightenment and as one of the founders of Romanticism.

———, ed. *The Age of Enlightenment*. New York: New American Library, 1956. This collection of essays discusses primarily the principal English philosophers, such as Locke, Berkeley, and Hume, who in turn influenced the French Enlightenment.

Boas, George. "In Search of the Age of Reason." In *Aspects of the Eighteenth Century*, pp. 1–20. Edited by Earl R. Wasserman. Baltimore: Johns Hopkins University Press, 1965. Explores the complex diversity of ideas during the Enlightenment, with particular reference to changing uses of the term "reason" from the followers of Cartesian rationalism to the proponents of Lockean and Newtonian experimental methods.

Cassirer, Ernst. *The Philosophy of the Enlightenment*. Translated by Fritz C. A. Koelln and James P. Pettegrove. Boston: Beacon Press, 1951. This is a standard interpretation of the Enlightenment's various issues from the nature of the mind to the nature of aesthetics. Although extensively critiqued by more recent scholars, it remains an important work.

Eliot, Simon, and Beverley Stern, eds. *The Age of Enlightenment*. 2 vols. Totowa, NJ: Barnes and Noble, 1979. A comprehensive collection of sources focusing on art and culture as well as political, philosophical, and historical matters.

Foucault, Michel. *Discipline and Punish: The Birth of the Prison*. Translated by Alan Sheridan. New York: Pantheon Books, 1977. This famous French historian traces the growing rationalization of public institutions which were deeply affected by Enlightenment philosophy.

Fox-Genovese, Elizabeth. "Women and the Enlightenment." In *Becoming Visible:*

*Women in European History*, pp. 251–278. Edited by Renate Bridenthal, Claudia Koonz, and Susan Mosher Stuard. 2nd ed. Boston: Houghton Mifflin, 1987. A good introduction to both women's involvement in the Enlightenment and the Enlightenment debates about women and their roles.

Gay, Peter. *The Age of Enlightenment*. New York: Time, 1966. Although essentially a picture book, this introduction to the eighteenth century is valuable for its overview of the relationship among politics, culture, art, and society.

———. *The Enlightenment: An Interpretation*. 2 vols. New York: Alfred A. Knopf, 1967. The standard interpretation of the Enlightenment, although many historians have since critiqued Gay's evaluation.

Goodman, Dea. *The Republic of Letters: A Cultural History of the French Enlightenment*. Ithaca, NY: Cornell University Press, 1994. A recent work that emphasizes the central role of the salon in the development of the Enlightenment community.

Guerlac, Henry. "Where the Statue Stood: Divergent Loyalties to Newton in the Eighteenth Century." In *Aspects of the Eighteenth Century*, pp. 317–334. Edited by Earl R. Wasserman. Baltimore: Johns Hopkins University Press, 1965. Guerlac explores how Newton's scientific method worked and discusses the different ways in which Enlightenment *philosophes* appropriated and adapted Newton's ideas.

Hampson, Norman. *The Enlightenment*. Harmondsworth: Penguin Books, 1968. Volume 4 in the Pelican History of European Thought series, this is one of the best introductions to the history of the Enlightenment.

Hertzberg, Arthur. *The French Enlightenment and the Jews*. New York: Columbia University Press, 1968. An important book about a little discussed subject; the author finds both the development of modern (i.e., nineteenth- and twentieth-century) anti-Semitism and the toleration of Jewishness in the debates of the Enlightenment.

Hulliung, Mark. *The Autocritique of Enlightenment: Rousseau and the Philosophes*. Cambridge, MA: Harvard University Press, 1994. A recent work by an important scholar, this book critiques the contention that Rousseau was an anti-Enlightenment figure.

———. *Montesquieu and the Old Regime*. Berkeley: University of California Press, 1976. The author places Montesquieu's political works in the context of republican political philosophy.

Im Hof, Ulrich. *The Enlightenment*. Translated by William E. Yuill. Oxford: Basil Blackwell, 1994. A recent, excellent overview of the period that addresses political, social, economic, and cultural perspectives in creating a synthesis of the various elements of eighteenth-century history.

Jacob, Margaret C. *Living the Enlightenment: Freemasonry and Politics in Eighteenth-Century Europe*. New York: Oxford University Press, 1991. This work explores the development of freemasonry in the context of both Enlightenment ideas and the community of intellectuals who made up the Enlightenment.

———. *The Radical Enlightenment: Pantheists, Freemasons and Republicans*. London: George Allen and Unwin, 1981. Jacob traces the development of "radical" (i.e., antimonarchist and anti-organized religion) ideas from their Newtonian, Lockean, and Hobbesian origins to their acceptance in "mainstream" French Enlightenment thought between the 1770s and the French Revolution.

Jacob, Margaret C., and Wijnand W. Mijnhardt, eds. *The Dutch Republic in the Eighteenth Century: Decline, Enlightenment, and Revolution.* Ithaca, NY: Cornell University Press, 1992. A collection of essays that presents a variety of views regarding the influence on and the impact of the Enlightenment in the Dutch Republic.

Spencer, Samia I., ed. *French Women and the Age of Enlightenment.* Bloomington: Indiana University Press, 1984. This collection of essays is devoted to the contributions of and the intellectual debates about women in the period.

Steinbrügge, Lieselotte. *The Moral Sex: Woman's Nature in the French Enlightenment.* Translated by Pamela E. Selwyn. New York: Oxford University Press, 1995. Steinbrügge makes a convincing argument for finding the origins of modern-day misogyny in the work of the popularizers of French Enlightenment thought such as Diderot and the authors of the *Encyclopédie.*

Trumbach, Randolph. "Sex, Gender, and Sexual Identity in Modern Culture: Male Sodomy and Female Prostitution in Enlightenment London." In *Forbidden History: The State, Society, and the Regulation of Sexuality in Modern Europe*, pp. 89–106. Edited by John C. Fout. Chicago: University of Chicago Press, 1992. An important article on a controversial topic: the development, with the Enlightenment, of modern notions of male and female gender as referring exclusively to heterosexual beings, the demotion of male bisexuality to a third, inferior gender, and the development of female prostitution as a "necessary evil" which ensures that unmarried males will maintain their gender distinction.

Voltaire. *"Candide," "Zadig," and Selected Stories.* Translated, with an introduction by Donald M. Frame. New York: Penguin Books, 1961. One famous and several lesser-known works by the great popularizer of the French Enlightenment. *Candide*, especially, is a must-read for students of the period.

Wuthnow, Robert. "Part II: The Enlightenment." In *Communities of Discourse: Ideology and Social Structure in the Reformation, the Enlightenment, and European Socialism.* Cambridge, MA: Harvard University Press, 1989. Good study of the social, economic, and political contexts of the Enlightenment with an interesting theory on why it occurred in some European regions—England, France, Scotland, and Prussia—but not in others.

# 6

# The Agricultural Revolution, c. 1750

## INTRODUCTION

When the word "revolution" is mentioned, one usually thinks of tumult, chaos, and confusion in a rapidly changing environment frequently characterized by bloodshed and the use of great force. By those standards, the agricultural transformation of the eighteenth century does not qualify as a revolution. Rather, the changes that define the Agricultural Revolution came slowly and gradually over the decades. There was little disorder and no bloodshed, and reason rather than force prevailed. Nevertheless, few can deny that "an assertedly momentous change," the dictionary definition of revolution, did in fact occur.

The Agricultural Revolution comprised a new and radical approach to farming and animal husbandry. At the start of the eighteenth century, the vast majority of Europeans were engaged in agriculture. With the possible exception of Holland, at least 80 percent of Europeans farmed, and that percentage increased as one moved in an easterly direction across the Continent.

Farming in 1700 proceeded in a manner little different from how it had proceeded several hundred years earlier. Hordes of peasants worked the land, but they received only a meager bounty in return. Yields were low, and crop failure due to flood and drought remained common. When

In the eighteenth century, agricultural labor remained a backbreaking task; however, new farming techniques and tools greatly increased the yield and led to better nutrition for all. (Reproduced from the Collections of the Library of Congress)

that occurred, famine was a possibility. Fields, which were open as opposed to enclosed, were divided into numerous long, narrow strips and were farmed communally. The village as a whole decided what to plant, when to plant, and when to harvest. This open-field system meant that the peasants would usually be able to survive, but it precluded more efficient and hence more productive forms of agriculture. Soil exhaustion remained a major problem, and the eighteenth-century peasant, like his medieval counterpart, dealt with this by rotating crops so that every other year, or every third year, a field would lie fallow. While this preserved the soil, it also withdrew from production annually anywhere from 33 percent to 50 percent of the arable land. Each village had its common, or meadow and pasture lands, where a variety of animals—individually owned by the peasants—intermingled freely as they grazed.

This pattern was almost universal; only the Dutch farmed differently. Driven by the pressure of a large population crowded into a small area, and open to experimentation, the Dutch had developed techniques that allowed them to farm more intensively and efficiently than their neighbors. For example, they excelled at draining land and making it useful for crops. They also introduced new crops, rotated old crops, and enclosed their fields. When the Agricultural Revolution arrived, its greatest supporters, the English, copied the Dutch with enthusiasm and success.

To a large extent, the Agricultural Revolution emanated from the Scientific Revolution and the Enlightenment. The former, with its interest in practical concerns, provided a wealth of new knowledge about plants and animals that the eighteenth century subsequently put to good use. The latter spurred men to explore and experiment in the belief that rational undertakings could lead to substantial material benefits. Early Romanticism also contributed. By the middle of the century, an increasing number of wealthy landowners, lured by a newfound love of nature, abandoned the city for their country estates. There they became gentlemen farmers, conducting agricultural experiments and overseeing the rational exploitation of their property.

Perhaps the profit motive provided the greatest spur to agricultural change. From at least 1740, agricultural prices—but especially grain prices—moved upward, giving growers a real incentive to increase output. For the growers, new and more effective methods of raising crops meant bigger yields, and bigger yields meant a greater surplus for an expanding market and, hence, greater profits.

The Agricultural Revolution consisted of several interlocking parts. Placing more land under cultivation was an important feature. In England, many of the fens and marshes that dotted the countryside were drained and filled. As early as the middle of the seventeenth century, Dutch engineers had reclaimed 40,000 acres in Cambridgeshire; in the next century, native Englishmen continued and accelerated this process.

Even more important was the introduction of crop rotation, which did away with the fallow. Once again the English made exceptional progress, but they copied the Dutch. Grain crops tend to drain the land, thereby requiring a period of rest, or fallow, for the soil to recover. In order to eliminate the fallow, the Dutch—followed by the English—began to plant nitrogen-storing crops that replenished the soil. Peas, beans, turnips, potatoes, and clover all helped to restore the soil. The planting of these crops paid several important dividends. By eliminating the fallow, the amount of land given over to crop raising increased by 33 to 50 percent per year. Furthermore, many of the new crops provided food for the peasants, thereby augmenting their caloric intake and improving their nutrition. If the peasants did not consume the new crops, livestock did. With more fodder for animals, the need to slaughter livestock to avoid having them starve to death over the winter months disappeared. Consequently, there were more animals, and this meant not only more meat in the average human diet but also more fertilizer, which, in turn, meant healthier, more productive soil. The end result of better soil was another component part of the Agricultural Revolution—larger crop yields per acre.

Not only did the Agricultural Revolution witness an increase in the number of animals, but the quality of those animals improved dramatically thanks to better breeding methods, yet another part of the Agricultural Revolution. Between 1710 and 1795, the weight of the average animal sold at London's Smithfield market doubled. As with more animals, better animals resulted in more meat in the average person's diet.

New crop cultivation was also an important part of the Agricultural Revolution. In particular, the potato flourished. Brought to Europe from the New World, cultivation of the potato gradually spread across Europe. It could be grown virtually anywhere in Europe, and it soon became a staple in the diet of poorer Europeans ranging from Ireland to Russia. In *European History in a World Perspective* the historian Samuel B. Clough writes that "no other plant produces so much nutrition per acre at so low a cost and under so many and varied conditions of soil and climate."

Finally, new and improved tools figured prominently in the Agricultural Revolution. For example, modifications to the plow included the colter in front of the share to make more effective vertical cuts in the sod and the moldboard to turn the sod over more efficiently.

One of the Agricultural Revolution's great mechanical innovators was Jethro Tull (1674–1741), a landholder who was representative of the "improving landlords," a group of gentlemen farmers responsible for introducing important changes in English agriculture. Taking a cue from the French peasants of the Languedoc region, Tull perfected a horse-drawn hoe that effectively killed weeds between rows of crops. That crops were grown in rows rather than haphazardly is also traceable to Tull. In order to replace the wasteful and inefficient broadcasting of seed, Tull invented a seed drill that allowed for the planting of single seeds in rows at a uniform distance and depth.

Viscount Charles Townshend (1674–1738) also played a prominent role in the Agricultural Revolution. While serving as English ambassador to Holland, Townshend observed the crop rotation practiced by Dutch farmers. Upon his return to England and retirement from diplomatic service, Townshend applied the Dutch lessons to his estates in Norfolk. Instead of letting his fields lie fallow, Townshend planted them with clover and turnips. These crops not only replenished the soil, but also provided fodder for his livestock. Townshend was so enthusiastic about the use of turnips as a crop that he earned the nickname Turnip Townshend.

Townshend's methods were further improved upon by Thomas William Coke (1752–1842), later earl of Leicester. Coke developed a four-crop rotation scheme that became known as the Norfolk System and was eventually adopted throughout much of England. By planting wheat, turnips, barley, and clover in succession, Coke eliminated the fallow altogether.

Coke also engaged in the selective breeding of pigs, but the most important figure in this sphere of the Agricultural Revolution was Robert Bakewell (1725–1795). Bakewell was determined to change the prevalent system of animal husbandry, which featured "the haphazard union of nobody's son with everybody's daughter." He advised against the prevailing practice of allowing animals to run loose on the common and urged that the best animals be segregated, stabled, and bred. Using this formula, Bakewell developed the Leicestershire breed of sheep. His experiments resulted in significant improvement in the size and quality of English cattle as well.

News of this revolution in agriculture was spread chiefly by Arthur Young (1741–1820), an indefatigable publicist and enthusiastic gentleman farmer. Young published more than 250 books and articles on scientific farming and edited the *Annals of Agriculture*, which included among its contributors King George III, who was nicknamed Farmer George.

Young, who traveled widely promoting the cause of modern farming, was instrumental in the creation of the British Board of Agriculture in 1793.

As the Agricultural Revolution gained momentum, it became apparent that the open-field system stood in the way of more efficient farming. The result in England was to accelerate the enclosure movement, which dated back to Tudor times. As its name implies, the enclosure movement called for the consolidation of farming strips and the erection of fences or hedges to distinguish one plot from another. It also required the division and hence disappearance of the common. Many smaller farmers objected to this, but during the eighteenth century Parliament bent to the wishes of the well-to-do who favored enclosure. Between 1700 and 1760, Parliament passed on the average four enclosure acts per year; between 1760 and 1792 that figure grew to forty per year, and between 1798 and 1815 it reached eighty per year.

George III was not the only famous figure to embrace the Agricultural Revolution. George Washington, Thomas Jefferson, Lafayette, Frederick the Great, and Catherine the Great all enthusiastically lent their support. Although the Agricultural Revolution initially appeared in England, the Low Countries, and France, it gradually spread throughout the world.

---

## INTERPRETIVE ESSAY
### *Robert D. Cornwall*

To speak of the Agricultural Revolution of the eighteenth century is not to speak of a technologically driven revolution. True technological innovation did not occur until the end of the eighteenth century with the beginnings of the Industrial Revolution. While the agricultural revolutions in the nineteenth century depended more on improvements in technology, the Agricultural Revolution of the eighteenth century relied largely on improved land usage, the development of new farming techniques, and the introduction of new crops. The absence of significant technological innovation has led some scholars to discount the existence of this revolution. However, the rate of growth in production on English farms suggests that some kind of revolution did occur.

European farmers as a whole made a variety of improvements in agriculture that led to a tremendous boost in productivity. Nowhere was this more true than in England. This revolution, however, did not begin with a recognizable bang. Scholars continue to disagree about when the revolution began. They also differ about its geographic extent. Nonetheless, all scholars agree that something important happened in the agricultural world of the eighteenth century.

Agricultural improvement could be found throughout Europe and the Americas during this period. However, only in England did production increases reach revolutionary proportions. During the nineteenth century, the progress achieved by England spread to its former colonies in North America and to the rest of Europe. England's farmers and landowners had begun to improve their lands even before the eighteenth century. The eighteenth century brought together all of the essential components for a substantial increase in agricultural productivity: demand for food, improved transportation, a growing population, progress in animal breeding, new crops, and better farming techniques. These improvements and the growing need for greater efficiency led to innovation. As the good harvests of the first half of the century drove down prices, landowners and farmers needed to find cost-effective ways to meet the demand for produce while remaining financially sound.

While the English revolution in agriculture occurred during the eighteenth century, Holland experienced the earliest stages of the revolution during the sixteenth and seventeenth centuries. As that tiny country moved from a rural to an urban population, it found it necessary to increase its agricultural productivity. At the beginning of the eighteenth century, England found itself in a similar situation. English farmers put into use farming techniques and new crops derived from Holland, thereby enabling the country to support an economy less dependent on a large rural and agrarian population. Similar pressures from population growth would help spread the revolution to North America, France, and the remainder of Europe during the nineteenth century.

The improvements and innovations of the revolution were highly interrelated. Improvements in stock raising and breeding joined with the introduction of new crops to help better use land that no longer could sustain the yields of earlier years. Throughout the century, considerable amounts of land were restored to productivity. The revolution began with the enclosure of previously open lands or wasteland. Since most of the wasteland consisted of bogs and swamps, the first step in the process of converting waste to arable land involved draining the land. From there the farmers could fence the land and begin cultivation. Before the introduction of systematic crop rotation, significant portions of the available arable land had to be left fallow, often for decades. As farmers planted the once fallow land with fodder crops such as clover and turnips introduced from Holland, or planted grasses that renewed and revitalized the soil, they restored the land to its primitive condition. The new crops not only restored the vitality of the soil, but also provided food for sheep and cattle, especially during the winter. Increased herd and flock sizes allowed for the production of more manure. As a result, farmers now had sufficient natural fertilizer to renew once fallow land. Since farmers and landowners no longer had to leave significant portions of their land fallow, they could increase the amount in agricultural production. This increase in productive acreage led to a substantial rise in the amount of food and agricultural products available for both domestic consumption and export.

Perhaps the greatest advance in the eighteenth-century revolution was the significant expansion of enclosure in England. Enclosure provided for a more efficient means of farming, as the land could be better managed. By the end of the century, 6 million acres, or one-quarter of the available open land, had been enclosed, much of it through acts of Parliament. By enclosing the land, farmers could keep a better balance between arable land and pasture. They could adopt new forms of husbandry and convert land to more profitable uses. Land that had been inefficiently farmed for centuries could be put to more efficient uses, and worn-out land could be converted to grass or clover for pasture, thus enriching and restoring it. As farmers converted fields to husbandry, the manure provided a natural fertilizer that further restored the soil for future planting. At the same time, lands long used as pasture or that had lain fallow for decades could be plowed and prepared for planting. Wastelands could be cleared, plowed, and improved by applying marl and manure. As farsighted landowners and farmers enclosed their fields and instituted new forms of crop rotation, the productivity of the land jumped significantly. The heart of the revolution was conversion from a system of permanent cultivation and permanent grassland to a flexible form of farming that alternated between tillage and grazing, eliminating fallow fields.

As important as new techniques and new crops were to the Agricultural Revolution, for a country to move beyond subsistence farming it would need to find a way to transport the surplus to market economically. Developments in French agriculture suffered from a lack of transportation. As a result, French farmers found it more difficult than their English counterparts to create a national market. French agriculture remained highly regionalized until the introduction of a rail network in the 1850s.

Although England and Holland relied on modes of transportation similar to those used in France, their smaller size, and the availability of water transport, enabled them to create national markets before France. Water was the most cost effective form of transportation before the introduction of the railroads. The development of a network of canals during the eighteenth century expanded the availability of this important resource to cities and regions that lay too distant from the coast or the rivers to take advantage of those routes. Water transportation was much cheaper than overland transportation, therefore farmers who could move their produce by water could sell it at a much lower price than could those dependent on wagon or packhorse. Water transportation proved to be highly beneficial for English farmers who relied primarily on river transportation, especially since few economically important areas in England were more than fifteen miles from the nearest river. Rivers would continue to be the primary means of transportation during the century, especially for large amounts of material.

The most important development leading toward a national market was the creation of a network of canals, which had begun in the seventeenth century. By the mid-1700s a major move was made to expand the canals, bringing the farmers even greater access to water transportation and allowing them to move large amounts of produce quickly and efficiently. Canals further benefitted farmers by reducing the cost of their products.

The other major mode of transportation was road. At the beginning of the century, England's meager road system, built and maintained by local communities, was in poor condition. During the eighteenth century, Parliament created a network of turnpikes that significantly improved overland transportation. Instead of taxing parish property owners to finance the roads, Parliament made the users of the roads pay tolls. Although the carriers objected to the tolls, which they claimed were punitive, the new roads made it easier and faster to transport goods. Despite the tolls, the turnpikes and the gradual replacement of packhorses with four-wheeled wagons brought a decline in overall costs. Improved transportation lowered the expense and shortened the time needed to transport items, especially perishables. Consequently, merchants could pass on the savings, thereby stimulating demand.

Improvements in the maritime industry encouraged trade in agricultural goods. Piracy declined, and better ships helped to lower insurance rates. Modern sailing techniques and more efficient organization shortened voyages and made better use of ports. Only the warfare of the 1770s put a halt to the decline in maritime costs.

One can see the impact of the revolution in agriculture in two related areas, population growth and urbanization. England's population nearly doubled during the eighteenth century, growing from just over 5 million in 1700 to more than 9 million in 1800. Whereas the urban population of England in 1520 stood at less than 6 percent of the total, by 1800 it had risen to almost 28 percent. As the revolution progressed, a considerable part of the rural population itself moved from agriculture-related activities to other forms of employment. By the end of the century, the numbers involved in agriculture decreased from approximately 80 percent of the rural population to 50 percent. Though agriculture remained labor intensive, the land could now support a much larger nonagricultural population than before. Another sign of England's revolution in agriculture was the increase in the number of towns with populations over five thousand, which was the dividing line between rural and urban life. If London is excluded, the population share of cities with a population over five thousand increased from 6 percent to 17 percent.

London remained the unchallenged urban center of England. No city approached the capital in size or prestige. Its influence also extended well beyond England's boundaries, for during the eighteenth century London became one of the most important cities in Europe. A few centuries earlier, London did not stand among the ten largest cities in Europe, but by 1800 it was the largest city in the world and the center of a worldwide empire. Its population, which had already begun to increase substantially during the seventeenth century, nearly doubled during the eighteenth century, rising from 575,000 in 1700 to 960,000 in 1800.

London was not alone in urbanizing. Cities such as Manchester, Liverpool, and Birmingham, which had not been among the largest in England in the seventeenth century, emerged as leading cities. With populations increasing a hundredfold or more during the century, new urban centers emerged that surpassed in importance older regional centers such as Norwich and York. Manchester, whose population grew from approximately 8,000 in 1700 to almost 90,000 a century later, and Liverpool, which increased from approximately 7,000 to 83,000, soon became industrial and commercial giants second only to London among England's cities.

Even more important, these cities would become leading centers of the Industrial Revolution. This growth could not have occurred without an ever-increasing supply of agricultural products. By contrast, except for Holland the Continent remained largely rural, as did North America. Philadelphia was the largest American city, with a population of around 35,000 in 1776. Only port cities such as Boston, New York, Newport, and Charleston stood out in rural and agrarian colonial America. Plentiful land and an independent spirit among the people served as deterrents to urbanization. France had been a much larger and much more urbanized country than England in 1500, but England's urban population grew to three times the size of France's by 1800. The difference between England and its neighbors was largely due to its greater agricultural productivity. Only England and Holland had the resources to support a large urban population.

Significant population growth and urbanization cannot occur if a nation remains dependent on subsistence-level farming and cannot provide sufficient foodstuffs at reasonable prices for its nonagricultural population. In spite of the tremendous strides made during the eighteenth century to increase production, by the end of the century England had moved from being an exporter to an importer of agricultural goods. Nevertheless, England stood alone among its neighbors in its ability to move beyond subsistence farming to the development of a national market.

The English saw significant improvements in their diet. A combination of lower prices and greater availability allowed even the lower classes greater access to more nutritious food, including the once expensive but more nourishing wheat and protein-rich meat. Improvements in breeding, together with more effective ways of providing feed during the winter, allowed farmers to keep their animals longer, producing more cattle and sheep. The animals were not only more numerous, but because they did not have to be slaughtered as young as before, they could become larger. The key to feeding animals in the winter was the introduction of fodder crops such as turnips. Therefore, the price of meat decreased, making it more available to the general population, leading to better nutrition for the population as a whole.

That a revolution in productivity occurred during the eighteenth century is demonstrated by the fact that the portion of the English population directly involved in agriculture dropped from 60 percent to 36 percent. While the number of people involved in agriculture rose by almost 9 percent, the population as a whole increased more than 80 percent.

At the same time, with the exception of Holland, the agricultural labor force on the Continent and in America remained at levels of 55 percent to 60 percent or more of the population. As a result, serfdom and peasant farming continued to dominate central and eastern Europe, as well as much of western Europe. In eastern Europe, but especially Russia, only the nobility owned land, which was farmed by serfs who were essentially slaves. Russia did not abolish serfdom until the middle of the nineteenth century. Western Europe allowed the peasantry greater freedom, but there was little incentive for significant agricultural improvement, and agricultural techniques remained virtually unchanged from the Middle Ages. Even France continued to rely upon peasant-based farming. Colonial American agriculture, especially in the American South, depended not only on small farmers but also on larger estates worked by great numbers of black slaves. Slavery would not end in the American South until 1865, long after England had abolished the institution.

For England to have the percentage of its population involved in agriculture diminish significantly while remaining able to feed its growing population required determination and capital. Both came from wealthy gentry who recognized the commercial benefits derived from agrarian expansion. Through enclosure, crop rotation, and reclamation of wastelands, England realized a significant gain in productive agricultural lands. At the same time, small farms gave way to great estates worked by tenant farmers and wage laborers.

In moving to larger estates, England differed from much of continental Europe. Parliament limited the breakup of estates and larger farms by passing strict laws on primogeniture, which kept land in the hands of the oldest son, whereas most European legal systems allowed a more diffused inheritance. Parliament also passed mortgage laws that enabled landowners to borrow against their land to buy more land or to improve existing lands without the risk of forfeiture. Further incentive to borrow came from decreases in interest rates, which fell to as low as 4 or 5 percent.

Owners of large estates often had made their wealth in other fields, such as mining or commerce. Yet the land and its privileges drew them and their resources. Even the expansion of industry did not diminish the prestige of landownership. Therefore, with capital gained from other ventures, a significant number of landowners possessed the necessary financial resources to make improvements to their holdings. These improvements not only led to greater efficiency in farming, but well-endowed estates had the financial strength to survive fluctuations in the market. During the early years of the revolution, expanded agricultural output led to significant price decreases. Landowners with adequate capital resources survived the immediate cash flow problems from decreased prices and found themselves well positioned to take advantage of price increases during the second half of the eighteenth century.

Other landowners used their profits to enter other kinds of businesses, especially mining and canal and turnpike speculation. Between 1760 and 1815, wealthy landowners held approximately one-third of the shares in the canal companies. The landed gentry not only contributed financially, but also helped encourage transportation developments through its influence in Parliament. Thus, there seems to have been a mutually beneficial relationship between the land and the economy.

During the eighteenth century, landed estates gradually overshadowed small independent farms. The landed elite, in turn, leased their property to tenant farmers who worked the lands, paid rent, and reaped the benefits of bountiful harvests. The landowners often depended on their stewards, who had the responsibility of ensuring that the tenants were efficient and productive farmers. Although their influence was diminished, small farmers did not disappear altogether. Many continued to survive and even thrive; however, many small and middle-sized farms gave way to the more efficient large estates. This fact made the many enclosure acts passed by Parliament controversial. Most small farmers could not afford the cost of fences and hedges; many did not even have sufficient lands to enclose profitably. Enclosure also affected cottagers, who made their living in trades other than agriculture, such as nail making or spinning and weaving. Although they were not farmers, the cottagers often depended on the commons and open fields to graze a cow or pig or to grow potatoes or beans. Enclosure reduced the amount of land available to them. Perhaps the squatters who lived in shacks in the wastelands and eked out a living from farming and hunting were hit the hardest. Enclosure drove them off the land, making them both destitute and homeless.

Enclosure was, however, a boon for the landed elite. Their estates grew larger and more productive. It also attracted investment from those who had made their money in other fields and found it politically and socially beneficial to invest in land. Even as the cities grew and a new class of wealthy merchants emerged, political power remained in the hands of the landed elite. Parliament had become a much more important institution in the wake of the Glorious Revolution of 1688–1689, and membership in Parliament depended on ownership of land. Furthermore, Europe in the eighteenth century remained largely patriarchal and tied to old traditions. The Enlightenment may have begun eroding some traditional aspects of life, but the landed elite remained the leaders of society. In short, ownership of land meant power and prestige.

Enclosure not only provided the opportunity for economic gain, but also allowed landowners to explore aesthetic possibilities. The willingness of some aristocrats to devote prime farmland to creating gardens offers another example of England's ability to feed its growing population. As a result, during the course of the century the English garden came into its own. Though based on models brought from the Continent,

English gardens sought to create the illusion of a natural world tamed by man. One could enjoy the benefits of the outdoors in a controlled and "civilized" context.

Taken as a whole, the Agricultural Revolution gave a tremendous boost to England's economy. Though England became a net importer of food by the end of the century, until 1760 English farmers produced a surplus, so that 10 percent of their produce could be exported each year. The primary cause of the change from exporter to importer status was the increased population. Though English farmers attempted to keep up with demand, population increases at the end of the century, combined with war and several bad harvests, placed great pressure on them. However, both exports and imports remained a small fraction of the agricultural produce reserved for home consumption.

Perhaps the most important beneficiary of the rise in agriculture was the Industrial Revolution. It is unlikely that the Industrial Revolution, which took root after the middle of the eighteenth century and blossomed near the end of the century, could have occurred without the prior revolution in agriculture. Again, revolution came first to England, a nation that had the infrastructure and population to become industrialized.

The roots of the Industrial Revolution can possibly be found in the decrease in the price of grain and other agricultural products during the early years of the century, which caused real income levels for workers to increase. Even low-paid workers, who had once devoted almost 70 percent of their income to food purchases, began to have sufficient surplus income to buy manufactured goods. The resulting development of a mass market for manufactured goods spurred industrial development and investment. Although food prices increased over the last half of the century, transportation improvements kept these increases within bounds. Thus, the foundations for a new era had been laid; as the demand for agricultural goods increased, the need for innovation in industrial technology increased likewise.

Agricultural developments also affected the regionalization of industry. Since southern England possessed better and lighter soils than the north, the south became England's agricultural center, whereas the north became the center for industrial development, especially the cities of Manchester, Liverpool, and Birmingham.

Agriculture also provided the raw materials for industrialization, especially for the textile industry, which was the pacesetting industry during the early years of the Industrial Revolution. Cotton became an important commodity during the later years of the eighteenth century, and improvements in stock breeding and greater opportunities for grazing led to an increase in the availability of wool. As the textile industry grew, it demanded more raw materials, which in turn encouraged increased production of wool and cotton.

Agriculture not only influenced the development of the modern industrial age, but also benefitted from increased technology. While the earlier innovations had largely been tied to land usage, by the end of the century new tools started to aid agriculture. English farmers began to replace wood and stone tools with cast iron and standardized, factorymade ones. Eli Whitney's cotton gin, developed late in the eighteenth century, revolutionized the cotton industry, especially in the American South. In 1790 America was an insignificant producer of cotton, but by 1821 it had surpassed India as the world's leading cotton producer. Agricultural developments in the nineteenth century would be much more technologically driven than those of the eighteenth century.

The Agricultural Revolution, like many revolutions, had both ups and downs. In some ways it was more a gradual process than a dynamic revolutionary event. War, drought, and overproduction often interrupted efforts at improvement. Yet, throughout the eighteenth century English farmers adapted and innovated in ways that enabled the nation to expand its population base, urbanize, and develop industrially. In time, the innovations of the English and the Dutch were passed on to other nations, leading to further revolutions in agriculture, population growth, and industrialization in those countries.

## SELECTED BIBLIOGRAPHY

Beckett, J. V. *The Agricultural Revolution*. London: Basil Blackwell, 1990. Brief, readable overview of the Agricultural Revolution in Britain.

Chambers, J. D., and G. E. Mingay. *The Agricultural Revolution: 1750–1880*. New York: Schocken Books, 1966. Classic description of the key developments in English agriculture during the eighteenth and nineteenth centuries.

Clark, J. C. D. *English Society, 1688–1832*. Cambridge: Cambridge University Press, 1985. Revisionist study of English society suggesting that traditional religious and social attitudes prevailed during the eighteenth century.

Eversley, D. E. C. "The Home Market and Economic Growth in England, 1750–1780." In *Land, Labour and Population in the Industrial Revolution: Essays Presented to J. D. Chambers*, pp. 206–259. Edited by E. L. Jones and G. E. Mingay. London: Edward Arnold, 1967. Essay proposes that agricultural expansion lasted throughout the eighteenth century and corresponded to the creation of a national market for agricultural products during the second half of the century.

Ford, Boris, ed. *Eighteenth-Century Britain*. Cambridge: Cambridge University

Press, 1992. Series of essays on cultural life of eighteenth-century England, with sections on landscaping and gardening.

Fussell, G. E. *The Classical Tradition in West European Farming*. Rutherford, NJ: Fairleigh Dickinson University Press, 1972. Historical survey of farming developments, with a chapter on the eighteenth century.

Grigg, David. *The Dynamics of Agricultural Change: The Historical Experience*. London: Hutchinson, 1982. General survey of agricultural change in history that sets the revolution of the eighteenth century in its broader context.

John, A. H. "Agricultural Productivity and Economic Growth in England, 1700–1760." In *Agriculture and Economic Growth in England, 1650–1815*, pp. 172–193. Edited by E. L. Jones. London: Methuen, 1967. Essay suggests that agricultural expansion corresponded to the price decreases of the first half of the eighteenth century.

Jones, E. L. "Agriculture 1700–80." In *The Economic History of Britain since 1700*, pp. 66–86. Edited by Roderick Floud and Donald McCloskey. Cambridge: Cambridge University Press, 1981. Good starting point for understanding the economic impact of the Agricultural Revolution.

———. "Agriculture and Economic Growth in England, 1660–1750: Agricultural Change." In *Agriculture and Economic Growth in England, 1650–1815*, pp. 152–171. Edited by E. L. Jones. London: Methuen, 1967. Important essay, first published in the *Journal of Economic History*, focusing on the impact agricultural growth had on England's economy.

———, ed. *Agriculture and Economic Growth in England, 1650–1815*. London: Methuen, 1967. Series of essays on the relationship of agriculture and economic growth.

Kerridge, Eric. *The Agricultural Revolution*. London: George Allen and Unwin, 1967. Places date for England's Agricultural Revolution during the sixteenth and seventeenth centuries.

Langford, Paul. *Public Life and the Propertied Englishman, 1689–1798*. Oxford: Clarendon Press, 1991. Substantial but readable history of eighteenth-century England's propertied classes.

Mathias, Peter. "Agriculture and Industrialization." In *The First Industrial Revolutions*, pp. 101–126. Edited by Peter Mathias and John A. Davis. Cambridge, MA: Basil Blackwell, 1989. Author maintains that a revolution in agriculture was necessary before rapid industrialization could occur.

Porter, Roy. *English Society in the Eighteenth Century*. Rev. ed. New York: Penguin Books, 1990. Social history of England that demonstrates the impact of agriculture on economic and social life.

Price, Roger. *An Economic History of Modern France, 1730–1914*. Rev. ed. London: Macmillan, 1981. Shows why eighteenth-century France failed to experience the same agricultural expansion that England did.

Van Houtte, J. A. *An Economic History of the Low Countries, 800–1800*. London: Weidenfield and Nicolson, 1977. Includes a discussion of agricultural developments from 1670 to 1800 in the context of Holland's and Belgium's broader economic history.

Wrigley, E. Anthony. "Urban Growth and Agricultural Change: England and the Continent in the Early Modern Period." In *Population and Economy: From the Traditional to the Modern World*, pp. 123–168. Edited by Robert I. Rotberg and Theodore K. Rabb. Cambridge: Cambridge University Press, 1986. Valuable discussion of the relationship between agricultural developments and urban growth in England and continental Europe from the sixteenth century through the eighteenth century.

Revolt in Great Britain's North American colonies culminated in the creation of the United States of America. The American victory over General John Burgoyne at the Battle of Saratoga in 1777 helped to convince France to aid the revolutionaries. (Reproduced from the Collections of the Library of Congress)

# 7

# The American Revolution, 1763–1783

## INTRODUCTION

In 1763 the Seven Years' War came to an end. Truly a global conflict, the North American phase of the war was called the French and Indian War. Great Britain was one of the war's big winners, gaining France's colonial empire in Canada as well as all French claims east of the Mississippi River. However, the cost of the war had severely burdened the British treasury, leaving Great Britain heavily in debt. Furthermore, defending and administering its North American colonies also drained the British treasury, especially when at the end of the war Britain decided to station 10,000 troops in the colonies to preserve the peace. In order to alleviate these fiscal pressures, Great Britain determined to make its American colonists pay a larger share of the costs of empire.

The American colonists, many of whom fought in the French and Indian War, regarded themselves as loyal subjects of the king. They believed that they shared in the rights and privileges that accrued to all Englishmen, and they recognized the authority of the British Parliament. However, they worried about their own economic well-being and opposed sending more to the British treasury than they were already contributing. Furthermore, the French and Indian War had fostered a spirit of unity among the diverse colonials, some of whom now took a more "continental" point of view and began to refer to themselves as Americans.

At the close of the French and Indian War, the British government, led by George Grenville, who did the bidding of an energetic King George III, introduced a series of acts designed to achieve British objectives in North America. To maintain peace with the Indians, the Proclamation of 1763 set the westward limit of colonial expansion at the Appalachian Mountains. The Sugar Act of 1764 provided for a vigorous collection of tariff duties in America—especially on molasses—with the proceeds destined for the British treasury. It also included measures designed to destroy the widespread and profitable smuggling operations engaged in by many colonial merchants. In the same year, the Currency Act prohibited the colonies from issuing paper money. Although Americans opposed these measures, they reacted moderately. However, some Americans objected to taxes being levied without the consent of those who were taxed, and a boycott of British goods begun in Boston showed signs of spreading to other colonies.

Determined to carry out the king's program, Grenville pushed the Stamp Act through Parliament in 1765. The Stamp Act departed radically from the norm in that it levied a tax not on imports but on transactions undertaken within the colonies. It called for taxing such items as newspapers, playing cards, legal documents, and almanacs, with the proceeds going to Great Britain to offset the cost of maintaining the colonies.

The Americans reacted strongly to the Stamp Act. Destructive riots aimed at royal agents and tax collectors swept the colonies. Under the leadership of the young lawyer Patrick Henry, the Virginia House of Burgesses passed the Virginia Resolves proclaiming that the right to levy taxes rested solely with Virginians themselves and that Virginians were not obligated to submit to taxes levied by Parliament. Other colonies took up the cry of "no taxation without representation." Organizations known as the Sons of Liberty formed to protest British behavior, and a Stamp Act Congress drawing delegates from nine colonies met in New York City in late 1765 to raise formal objections to the Stamp Act.

The most effective weapon against the Stamp Act proved to be a boycott of imported British goods. Organized chiefly by colonial merchants, the boycott proved so effective that British exporters and merchants, seeing their income falling dramatically, raised a hue and cry of their own in Parliament. Grenville fell from office and was replaced by Lord Rockingham, who in 1766 brought about the repeal of the Stamp Act. However, Parliament also passed a Declaratory Act in which it maintained its absolute right to tax the colonies as it saw fit.

Tensions rose again in the following year when Parliament passed the Townshend Acts, which subjected the colonies to import duties on a variety of goods including lead, paper, paint, glass, and tea. In order to achieve vigorous enforcement, the acts also provided for writs of assistance, or general warrants, and admiralty courts to try cases without the benefit of juries.

The colonists reacted as one might expect. Denouncing the Townshend Acts as a violation of their rights as Englishmen, the colonists once again resorted to a boycott of British goods. The boycott was effective; the value of British imports into the colonies dropped by 41 percent between 1768 and 1769. However, in March 1770 a scuffle in Boston between British soldiers and a stone-throwing crowd led to the firing of shots during which five Americans died. Known to colonists as the Boston Massacre, this confrontation occurred, ironically, on the very day that Parliament repealed most of the Townshend Acts, keeping only a tax on tea.

A period of quiet now followed. However, Massachusetts radical Sam Adams established a Committee of Correspondence to trade information and to provide news of what was taking place in the various colonies. Committees of Correspondence quickly sprang up throughout the colonies, bringing greater cohesion among the Americans as the drift to revolution continued.

The period of quiet ended in 1773 when Lord North, the new leader of the British government, pushed the Tea Act through Parliament. Because the Townshend Acts' tax on tea had not been repealed, the colonists had continued to boycott British imported tea. The Tea Act now lowered that tax to an inconsequential three pence per pound as North tried both to break the boycott and to reinforce the principle that Parliament had the right to levy taxes on the colonies.

Colonial radicals clearly saw the significance of the Tea Act and renewed their protests. They were joined by a number of merchants who objected to the British scheme to award the right to sell the imported tea to a handful of carefully selected individuals who were known for their support of the British position. Opposition to the Tea Act reached a climax in December 1773 when several dozen Bostonians dressed in Indian garb boarded a merchant ship at anchor and dumped its cargo of tea into the harbor.

The Boston Tea Party outraged Parliament, which responded in April 1774 with the so-called Intolerable Acts, a collection of laws that seemed to strike at the very heart of colonial liberties. The Intolerable Acts closed the port of Boston, consigned many of the powers of the elected Mas-

sachusetts legislature to the royally appointed governor, and circum-
scribed the freedom of Massachusetts town meetings. Furthermore, the
Quartering Act allowed the British to house their troops in private homes
at the expense of the colonists, and the Quebec Act, which bound Canada
more closely to Great Britain, seemed to foreshadow further British attempts to diminish American autonomy.

The American colonies condemned the Intolerable Acts, and in September 1774 the First Continental Congress assembled in Philadelphia,
where it protested to the king a number of parliamentary measures enacted since 1763 and called for a total cessation of commercial activity
between the colonies and Great Britain. The congress agreed to hold a
second meeting in May 1775 if Britain failed to change its ways.

However, before the Second Continental Congress could meet, blood
was shed. During the winter of 1774–1775, sentiment for independence
grew rapidly in virtually every colony. Increasingly, the colonists ignored royal authority and took over civil administrations. Loyalists, or
Tories, were tarred and feathered, and their homes looted and burned.
Colonial militias formed, drilled openly, and began to collect arms and
munitions. In Massachusetts, "Minute Men" pledged to assemble fully
armed at a minute's notice, and in Virginia Patrick Henry uttered his
famous "give me liberty or give me death."

In April 1775 a force of British soldiers, or Redcoats, left Boston to
seize colonial stores hidden at Concord. At Lexington, armed colonists
confronted them and shots were fired. As the British continued on to
Concord, they encountered more armed resistance. Retreating to Boston,
they came under withering fire at times and replied in kind. By the end
of the day, 73 Redcoats lay dead and 202 were wounded or missing. The
colonials suffered 95 casualties.

If there was any doubt that a rupture had occurred between Great
Britain and the thirteen colonies, it was soon dispelled. In May 1775
American rebels seized the British garrison at Fort Ticonderoga, and in
June the Battle of Bunker Hill resulted in more than 400 dead and over
1,000 wounded. In August George III declared the thirteen colonies to
be in a state of rebellion.

The Second Continental Congress, meeting since May 1775, now
moved inexorably toward a declaration of independence from Britain. In
June 1775 it named George Washington commander in chief of the Continental forces, and several months later it authorized the creation of an
American navy. In January 1776 Thomas Paine published *Common Sense*,
a pamphlet that argued forcefully and effectively for independence from
Britain. Finally, on July 4, 1776, the Congress approved the Declaration

of Independence, a stirring document written chiefly by Thomas Jefferson.

With the Declaration of Independence, the focus of the American Revolution moved to the battlefield and the diplomatic front. It soon became clear that the neophyte American forces could not consistently beat the British regulars; but it also became apparent that as long as the Americans avoided set battles, the British could not defeat them and destroy the revolution. Consequently, throughout the course of the war the British controlled those areas where their troops were present, but the rest of the colonies remained in the hands of the rebels, who moved freely in the countryside.

In 1776 the colonials lost the Battle of Brooklyn Heights and retreated through New Jersey; but on Christmas Eve they turned the tide and successfully attacked British mercenaries encamped at Trenton. Several days later, Washington scored another success at Princeton. In 1777 the British moved from New York to Philadelphia. Washington resisted at Brandywine Creek and Germantown, but the British were triumphant, and the colonials went into winter camp at Valley Forge.

On the diplomatic front, the Americans scored an early triumph in 1776 when both France and Spain agreed to send war materials to the rebels and to extend loans as a way of undermining their rival, Great Britain. In late 1776 Benjamin Franklin was dispatched to France to convince the French to enter into a formal alliance with the Americans. Despite Franklin's personal charm, the French hesitated to commit themselves. However, when news of the stunning American victory at the 1777 Battle of Saratoga reached France, the French entered the war in 1778 on the side of the Americans. In 1779 Spain followed suit.

Stalemated in the northern colonies, the belligerents shifted their attention southward late in 1778. Hoping to exploit significant Loyalist sentiment in the southern colonies, the British won victories at Savannah, Charleston, and Camden; however, the Americans countered with important wins at Kings Mountain and Cowpens. After a draw at the Battle of Guilford Court House, the British commander, Lord Cornwallis, marched north into Virginia, where he allowed himself to be trapped at Yorktown. Bottled up on land by a Franco-American force commanded by Washington, and cut off from the sea by the French fleet under the Comte de Grasse, Cornwallis surrendered his army of 7,000 troops in October 1781. With Cornwallis' defeat, the military phase of the American Revolution ended.

Peace negotiations between the Americans and Great Britain opened in 1782, and the Treaty of Paris was signed on September 3, 1783. By the terms of the treaty, Great Britain recognized the independence of its thirteen North American colonies and agreed to set the Mississippi River as the new nation's western boundary.

---

# INTERPRETIVE ESSAY
## *Rick Kennedy*

The importance of the American Revolution for world history is found not in the war but in the implementation of political ideas. Of course the war was much more than just ideas: people died; rich merchants got richer; generals drew lines on maps. But the greatness of the Revolution, the reason the American Revolution holds an important place in every modern world civilization textbook, is in the construction of a stable new country based on the Declaration of Independence's individualistic and democratic ideals. The greatness of the Revolution is in the creation of the United States—a political system that links individual freedom with strength and stability, a political experiment that is often considered the world's first and oldest modern country.

Most of the world today defines "modern government" by what the United States implemented after the Revolution: a government specifically designed to respond to the will of "the people" for the protection of "the people's" rights; a government that structurally diffuses its own power in such a way that checks and balances exist; a government that protects against the concentration of power; a government that exalts freedom while enforcing stability and domestic tranquility; a government that glorifies and fears democracy.

Historians have long argued whether the American Revolution was radical or conservative. The fact is it was both. The historian Gordon Wood calls the Revolution "the greatest utopian movement in American history" and argues persuasively that the Revolution was fought in order to create a radical new society based on equality, freedom, and democracy—ideals that were best stated in the Declaration of Independence. Yet Wood also notes that "the ink on the Declaration of Independence was scarcely dry before many of the revolutionary leaders began expressing doubts about the possibility of realizing these high hopes." The American Revolution was radical and utopian, but those who crafted the new political system tried their best to moderate the radicalism, especially the power of democratic impulses expressed in the Declaration of

Independence. The Founding Fathers wanted stability. They felt it their virtuous responsibility to make the United States into a "more perfect union" than anything that had ever existed; however, the new country was to be only "more perfect"—the United States was not to be the democratic utopia of equality and pursuits of happiness. Liberty was the goal of the Constitution, but it was a liberty preserved for posterity, a stable liberty, a liberty protected from democracy.

The Declaration of Independence is a bit of an embarrassment. On many important facts it is wrong: most importantly on the matter of why Americans had the right to declare independence. The key statement— "But when a long train of abuses and usurpations, pursuing invariably the same object, evinces a design to reduce them under absolute despotism, it is their right, it is their duty, to overthrow such government"— is wrong. The British pursued no invariable object. They might have been bumbling in their colonial policies, but they had no design to subject the colonists to tyranny. That so many intelligent Americans such as John Adams and Thomas Jefferson could really believe such a thing is a mystery to historians.

What is important about the Declaration of Independence is that it said nothing that astonished its signers. When the Declaration was presented to the Second Continental Congress for approval, many small matters were changed, but the wild preamble about the self-evident truth that all men are created equal with unalienable rights of life, liberty, and the pursuit of happiness was agreed on without debate. That "governments are instituted among men, deriving their just powers from the consent of the governed" was a common assumption among progressive-minded British citizens. The Declaration of Independence condemns the British king for being un-British. The freedoms demanded at the beginning of the Revolution were British freedoms, and the American Revolution was fought to further British political ideas.

These ideas are evident in British mythology. King Arthur ruled from a Round Table symbolizing that the king was first among equals, not an absolute monarch. Robin Hood, a nobleman, defended Anglo-Saxon values of reciprocal responsibilities between monarch and people symbolized in taxation. The lesson of Robin Hood was that revolt against a tyrant is the right and duty of citizens. The rightful goal of such a revolt is to restore the proper relationship between king, nobles, and people. At the end of the Robin Hood story the good king is restored, Robin is returned to his rightful place in the aristocracy, and taxes are returned to a "fair" rate.

British school children were long taught that deep in Anglo-Saxon history a representative legislature existed called the Witan, which was the ancestor of Parliament. Every young American student of the time would have been told that Magna Carta in 1215 reaffirmed the rights of the nobles to be consulted before headstrong kings rashly leaped into wars. Kings in Britain were limited monarchs who required the consent of the governed. Royalty who did not understand this, such as Charles I or James II, could find themselves dethroned.

The grandparents and great-grandparents of American revolutionaries believed in the British right to overthrow kings. Young Thomas Jefferson in his first revolutionary tract brashly declared that he was going to "remind" the king of the history of the rights of British citizens: "that our ancestors, before their emigration to America, were free."

The freedom that Jefferson thought important to remind the king of was one of the core values professed by America's Founding Fathers. The early constitutions of the United States were in many ways more concrete, systematic, and institutionalized versions of the vague unwritten British constitution, which was itself often seen as modeled on the ancient Roman republic. This is an important point. The modernity of the United States is constructed on old principles developed in Britain and originating in Germanic customs and ancient Roman political theory. The two key terms are "democracy" and "republic."

A republic, as understood by our Founding Fathers, is a three-part mixed government. The Roman theory was that kings naturally become tyrants, and tyrants get overthrown by their nobles, who in turn eventually begin to misuse their power. Aristocracies are then overthrown by the people, who set up democracies. Democracies are governments ruled by the people but are very unstable because power eventually falls into the hands of mobs and demagogues. Chaos ensues. The people fear for their lives and safety until some very powerful person comes along who can bring order to the chaos. That person then gets made king—and the cycle begins all over again. The theory is that the three main types of government—monarchy, aristocracy, and democracy—are naturally unstable. Each tends toward corruption. A republic, however, solves the problem of instability by mixing the three types of government into a single government of checks and balances (see Figure 7.1).

The ideal of three-part mixed government was most clear in the government of every American colony where governor, council, and assembly ruled. Every colony was a little "republic." For the British, America was a land of political experiments where old ideas got extended or transformed. Virginia was given a republican structure in 1619. At the founding of Massachusetts in 1629, Puritans transformed what was le-

**Figure 7.1**
**A Republic**

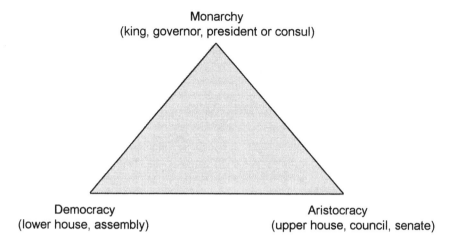

Monarchy
(king, governor, president or consul)

Democracy
(lower house, assembly)

Aristocracy
(upper house, council, senate)

gally a company with a relatively autocratic organization into a little
republic. In many respects, American colonists lived under governments
that were more representative than those of their English cousins; more
open, just, and free than the old country with its over-mighty nobility.
The "balance" of mixed government was *more* balanced in America than
it was in England and had ever been in Rome. White Americans in the
1760s and 1770s lived in colonial republics under a British constitution.
They were more free and less oppressed than most Europeans.

So why rebel? Why should a group of colonies, full of people who loved
their British traditions, whose quality of life was better than that of most
other people in the world, and who lived mostly under enlightened self-
government, declare war on the country that founded their traditions, encouraged their happiness, and gave them more self-government than
might be expected?

There is a different answer for every person who supported the Revolution; however, the unifying factor is simple: a misguided fear that the
king and Parliament in England desired to reduce the extensive rights
and freedoms in the colonies to such an extent that the Americans would
not even have ordinary British rights and freedoms. The American Revolution was a preemptive strike against those whom the rebels thought
were eventually going to oppress them.

The Declaration of Independence was written because "a decent respect to the opinions of mankind requires that [the revolutionaries]
should declare the causes which impel them to separation." The Decla-

ration was designed to tell people in Europe why Americans were fighting and to tell Americans why they should rebel. The Declaration's wild rhetoric about government's responsibility to protect every individual's right to "life, liberty, and the pursuit of happiness" promulgated a radical democratic vision. Most people died for this vision during the Revolution, and, accordingly, the first governments of the United States, which were organized to run the war, were much more democratic and dangerous than our Founding Fathers would later want.

The first government of the United States evolved out of the necessity of organizing independent states and uniting those states with one foreign policy. The colonies began writing state constitutions soon after the Revolution began. These state constitutions usually followed the model of the colonial governments—three-part republics with a strong assembly and a weak governor. Because of the strong assemblies, the state constitutions can be characterized as very democratic. The new governments sent delegates to the Continental Congress. Eventually the Articles of Confederation were enacted to solidify a system where states held the majority of power and the federal government was similar to today's United Nations. The most important fact of the first government of the United States is that it gave lots of power to "the people." The United States was more of a democracy then than it ever has been since, and this fact scared our Founding Fathers.

But why was the first government of the United States more of a democracy than later governments? To understand the first government of the United States, one must imagine thirteen separate republics sending ambassadors to a joint congress in order to create a unified foreign policy. Since each of the separate republics gave extensive power to the democratic branch of the triangle and weakened the power of the monarchical branch, the cumulative effect was that "the people" through their state legislatures had great influence on the federal government. Since the federal government did not have the power to tax or even to have its own army, it had to rely on state legislatures supplying money and men. "The people"—meaning the majority of propertied male adult voters from the farms and villages throughout America who sent their local leaders to the state legislatures—were very powerful—too powerful from the viewpoint of the rich men of the cities and plantations, who were concerned that eventually too much democracy would lead to mobs, riots, and demagogues.

Soon enough, the mobs, riots, and demagogues began to appear. In 1783 the Continental Congress in Philadelphia was surrounded by a threatening group of former soldiers. In 1787 a much bigger revolt of ex-soldiers appeared in western Massachusetts led by Daniel Shays, a farmer and Revolutionary War veteran. To many, Shays looked like a demagogue leading a private army. Imagine the problem: the government of Massachusetts calls for the Continental Congress to send an army to put down Shays' Rebellion; the Continental Congress explains that it has no army and that Massachusetts should use its own militia; the leaders of Massachusetts then try to explain that those rebelling are, in fact, the Massachusetts militia. Eventually the rich leaders of eastern Massachusetts hired mercenaries to help quell Shays' Rebellion.

This is exactly the corruption of democracy that our Founding Fathers feared. James Madison and Alexander Hamilton had already started the process of overthrowing the present government of the United States in order to create a more perfect government. Shays' Rebellion only confirmed what they already believed: the United States was too much a democracy; that people were talking too much about their own rights of life, liberty, and happiness; and such a government and society could not remain stable. The values of the Declaration of Independence had to be moderated by a new constitution that would diminish the power of individuals in government in order to protect individual liberty.

The creation of the Constitution is where most historians see a conservative revolt against the radicalism of the Revolution. Truly it was a sneaky affair perpetrated by rich elites to make sure that democracy did not overwhelm their own status and property. In their own minds, however, the Founding Fathers were virtuous protectors of stability. They were the well-educated who understood that democracy had to be moderated by the checks and balances of a republic in order to fend off democracy's own natural tendency to destroy itself. It was the rich elites who paid for the mercenaries to save Massachusetts from its own citizens. These men were sneaky, but they believed they were being sneaky for the higher calling of perfecting the American experiment.

James Madison was the model moderate revolutionary. Neither gun-toting or fist-pounding, Madison was the ultimate committee man. Unmarried and bookish, he thought long and hard about matters on which more showy politicians only made statements. The frail and pampered son of a rich plantation owner, little ''Jimmy'' Madison is one of the greatest figures of modern world history. He was a man of action. His actions, however, were not on the battlefield or even in the public forum; rather, he spent his evenings reading books and his days leading small committees of politicians. He is rightly considered the ''Father'' of the American Constitution, but he did not preside at the Constitutional Convention or even dominate the discussion. He mostly sat taking notes. His work was done before the convention in well-argued letters to potential delegates, at night after convention meetings when he would draw from his study of political history to convince wavering delegates, and after the convention when he wrote essays to newspapers explaining the Constitution's structure. The pen isn't necessarily mightier than the sword; rather, in the case of the American Revolution, Madison's pen, his soft-spoken thoughts, and his steadfast attention to a goal gave purpose to the work of the sword. George Washington knew this well and relied on the wisdom of the small young man who sent him letters and convinced him to come out of retirement.

Madison's clearest conviction was that too much democracy would destroy the United States, but that too little would destroy the liberty fought for in the Revolution. In eighteenth-century fashion, Madison spoke at the Constitutional Convention of "the inconveniences of democracy" and how, whatever the virtue of individuals, those virtues diminish in groups. "These observations," he told the convention, "are verified in the Histories of every Country ancient and modern." He had long before come to the conclusion that the democracy of state governments was hampering the work of the United States. As a young congressman during the Revolution, Madison came to every committee meeting prepared and participated in the great achievements of the Articles of Confederation congress: winning the war with Britain and writing the Northwest Ordinance, which stands as America's rational and egalitarian system for expansion. However, he believed that the federal government was too weak and the states too strong. James Madison's greatness began when he decided to overthrow his government.

This is one of the defining moments of the American Revolution—as important a moment as when Minute Men started shooting at the battles of Lexington and Concord. But how does a young, obscure hypochondriac overthrow a government? The answer was to ask the Articles of Confederation congress to call a committee meeting to discuss interstate commerce on the Potomac River. Each state legislature would send delegates to such a meeting, and Madison lobbied his friends to seek membership on the committee. The first meeting in 1786 failed, but Madison persuaded George Washington to allow the Virginia legislature to appoint him to the next meeting, scheduled for Philadelphia in 1787. With the famous general present, Madison could be sure that everybody would take the meeting seriously. Thus the pieces were in place to transform a meeting to discuss interstate commerce into a meeting to overthrow the government—and Madison already had in mind a basic plan for a new government.

Madison alone could not have turned a meeting to discuss interstate commerce into a drive to overthrow the existing government and create a new one in its place; the eventual support of well-known and trusted leaders such as George Washington and Benjamin Franklin proved crucial. Nevertheless, the only authority for what came to be called the Constitutional Convention was the vague wording of the commission to some of the delegates and the delegates' individual reputations for virtue and patriotism. That the delegates knew they were acting without proper authorization and that their behavior could easily be interpreted as improper is evident from their first-day vote to make their sessions secret.

Basically, the Founding Fathers in their secret sessions decided to create a federal government that structurally looked like the state governments and followed the old republican model which was designed to give democracy a place but keep it in check. A three-part mixed government was formed of the one, the few, and the many: a powerful president who commanded a federal army; a Senate of aristocrats; and a House of Representatives which would be democratic. That democracy was to be restricted is evident from the fact that "the people" voted only for the representatives. Senators were elected by states, not by "the people," and the president was elected by an electoral college. That the Founding Fathers did not want to destroy the power of democracy is evident from the fact that the House of Representatives was given special power over taxation and money. British traditions demanded that the people have some power over the purse to protect themselves against unjust taxation.

However, the Constitution was not just a rehash of old British republican ideals. The most creative act was to institute another level of checks and balances over the old level of one, few, many. A three-part structure of executive, legislative, and judiciary overlay the other three-part structure of monarch, upper house, and lower house, creating a new configuration (see Figure 7.2).

Look what happened to democracy in this new configuration. The House is shunted off to one corner, and the Senate, executive, and judiciary are arrayed to check and balance it. The judiciary is especially undemocratic, and the House of Representatives has no control over appointments to the federal courts; judges have lifetime tenure and are appointed by the president with the consent of the Senate.

The federal judiciary section was the wild card of the Constitution. It was the branch least accountable to the will of "the people" and was the

**Figure 7.2**
**Checks and Balances**

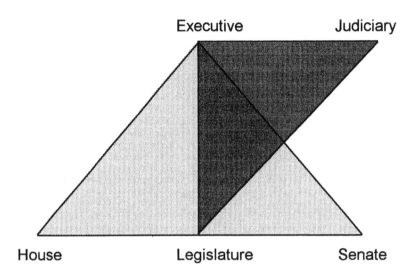

most vaguely constructed. Madison desired to keep the powers of the judiciary vague. He wrote to Jefferson on the general subject of judicial power that "much detail ought to be avoided in the Constitutional regulation of this Department, that there may be room for changes which may be demanded by the progressive changes in the state of our population." The power of unaccountable federal courts to work against democracy was apparently an option understood by the Founding Fathers.

Although democracy was greatly hindered by the new Constitution, the will of "the people" was not blocked; however, it was hemmed and fixed. Madison hoped the structure would encourage docility among the people. He especially hoped that the structure would create inefficiency. Madison believed that inefficiency was good in that it countered the kind of quick changes and demagoguery that afflict democracy. The new Constitution would enhance stability through inefficiency. Look again at the structure of government in Figure 7.2. Would anyone wanting to make money structure their business this way? Of course not. But making money and being quick to respond to markets or "the people's" will was not the goal of the Constitution. The goal was and is stability, achieved by diminishing the role of democracy.

But how did the Founding Fathers overthrow the Articles of Confederation and fulfill the hope of the Declaration of Independence for a stable government that protects individual rights from a tyrannous government? How did they get America to adopt the Constitution?

The answer, for which there was a precedent in Massachusetts history, was to call for specially elected "ratification conventions." These ratification conventions could be more easily controlled by the elite members of society and were less subject to democracy. Nevertheless, even with the ratification convention strategy, the Founding Fathers knew that they faced an uphill struggle.

Eventually, the big states ratified the Constitution; but there was plenty of dissent, and bloodshed was possible. It is at this juncture that the American Revolution is most amazing. At roughly the same time that the French Revolution was descending into violence and chaos, America remained calm. The reason was the trustworthiness of George Washington, a man whose sterling character generated a consensus of confidence that overpowered any move to bloodshed.

The power of George Washington's reputation cannot be overestimated. At the conclusion of the Revolutionary War, he had the chance to declare martial law. Many powerful and conscientious people wanted him to do so, but he retired instead. He stands among the greatest leaders of world history because at this crucial moment he chose not to seize power. Like Cincinnatus of Roman history, Washington forced "the people" to accept responsibility for the future by refusing to be their king. When he showed up at the Constitutional Convention, stood by the Constitution in debate, and accepted the first presidency, "the people's" fears were largely quieted. They trusted Washington to do the right thing—and he did not let them down.

But "the people" did demand something more from the new government: a Bill of Rights. Just as we cannot overestimate the trust people had in George Washington, we should not underestimate the fear of the new Constitution. Its famous preamble was enough to make a farmer in western Pennsylvania fear for his rights. The American people demanded a Bill of Rights to protect them from the Constitution. James Madison, as leader of the first Congress of the United States, wrote the Bill of Rights against his own best judgment because he knew it had to be done in order to calm the fears of "the people."

The Constitution says nothing about every individual's right to "life, liberty and the pursuit of happiness." It says nothing about government's duty to protect the inalienable rights of citizens. Unlike the Declaration of Independence, it does not allow for justified revolt against the government. In fact, the preamble of the Constitution clearly threatens those who disrupt society in the way the revolutionaries had disrupted society in 1775–1776. The preamble states right off that the new government will "insure domestic tranquility" and "provide for the common defense." This is achieved by creating a federal army under the leadership of the president. The *first* duty, in fact, of the new federal army was to attack farmers in western Pennsylvania who were disrupting "domestic tranquility." The threat of the Constitution was real.

So what did Madison include in the Bill of Rights, the first ten amendments to the Constitution? Amendment one declares the inalienable rights of individuals. Amendment two gives "the people" the right to bear arms in order to protect themselves—implied is that "the people" can protect themselves from the new, more powerful federal government. Amendments three and four tell of more rights the new government cannot deny, while five through eight respond to those vague constitutional statements creating a court system not touched by democracy. Finally, amendments nine and ten promise individuals and states that the new Constitution will only take a few new responsibilities, that individuals and states will retain the wide-ranging liberties and powers that they had had under British colonial rule.

The Bill of Rights calmed many people's fear of the new Constitution. George Washington was trusted by an overwhelming majority of citizens. The Revolution, a shooting war full of ringing declarations, had been turned into a government strong enough to enforce domestic tranquility. All the revolutionary rhetoric about universal equality and individual rights of life, liberty, and pursuit of happiness, about the government's responsibility to look out for individual rights, and the right and duty of citizens to overthrow governments that don't, all those exalted sentiments had inspired states to enhance democracy in their new constitutions. The very democratic states then made a very democratic federal union under the Articles of Confederation. But sober men educated in the republican tradition and fearful of too much democracy were common in every state. These sober men appreciated the great ideals of the Declaration of Independence, but they wanted those ideals structured in stable form. As far back as 1776, John Adams, one of the great sober men of the Revolution, received a letter from his wife asking that he "remember the ladies" as he and his friends were designing governments. Men, she wrote, will be tyrants over women just as kings are over colonies. Adams had no desire to complicate matters by raising the gender issue. Nor did he and his compatriots have any interest in raising the slavery issue. Rather they were intent on stabilizing their gains.

Right from the start, the words of the Revolution were being compromised in the name of stability. Such compromises made for the success of the American Revolution. When the Founding Fathers met in secret to overthrow the Articles of Confederation, they did so with the humility of compromisers, not the hubris of revolutionaries.

The Constitution they created has no wild rhetoric. Look to the timidity of its statement of purpose: "in order to form a more perfect union." More perfect! What does that mean? The two words together are baldly meaningless, but those two words are a window into what made the American Revolution one of the greatest events in world history. The American Revolution was conservatively radical. It changed the course of history, proving the possibility of large republics sustaining extensive democracy while inhibiting the negative tendencies associated with democracy. "More perfect" symbolizes the hesitant idealism for government "of the people, by the people, and for the people" that worked its way out in the American Revolution.

"Modern" countries today strive for a mixture of democracy and stability. The writing of constitutions has become a standard form of government creation if a country wishes to have the respect of the rest of the world. America led the pursuit of being "modern" with the creation of the United States. Many other countries sought the goal soon after the success of the United States was evident. The French Revolution, the Haitian Revolution, the Mexican Revolution, the revolutions of 1848—all were early attempts at modernity. In the 1990s South Africans approved a new constitution creating a more democratic and stable country. Their president, Nelson Mandela, is a man like George Washington, a sober man of idealism, a man proven trustworthy. Such people create out of the killing and suffering of war the political revolutions that can stand the test of time. The most influential model in world history of a successful political revolution is the American Revolution of the eighteenth century.

## SELECTED BIBLIOGRAPHY

Bailyn, Bernard. *The Ideological Origins of the American Revolution*. Cambridge, MA: Harvard University Press, 1967. The classic work detailing the intellectual history of the Revolution.

Breen, T. H. *Tobacco Culture: The Mentality of the Great Tidewater Planters on the Eve of the Revolution*. Princeton, NJ: Princeton University Press, 1985. A study of British agrarian ideas of freedom and indebtedness that helps to explain why slave owners embraced the Revolution.

Brookhiser, Richard. *Founding Father: Rediscovering George Washington*. New York: Free Press, 1995. The newest and most readable of the many biographies that identify Washington's character as crucial throughout the Revolution.

Frey, Sylvia. *Water from the Rock: Black Resistance in a Revolutionary Age.* Princeton, NJ: Princeton University Press, 1991. Careful study indicating that the fear of a slave uprising was an important factor in the minds of Southerners.

Gross, Robert A. *The Minutemen in Their World.* New York: Hill and Wang, 1976. An excellent study of revolutionary life in Concord, Massachusetts.

Kammen, Michael. *A Machine that Would Go by Itself: The Constitution in American Culture.* New York: St. Martin's Press, 1994. The Constitution as it has been interpreted throughout United States history.

Kelsey, Isabel T. *Joseph Brant, 1743–1807: Man of Two Worlds.* Syracuse, NY: Syracuse University Press, 1984. Brant was an Iroquois war leader fighting with the British.

Kerber, Linda K. *Women of the Republic: Intellect and Ideology in Revolutionary America.* Chapel Hill: University of North Carolina Press, 1980. The idea of the republican woman as key to the success of creating the American character.

Madison, James. *The Mind of the Founder: Sources of the Political Thought of James Madison.* Edited by Marvin Meyers. Hanover, NH: University Press of New England, 1981. Madison's thoughtfulness and comprehensive mind are evident in this collection.

Maier, Pauline. *The Old Revolutionaries: Political Lives in the Age of Samuel Adams.* New York: Alfred A. Knopf, 1980. Maier shows the diversity of revolutionary convictions and motivations in six men.

Main, Jackson Turner. *The Antifederalists: Critics of the Constitution, 1781–1788.* New York: W. W. Norton, 1974. The process of creating the Constitution from the perspective of those more democratically oriented.

Matthews, Richard K. *If Men Were Angels: James Madison and the Heartless Empire of Reason.* Lawrence: University Press of Kansas, 1995. Matthews' position is that Madison, not Jefferson, is the founder who best states America's ultimate values.

McDonald, Forrest. *Alexander Hamilton: A Biography.* New York: W. W. Norton, 1979. An excellent study of the virtuous ideals and brilliance of a founder too often taught only from the perspective of Jefferson.

Middlekauff, Robert. *The Glorious Cause: The American Revolution, 1763–1798.* New York: Oxford University Press, 1982. The best of recent, in-depth narratives of the event.

Morgan, Edmund S. *Inventing the People: The Rise of Popular Sovereignty in England and America.* New York: W. W. Norton, 1988. A thoughtful analysis of the American abstraction of "the people" in the Constitution.

Morris, Richard B. *Witnesses at the Creation: Hamilton, Madison, Jay, and the Constitution.* New York: Plume, 1985. The three authors of the *Federalist Papers* and their interpretation of the Constitution.

Norton, Mary Beth. *Liberty's Daughters: The Revolutionary Experience of American Independence, 1750–1800.* Boston: Little, Brown, 1980. Women were, of course, intricately involved in the Revolution, but were kept out of the political arena.

Peterson, Merrill D. *Thomas Jefferson and the New Nation: A Biography.* New York: Oxford University Press, 1970. The fullest biography and analysis of the author of the Declaration of Independence and war governor of Virginia.

Richard, Carl J. *The Founders and the Classics: Greece, Rome and the American Enlightenment.* Cambridge, MA: Harvard University Press, 1994. A study of the classical influences on American politics; especially important are the models of mixed government.

Rosswurm, Stephen. *Arms, Country, and Class: The Philadelphia Militia and the "Lower Sort" during the American Revolution.* New Brunswick, NJ: Rutgers University Press, 1988. Focuses on important issues of class in the Revolution's key city.

Wood, Gordon S. *The Creation of the American Republic, 1776–1787.* New York: W. W. Norton, 1972. A classic work on the intellectual conflicts and contrasting ideologies of the period.

———. *The Radicalism of the American Revolution.* New York: Alfred A. Knopf, 1992. Emphasizing radicalism, Wood shows the internal tendencies of the Revolution's political thinkers.

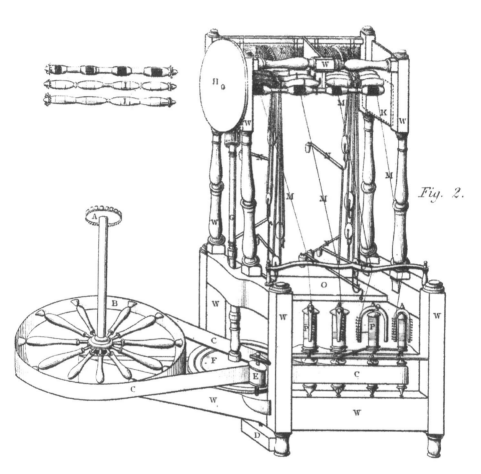

Richard Arkwright's spinning machine typifies the technological advancements that lay at the heart of the Industrial Revolution, a stunning transformation that saw machine production of goods supersede hand production. (Reproduced from the Collections of the Library of Congress)

# 8

# The Industrial Revolution, c. 1775

## INTRODUCTION

The Industrial Revolution was hardly a revolution in the conventional sense of the word. It was not a sudden overthrow of the prevailing status quo; the streets were not filled with revolutionaries. However, it did result in a drastic change in the way human beings produce goods. The transformation from producing goods by hand to producing them by power-driven machines lies at the heart of the Industrial Revolution.

There is no precise date to mark the beginning of the Industrial Revolution, although the first signs of the monumental transformation from hand production to machine production had clearly appeared by the latter decades of the eighteenth century. Moreover, the Industrial Revolution continues today as nonindustrialized countries struggle to industrialize and already industrialized ones adopt new and more efficient technologies.

The home of the Industrial Revolution was Great Britain. There, a fortuitous set of circumstances gave the British both the necessary impetus and the tools to develop new or improved methods of production. Great Britain was blessed with abundant natural resources, especially coal and water, which supplied much of the Industrial Revolution's energy. Great Britain also had a sufficient population base to man the new machines, and this supply of cheap labor expanded as the Agricultural Revolution freed up countless British farm laborers for work in the Industrial Revolution's factories.

An entrepreneurial spirit also characterized British life. For many generations, a significant number of Britons had engaged in commercial activities. They had become accustomed to taking chances in order to secure large financial rewards. Risk taking for profit had become ingrained, and the British had prospered. Its entrepreneurial spirit and its favorable Atlantic location combined to bring wealth to Great Britain. In turn this meant an abundance of surplus capital for investment in new but potentially lucrative ventures such as the invention and perfection of machines. It also meant that many Britons understood the complexities of banking and finance, necessary elements for any economic expansion.

Great Britain was also fortunate in that its large and expanding colonial empire provided ready markets for British production. The demand for goods emanating from the colonies stimulated British producers to seek ways to increase their output. Furthermore, the colonies also supplied Great Britain with inexpensive raw materials such as cotton for the new machines of the Industrial Revolution.

Finally, after the upheavals of the seventeenth century, Great Britain in the eighteenth century provided the model of governmental stability for the world. This stability gave the British entrepreneur a sense of confidence that encouraged him to experiment and to explore new ways to produce goods. This attitude was further bolstered by the fact that the British government viewed commercial and business interests with sympathy and that social mobility in Great Britain was much more of an accomplished fact than on the Continent. A bright, innovative, hardworking man could expect to ascend the British social ladder, although in the eighteenth century the traditional elite continued to occupy that ladder's top rungs.

The Industrial Revolution first appeared in the textile industry. For centuries Great Britain had manufactured and exported woolen cloth. Cloth production took place in innumerable cottages in the British countryside according to the "putting out" or "domestic" system. This system featured merchants or entrepreneurs who delivered raw materials and sometimes supplied equipment to farm households which would spin thread or weave cloth in their spare time. The merchant or entrepreneur would periodically pick up the finished product from the spinner or weaver, pay the family for their work, and sell the product at a profit.

By the early eighteenth century, the popularity of woolen cloth was declining as consumers sought the more comfortable cotton cloth imported from India. The British Parliament imposed high import duties to dampen demand for cotton and thereby protect the woolen industry. The tariffs did not lower demand, which remained as high as ever; but they did open up great possibilities for British producers of cotton cloth. With Indian cottons now prohibitively expensive but the demand for cotton still strong, opportunities for British cotton producers to reap huge profits seemed limitless.

However, technological problems created difficulties. Neither the spinning of cotton thread nor the weaving of cotton cloth could keep up with demand. The latter problem was partially solved in the 1730s when John Kay, a craftsman, invented the flying shuttle, a device that allowed a single weaver sitting at a loom to throw the shuttle from side to side through the warp (the threads running the long way) of the cloth. This simple device greatly accelerated the weaving process and also reduced the number of workers required to produce cotton cloth, because a second person was no longer needed to throw the shuttle.

While the flying shuttle aided the weaving process, spinning of thread lagged behind until James Hargreaves, a weaver and millwright, invented the spinning jenny in the 1760s. Named for his wife, Hargreaves' spinning jenny operated on the same principle as the spinning wheel but at an expanded level that allowed a single spinner to produce six, eight, and then sixteen times as much thread as before.

The next step followed shortly thereafter when in the late 1760s Richard Arkwright invented the water frame. Arkwright's water frame was a larger version of the spinning jenny, but it replaced hand power with water power. However, water power was not entirely reliable, and in 1785 Arkwright substituted a refined version of the steam engine to drive his machines. In requiring first water and then steam to power the frame, it was necessary to move the spinning process from the individual cottage into a larger facility, usually adjacent to a stream. The birth of the factory, where many workers from different locales congregated to produce, with the help of machines, goods that had once been produced in cottages by hand, was now under way.

A further refinement of the spinning process occurred when the weaver Samuel Crompton perfected the spinning mule in 1779. Eventually powered by steam, the mule combined features of the spinning jenny and the water frame to produce copious amounts of a superior thread.

With demand for cottons showing no signs of abating, a new bottleneck had been created as the production of thread exceeded the ability of weavers to make cloth. Edmund Cartwright, a clergyman and amateur inventor, brought the spinning and weaving processes back into balance in 1784 when he invented the power loom. Driven by animal power, water, or steam, the power loom greatly accelerated the weaving of cloth. Although it took some time to catch on, by 1833 there were more than 100,000 power looms operating in Great Britain alone.

The cotton textile industry also faced a problem with the raw material itself. Separating the seeds from the fiber of a cotton boll was tedious, time-consuming, and labor-intensive; but in 1793 the American Eli Whitney invented the cotton gin, which greatly speeded up this process while reducing the required number of workers. Planters, especially in the southern portions of the United States, turned to growing cotton, and the textile factories in Great Britain now had an adequate supply of the raw material. By 1800 cotton cloth production in Great Britain was eight times what it had been only twenty years earlier; and by 1820 cotton exports made up 46 percent of Great Britain's export trade.

Power driven machinery proved to be essential for the expansion of the textile industry; and while water as a source of power was important, steam—in the form of the steam engine—soon occupied a position of primacy. The power of steam was known to the ancients—Hero of Alexandria had invented something resembling a steam engine—but it was only in the seventeenth century that modern man seriously turned his attention to the possibilities of steam.

As Europe's forests dwindled and charcoal became more difficult and expensive to obtain, the demand for coal as a source of heat for smelting iron and forging metal increased. However, when coal-mining shafts dropped below the water table, coal mines tended to fill with water. It soon became clear that the continued exploitation of coal as a source of energy depended upon the development of an efficient way to bail water from mines. An answer of sorts was provided during the first decade of the eighteenth century when Thomas Newcomen, an ironmonger, harnessed the power of steam to produce an engine capable of driving a pump. However, this Newcomen engine was clumsy, costly, and not particularly efficient.

In 1763 James Watt, a technician at the University of Glasgow, began to tinker with Newcomen's engine. Watt made the device more efficient and provided for the rotary power required of most machines through a system of gears dubbed the "sun and planet." He patented his new steam engine in 1769, but it was not an immediate success. By the 1780s, however, Watt's steam engine was gaining popularity as a source of constant, forceful power for driving machines. The power that the Industrial Revolution required was now at hand.

Iron was the most important building block of the Industrial Revolution. Compared to iron, machines and engines constructed of wood lacked durability; but iron was difficult to produce. Specifically, the smelting of iron ore to retrieve the metal required large amounts of charcoal, and by the eighteenth century many European countries, including Great Britain, had used up the forests that served as the raw material for charcoal.

Substituting coal, which was cheap and plentiful, for charcoal had proven unsatisfactory because the mineral impurities present in coal tended to be absorbed into the molten iron during the smelting process. However, in 1709 Abraham Darby, an ironmaster, partially solved this problem when he smelted iron ore with coke, or coal whose impurities had been burned off in a baking-like process. The resulting product—pig iron—although good for casting, still contained too many impurities and had to be smelted further with charcoal to produce wrought iron or steel, a costly and time-consuming procedure.

With an increasing demand for iron, new technologies appeared to accelerate the iron-making process. It was discovered that jets of air applied to the coke during the smelting process would increase the temperature and burn off more impurities. Then in the 1780s Henry Cort hit upon the puddling process. He discovered that by stirring, or puddling, the molten iron ore as it was being smelted with coke, even more impurities would be burned off. The resultant product could be made into wrought iron or steel without additional charcoal smelting. Cort further perfected iron making in the 1780s when he invented the rolling mill, a device similar to the rollers found on an old-fashioned wringer washer that squeezed even more impurities from the molten metal and produced sheets of iron that were more easily applied to industrial use. The great building block of the Industrial Revolution had arrived.

---

## INTERPRETIVE ESSAY
*David Mitch*

The economy of Britain in 1850 produced over 50 percent more per person than it had in 1750. This implies an average rate of growth of about half a percent per year over this period. By late twentieth-century standards, such increases in economic productivity seem quite modest. Since 1950, output per person has grown at a rate of about 2 percent a year in the United States, 4 percent a year in western Germany, 5 percent a year in South Korea, 6 percent a year in Japan, and almost 8 percent a year in Singapore. Moreover, the human race, due to its inherent intelligence, has always had the capability of improving its living standards. And there is evidence of technological advance and consequent advances in economic productivity from the Stone Age onward.

However, in the late eighteenth and early nineteenth century, sustaining a continued increase in output per person with population growing at 1 percent per year, as the British economy of the time in fact did, was unprecedented. The possibility of output per capita growing at a rate of half a percent per year in the face of rising population levels for any sustained period of time would appear highly unlikely prior to 1750. Projecting growth at this rate back in time for several decades or more would imply that levels of output prevailing earlier in time would have been too low to sustain human life. Based on pessimistic expectations of the possibility for improvements in productivity, Thomas Malthus, in his *Essay on Population*, published in 1798, put forth the argument that population growth continually threatened to outstrip the growth of the food supply and hence consign the bulk of the human race to survival at a subsistence level. In the words of T. S. Ashton, whose book *The Industrial Revolution* is an influential account of the British Industrial Revolution:

> The central problem of the age [the late eighteenth and early nineteenth century] was how to feed and clothe and employ generations of children outnumbering by far those of any earlier time. . . . If England had remained a nation of cultivators and craftsmen . . . the weight of a growing population must have pressed down the spring of her spirit. She was delivered, not by her rulers, but by those who, seeking no doubt their own narrow ends, had the wit and resource to devise new instruments of production and new methods of administering industry. There are today on the plains of India and China men and women, plague-ridden and hungry, living lives little better, to outward appearance, than those of the cattle that toil with them by day and share their places of sleep by night. Such Asiatic standards, and such unmechanized horrors, are the lot of those who increase their numbers without passing through an industrial revolution.

That the growth rates achieved by the British economy between 1750 and 1850 were unprecedented in human experience is also suggested by the assessment of the distinguished English historian and member of Parliament Thomas Babington Macaulay. Writing in 1830, toward the end of the Industrial Revolution, Macaulay declared: "If we were to prophesy that in the year 1930 a population of fifty million, better fed, clad, and lodged than the English of our time, will cover these islands, that Sussex and Huntingdonshire will be wealthier than the wealthiest parts of the West Riding of Yorkshire now are . . . that machines constructed on principles yet undiscovered will be in every house . . . many people would think us insane."

Macaulay's forecast in the event was remarkably accurate, even to the level of population, which, if Ireland is included, was off by less than 2 percent.

An English schoolboy wrote the following in answer to an examination question on the Industrial Revolution: "About 1760 a wave of gadgets swept over England." Inventions and new technologies such as the mechanization of cotton spinning, the power loom, the puddling process for making iron and steel, and the steam engine were certainly central to the Industrial Revolution. Over two-thirds of the increase in output per capita achieved by the British economy between 1760 and 1830 can be attributed to improvements in productivity rather than to the accumulation of labor and capital. Technological advance occurred far more rapidly in some industries than in others in the late eighteenth-century British economy. But industries experiencing rapid technological advance were diverse in character, ranging from textile manufacture and iron and steel to railroads, ocean shipping, and agriculture. Thus the British Industrial Revolution could be interpreted as an instance of technological advance setting in motion profound economic and social change.

But why was the pace of technological advance so rapid in late eighteenth-century England? The advance of scientific knowledge, such as Isaac Newton's fundamental contributions to physics earlier in the eighteenth century, surprisingly did not play a role. The inventions of the British Industrial Revolution all originated from trial and error tinkering rather than from the insight provided by scientific principles. The few formal scientific principles that late eighteenth-century British inventors did employ appear in retrospect to have been erroneous.

In general, simple, single-cause explanations of British technological advance and of why the Industrial Revolution occurred first in Britain are unsatisfactory. This point is exemplified by the most obvious of explanations as to why Britain would have been a technological leader in the eighteenth century, the presence of a superior educational system. In fact, British educational institutions at all levels in the eighteenth century were at best mediocre. Roughly half of all English men and women in the eighteenth century were unable to even sign their names. Oxford and Cambridge, the major English universities, were notoriously stagnant and decrepit compared with the far more vibrant Dutch and Scottish universities of the day.

Nor are other commonly offered explanations for Britain's early industrialization any more satisfactory. Britain was blessed with abundant coal and iron deposits, and its island position afforded it ready access to cheap transport by water. However, natural resource constraints could be overcome by importing resources in scarce supply domestically. Indeed, Britain imported a good deal of iron ore during the nineteenth century. If Belgium, with its abundance of coal and iron ore, was relatively quick to follow the British course of industrialization, so was Switzerland, where coal and iron had to be imported. That reliance on importation of key resources from abroad was no barrier to sustained industrial growth is clearly illustrated by British cotton production. The British cotton textile industry imported the entirety of its raw cotton from abroad, and yet was one of the fastest growing manufacturing sectors during the British Industrial Revolution. Similarly, although Britain appears to have experienced substantial improvement in its agricultural productivity just prior to the Industrial Revolution, its ability to import food from abroad tends to minimize the importance of this factor. Finally, to turn to another common explanation of early British industrial leadership, it has often been observed that the proprietors of Britain's new industrial enterprises were disproportionately from nonconformist Protestant faiths. Yet similar faiths were practiced with equal intensity in Holland and Prussia without resulting in the same flourishing of manufacturing establishments.

Even if no one cause can account for why the Industrial Revolution occurred first in Britain, a number of factors did enable the British economy to profit considerably from late eighteenth-century inventions. Over the previous century and a half, British merchants had been establishing increasingly regular trade routes throughout the world. As production of cotton cloth burgeoned, British manufacturers could draw on extensive experience and well-developed world networks in finding foreign buyers for the product. The development of a constitutional monarchy in the later seventeenth century and the early eighteenth century meant that the power of any British king or queen was in large part balanced and offset by the power of Parliament. This limited the power of the king or queen to tax the profits of the increasingly prosperous enterprises engaged in manufacturing textiles, iron, steel, and similar products. Those who were investing funds in manufacturing enterprises were further assured of retaining a significant proportion of the profits by the gradual evolution of a system of common law in England that had come to establish definite ownership and rights of control over property. Furthermore, compared with other European societies, wealth carried more inherent social status in Britain. There was more direct incentive in English society to pursue the accumulation of wealth rather than to pursue other routes to prestige such as the acquisition of an aristocratic title or a landed estate. Another contributing factor was that England was relatively tolerant, though hardly entirely so, of diverse religious and cultural traditions. This toleration allowed diverse sources of talent and ideas to contribute to the innovation and development of new technologies and enterprises.

Thus, on the one hand the British Industrial Revolution established that sustained long-term economic growth was possible. On the other hand, an examination of its causes points to the complexity of the factors underlying long-run economic growth.

The Industrial Revolution offered the prospect of higher earnings for at least some British workers. A male cotton spinner in England around 1800 could expect to earn more than twice as much per week as a male farm worker. And Andrew Ure, a noted early nineteenth-century advocate of the advantages of the new technologies in manufacturing, argued in *The Philosophy of Manufactures* that these earnings were obtained under easier working conditions:

> In my recent tour . . . through the manufacturing districts, I have seen tens of thousands of old, young, and middle-aged of both sexes, many of them too feeble to get their daily bread by any of the former modes of industry, earning abundant food, raiment, and domestic accommodation, without perspiring at a single pore, screened meanwhile from the summer's sun and the winter's frost, in apartments more airy and salubrious than those of the metropolis in which our legislative and fashionable aristocracies assemble.

However, cotton spinning was one of the most highly paid of all textile occupations, and most cotton textile workers, whether male or female, had neither the skills nor the opportunity to enter such highly paid work and had to settle for much less. If the work force as a whole is considered and

full allowance given for the growth of particularly highly paid manufacturing occupations, average working-class incomes at best rose modestly
during the Industrial Revolution and by some accounts may have actually
fallen. Eventually the benefits of marked improvements in productivity
did reach all segments of the British labor force, and the average British
worker in 1900 probably could buy a mix of goods and services more than
double the value of that of his counterpart in 1850.

But whether working-class earnings changed for the better or the
worse, and no matter when this may have occurred, the conditions of
working-class life changed in other important dimensions throughout
the Industrial Revolution.

Perhaps the one most easily measured is the movement of people from
country to city. In 1760, four of every five inhabitants of Britain resided
in rural areas; by 1840, when, according to many historians, the Industrial Revolution in Britain had already come to an end, this proportion
had fallen to one out of every two. It was thus still the case that by the
end of the period commonly associated with the British Industrial Revolution, farm and related rural influences were pervasive in British society. But for the growing numbers of English men, women, and children
who moved from the countryside to the city, the contrast in sights,
sounds, and smells would have been striking. This is evident in the following account of the Hale family as it arrived in the fictional northern
manufacturing town of Milton after residing for years in a rural village,
as related in Elizabeth Gaskell's mid-nineteenth-century novel, *North and
South*:

> For several miles before they reached Milton, they saw a deep
> lead-coloured cloud hanging over the horizon in the direction
> in which it lay. It was all the darker from contrast with the
> pale gray-blue of the wintry sky. . . . Nearer to the town, the
> air had a faint taste and smell of smoke; perhaps, after all,
> more a loss of the fragrance of grass and herbage than any
> positive taste or smell. Quick they were whirled over long,
> straight, hopeless streets of regularly-built houses, all small
> and of brick. Here and there a great oblong many windowed
> factory stood up, like a hen among her chickens, puffing out
> black "unparliamentary" smoke, and sufficiently accounting
> for the cloud which Margaret had taken to foretell rain . . .
> every van, every wagon and truck, bore cotton, either in the
> raw shape in bags, or the woven shape in bales of calico. Peo-
> ple thronged the footpaths, most of them well-dressed as re-

garded the material, but with a slovenly looseness which struck Margaret as different from the shabby, threadbare smartness of a similar class in London.

Frederick Engels, the friend and collaborator of Karl Marx, painted an even starker picture than Gaskell in *The Condition of the Working Class in England*, written in 1844 and based on his travels in England:

> If we briefly formulate the result of our wanderings, we must admit that 350,000 working-people of Manchester and its environs live, almost all of them, in wretched, damp, filthy cottages, that the streets which surround them are usually in the most miserable and filthy condition, laid out without the slightest reference to ventilation, with reference solely to the profit secured by the contractor.... Here are long, narrow lanes between which run contracted, crooked courts and passages, the entrances to which are so irregular that the explorer is caught in a blind alley at every few steps, or comes out where he least expects to, unless he knows every court and every alley exactly and separately.... When the sanitary police made its expedition hither in 1831 ... they found in Parliament Street for three hundred and eighty persons, and in Parliament Passage for thirty thickly populated houses, but a single privy.

One important change in the worker's daily environment attributable to industrialization was the rise in the proportion of productive activity that occurred in factories rather than in cottages and workshops. The use of a central power source to drive machinery was the distinctive technological feature of the factory. But the factory also allowed increased control over work effort by centralizing the location of work. According to the noted nineteenth-century advocate of factory production, Andrew Ure: "The principle of the factory system ... is to substitute mechanical science for hand skill.... The grand object ... of the modern manufacturer is, through the union of capital and science, to reduce the task of his work-people to the exercise of vigilance and dexterity."

The development of the manufacturing sector, however, was not just confined to the large-scale factory. More traditional ways of organizing production such as craft and workshop operations continued to be important throughout the nineteenth century. According to the 1851 census of England and Wales, industries such as building, tailoring, and shoemaking, typically organized according to traditional craft and artisan principles, employed more male workers than industries such as cotton, wool, or iron manufacture, where the factory method of production was common. However, if female as well as male employment is taken into account, then the factory mode of organization was relatively more important. The nature of the urban and manufacturing environment would have taken on a particularly concentrated form in the hours the worker would have spent in a factory. As Engels describes it:

> The supervision of machinery, the joining of broken threads, is no activity which claims the operative's thinking powers, yet it is of a sort which prevents him from occupying his mind with other things . . . this work affords the muscles no opportunity for physical activity. . . . Moreover, he must not take a moment's rest; the engine moves unceasingly; the wheels, the straps, the spindles hum and rattle in his ears without a pause, and if he tries to snatch one instant, there is the overlooker at his back with the book of fines.

The difference between the manufacturing and agricultural districts of England was evident not only in bleak physical accounts of the environment in manufacturing districts but also in their higher rates of disease and mortality. The higher wages commonly paid in manufacturing districts to a large degree simply compensated workers for the health risks and lower life expectancy that came from living in such districts.

Despite the evident changes in physical environment that were associated with the rise of the manufacturing sector, there were also important aspects of continuity with traditional rural British society. If there was extensive geographical mobility in industrial areas, with large proportions of the population living their adult lives quite far from where they had been born, such also appears to have been the case in many preindustrial rural areas. If the family was an important source of security and assistance during periods of individual life crisis in preindustrial agrarian societies, it also served that role in mid-nineteenth-century manufacturing cities, even if family members were physically separated and living many miles apart. Employment opportunities for women and children may have increased somewhat during the Industrial Revolution. However, the employment of women and children was also common in agriculture. And the number of children under ten employed in any activity, whether on farms or in factories, was never more than a very small percentage of the total work force. Even in industrial areas, most married women were not employed full time.

The influence of traditional landed interests was more persistent than one might have expected during the British Industrial Revolution. To be sure, ever increasing numbers of workers found themselves working in factories rather than on farms, and manufacturing proprietors came to control an increasing share of British wealth. However, Parliament continued to be controlled by rural landed interests through at least the first third of the nineteenth century, as the Industrial Revolution in England was nearing an end. Despite occasional strikes and uprisings, the labor union movement did not build widespread momentum until later in the nineteenth century. The Labour Party emerged as a major force in British politics only in the twentieth century. Preindustrial British society was notable for its stratification into intricate layers of status. Although the nature of the layers and occupational groupings was to change with the Industrial Revolution, a similar complexity of layers remained. And this may well have been an obstacle to formation of broadly unified social groupings. Just as there was a fine gradation of status according to landholding in preindustrial Britain, similar gradations emerged according to the amount of capital invested in one's shop or factory, or according to the exact type of manufacturing skill one practiced.

The social and economic changes associated with the Industrial Revolution did set in motion important impulses for political reform. From the 1830s onward there were extensive series of investigations by Parliament and various civic groups into problems commonly thought to have been spawned by industrialization, such as crime, ill health, and poverty. A wide range of parliamentary legislation aimed at correcting these problems resulted. The so-called Factory Acts restricted the employment and hours of work of women and children in factories. The Public Health Act of 1848 was spurred by recurrent outbreaks of cholera in industrial cities and aimed at improving sewage disposal and purifying water supplies. Industrial areas were poorly provided with schools during the Industrial Revolution. In the last two-thirds of the nineteenth century, efforts to expand schooling were reflected in marked improvements in literacy rates. As awareness of the social problems associated with industrialization grew, so did the perception of the inadequacies of the free market and voluntary agencies in coping with these problems. Thus, government both at the national and the local level came to assume an ever-increasing responsibility for addressing them. This in turn led to efforts to improve the administration of government at all levels so that it was guided more by systematic policy than by the idiosyncratic, narrow interests of parish functionaries and country squires.

The British Industrial Revolution had repercussions throughout the rest of the world, and these continued long after 1850, when Britain's rise to preeminence as an industrial power had been completed. However, it should also be noted that important aspects of Britain's international influence cannot be attributed to industrialization. Britain already had extensive colonies in North America, India, and elsewhere in Asia by the mid-eighteenth century, when its full-scale industrialization got under way. Correspondingly, by this time British merchants had established networks for commercial dealings throughout the world. To be sure, the demand of British factories for raw cotton helped generate a demand for slaves in the American South to grow that cotton. But many slaves were used in the New World to grow products with nonindustrial uses, such as sugar and rice.

The influence of British industrialists may have been stronger in the promotion of free trade than in extending the British Empire. Over half of Britain's cotton textile production was exported abroad. And British industrialists also had an interest in eliminating high tariffs on imports of grain from abroad. Cheap grain prices meant that factory workers would be likely to settle for lower wages because bread prices would be lower. Adam Smith and David Ricardo, who developed the intellectual arguments for free trade, were not directly associated with industrial interests. Moreover, tariffs on grain imports were actually increased in the early nineteenth century when industrialization was in full swing. Only in 1846 were the tariffs on grain imports repealed, and the politics behind repeal were complex. But although repeal entailed more than simply industrial interests in Parliament prevailing over landed interests, industrial interests were well represented in the Anti–Corn Law League, one of the most visible lobbying groups pushing for repeal of the tariffs on grain imports. The introduction of the telegraph and the steamship in the later nineteenth century perhaps did more than the earlier rise of the manufacturing sector to integrate world markets. Nevertheless, British industrialization should be seen as a significant contributing factor in the ongoing formation of a global economy, attributable to the interest industrialists had in promoting their exports and in encouraging cheap imports of food for their factory workers.

The British Industrial Revolution is of enduring significance as one of the earliest economic episodes in which income per capita and population levels were able to rise simultaneously. However, other countries have been able to accomplish the same result in diverse ways. Belgium followed the British path fairly closely, with initial growth in cotton textiles and then in coal production. Indeed, Belgium's early industrialization rather consciously tried to imitate British practices by industrial espionage. A Belgian named Lieven Bauwens successfully smuggled British textile spinning machinery into Belgium to set up the first mechanized textile spinning factory outside of England. The mechanization of cotton textiles was also prominent in the industrialization of the United States and Japan. But other economies found alternative ways of achieving prosperity. In the late nineteenth century, Scandinavian countries were able to take advantage of strong international markets for dairy products, timber, and fish to achieve rapid economic growth without extensive industrialization. In the late twentieth century, Hong Kong and Singapore based the growth of their manufacturing sectors on their strength as trading centers.

The British Industrial Revolution did not define a standard course of economic development that all subsequent economies experiencing rapid economic growth were to follow. But it did establish a number of features that have become characteristic of modern economic growth, even if these features are by no means indispensable. The most obvious feature has been the shift in economic activity away from agriculture. Half of the male labor force in Britain in 1760, on the eve of its Industrial Revolution, was employed in agriculture. The same proportion was employed in agriculture in France and Germany as they began pronounced expansion of their industrial sectors in the mid-nineteenth century. By 1840, when the initial phase of its Industrial Revolution had been completed, Britain had just over one-fourth of its male labor force employed in agriculture, and by 1910 that proportion had fallen to 11 percent. The magnitude of the shift away from agriculture was unusually high in Britain in the course of its Industrial Revolution. Belgium, Germany, and France at the end of the nineteenth century, with their first phase of industrial expansion largely completed, still had, respectively, 32 percent, 36 percent, and 40 percent of their male labor force employed in agriculture. Nevertheless, a declining role for agriculture has been a common though by no means universal experience for economies undergoing significant economic growth over the last century and a half.

Another common accompaniment of modern economic growth has been urbanization, with all of the contrasts between city and country life that this entails. In Britain, as noted above, the proportion of the population residing in urban areas rose from about one-fifth in 1760 to one-half in 1840. In Germany and France in 1870, in their initial stages of industrialization, roughly one-third of the population resided in urban areas, a higher proportion than in Britain on the eve of its industrialization. But the continued shift into towns and cities proceeded at a slower pace than in Britain. By 1900, only 56 percent of the German population and 44 percent of the French population resided in urban areas compared with three-fourths of the British population.

As noted above, in one important dimension change was relatively modest during the British Industrial Revolution compared to subsequent instances of economic growth elsewhere. The increase of output per capita of half a percent per year experienced in Britain during its Industrial Revolution was exceeded by growth at double and even triple that rate in France, Germany, Japan, the Soviet Union, and the United States as these economies industrialized in the late nineteenth century and the early twentieth century.

In its mode of manufacturing production, Britain pursued an intermediate course compared with subsequent industrializing countries. Although the spread of factories during British industrialization drew much notice from contemporary commentators, traditional workshop and craft modes of production persisted in importance in Britain throughout its Industrial Revolution. France and Switzerland are generally viewed as having made more use of these traditional modes during their industrialization. It is in the United States, with the spread of the assembly line and other mass-production techniques, and in Germany, with its large industrial conglomerates, that new methods of organizing industry became especially prominent.

Conservative, rural interests retained substantial political influence in many industrializing countries. If Britain was only able to repeal sizeable tariffs on food imports in the mid-nineteenth century, other industrializing countries such as France, Germany, Japan, and the United States pursued far more protectionist tariff policies for a much longer time. And in these countries, as in Britain, truly influential organized labor movements emerged only in the very late nineteenth century and into the early twentieth century. Nevertheless, most industrializing countries followed Britain in recognizing that government intervention was required to cope with some of the adverse consequences of industrialization. First, regulation of the employment of women and children in factories, and later, provision of basic social insurance to ensure access to health care, unemployment compensation, and income in old age became established in most industrializing countries.

The British Industrial Revolution made the world aware of the complexity and depth of the changes set in motion by long-term economic change. In 1776, as the British Industrial Revolution was barely under way, Adam Smith published one of history's most influential books, *An Inquiry into the Nature and Causes of the Wealth of Nations*. Smith emphasized how government policy could influence economic performance. In two other influential books written about a century later, the emphasis was reversed. Karl Marx in *Capital*, written in 1867, and Arnold Toynbee in *Lectures on the Industrial Revolution of the Eighteenth Century in England*, published in 1884, both emphasized the profound ways in which the growth of the manufacturing sector had altered political and social relationships in Britain. It was thus after the events of the British Industrial Revolution had come to pass that writers such as Marx and Toynbee fully appreciated the potential for economic change to transform the general course of human history.

## SELECTED BIBLIOGRAPHY

Ashton, T. S. *The Industrial Revolution, 1760–1830*. London: Oxford University Press, 1948. A noted British economic historian's especially influential overview of the fundamental changes caused by the British Industrial Revolution.

Berg, Maxine. *The Age of Manufactures: Industry, Innovation and Work in Britain, 1700–1820*. London: Fontana Press, 1985. Argues for the importance of traditional craft, cottage, and workshop forms of production during the Industrial Revolution.

Brown, John C. "The Condition of England and the Standard of Living: Cotton Textiles in the Northwest, 1806–1850." *Journal of Economic History* 50 (1990): 591–615. Finds that higher wages paid in textile manufacturing districts compensated for higher mortality rates and other hardships in England's industrial areas.

Collier, Frances. *The Family Economy of the Working Classes in the Cotton Industry, 1784–1833*. Manchester: Manchester University Press, 1964. Considers the organization of the working-class family in cotton manufacturing areas during the Industrial Revolution.

Crafts, N. F. R. *British Economic Growth during the Industrial Revolution*. Oxford: Oxford University Press, 1985. An important quantitative history of the Industrial Revolution.

Crouzet, François. *The First Industrialists: The Problems of Origins*. Cambridge: Cambridge University Press, 1985. Examines the extent to which those who ran industrial enterprises tended to come from particular religious, social, and educational backgrounds.

Evans, Eric. *The Forging of the Modern State. Early Industrial Britain: 1783–1870*. London: Longman, 1983. A useful general history of Britain during the era of industrial revolution.

Floud, R., and D. McCloskey, eds. *The Economic History of Britain since 1700. Vol. 1: 1700–1860*. 2nd ed. Cambridge: Cambridge University Press, 1994. Essays by economists on specific aspects of the British Industrial Revolution.

Himmelfarb, Gertrude. *The Idea of Poverty: England in the Early Industrial Age*. New York: Alfred A. Knopf, 1984. An intellectual history of the efforts of eighteenth-and early nineteenth-century British social commentators and policymakers to address the problems of poverty associated with the British Industrial Revolution.

Kuznets, Simon. *Modern Economic Growth: Rate, Structure, and Spread.* New Haven, CT: Yale University Press, 1966. Surveys general patterns of economic growth and thus provides standards of reference for the British Industrial Revolution.

Landes, D. *The Unbound Prometheus: Technological Change and Industrial Development in Western Europe from 1750 to the Present.* Cambridge: Cambridge University Press, 1969. A comparative survey of the role of technological change in western European economic development.

Mantoux, Paul. *The Industrial Revolution in the Eighteenth Century.* Rev. ed. New York: Harper Torchbooks, 1961. A classic early history of the Industrial Revolution which puts particular emphasis on the impact of the factory and the role of organizational changes in the British economy.

Mokyr, J. *The Lever of Riches: Technological Creativity and Economic Progress.* Oxford: Oxford University Press, 1990. A survey of technological progress, including the Industrial Revolution period, aimed at a general audience.

———, ed. *The British Industrial Revolution: An Economic Perspective.* Boulder, CO: Westview Press, 1993. Contains surveys of technology, macroeconomic trends, agriculture, and human capital as well as a comprehensive overview by the editor.

Morris, R. J. *Class and Class Consciousness in the Industrial Revolution, 1780–1850.* London: Macmillan, 1979. A concise survey of the literature on the formation of social classes during the Industrial Revolution.

Pollard, S. *Typology of Industrialization Processes in the Nineteenth Century.* Chur: Harwood Academic, 1990. A systematic survey of industrialization in Europe, North America, and Japan.

Roberts, D. *Victorian Origins of the British Welfare State.* New Haven, CT: Yale University Press, 1960. An examination of the rise of bureaucratic administration in British government that ensued in the aftermath of the British Industrial Revolution.

Stearns, P. N. *The Industrial Revolution in World History.* Boulder, CO: Westview Press, 1993. Discusses the concept of the Industrial Revolution and its ramifications in comparative perspective.

Taylor, Arthur J., ed. *The Standard of Living in Britain in the Industrial Revolution.* London: Methuen, 1975. A collection of important articles debating whether working-class living standards rose during the British Industrial Revolution.

Thompson, E. P. *The Making of the English Working Class.* New York: Vintage, 1963. A classic study of the development of a working-class movement during the Industrial Revolution.

Toynbee, A. *Lectures on the Industrial Revolution in England.* London: Rivingtons, 1884. One of the earliest and most influential statements of the profound economic and social consequences stemming from industrialization in England.

Williamson, J. G. *Did British Capitalism Breed Inequality?* London: Allen and Unwin, 1985. A quantitative history of trends in income inequality in Britain in the eighteenth and nineteenth centuries.

# The Atlantic Slave Trade, c. 1780

## INTRODUCTION

Slavery is almost as old as mankind itself. Our earliest ancestors most likely engaged in slavery; certainly the ancient Mesopotamians and Egyptians held slaves. The much-praised Greek civilization of the fifth century B.C. featured the institution of slavery. The Roman Empire not only enslaved whites, but also imported slaves from Black Africa, or Africa south of the Sahara Desert. Later on, the Moslems continued this practice, and during the Middle Ages Europeans occasionally acquired a black slave or two from Arab traders. The first recorded instance of the direct importation of slaves from Black Africa to modern Europe occurred in 1441 when an enterprising Portuguese captain shipped home about a dozen Africans from the coast of Guinea as a gift to his sovereign, Prince Henry the Navigator. This marks the beginning of the modern slave trade, a business activity having great economic and social consequences that reached a climax in the eighteenth century.

To a large extent, the growth of the slave trade arose from the discovery of the New World and the economic pressures that ensued as the Europeans exploited this discovery. The nature of Europe's colonial holdings in the New World created a demand for labor that slaves from Africa would ultimately fill. The Spanish, followed at some distance by

Employing inhumane methods, the Atlantic slave trade peaked during the eighteenth century, when more than 5 million African slaves arrived in the New World. (Reproduced from the Collections of the Library of Congress)

the Portuguese, carried out the initial exploitation of the New World. At first the Spanish focused on extracting precious metals, especially gold and silver; later they turned to large-scale agricultural production.

In both cases there was a significant demand for labor. Since the Spanish themselves would not meet that demand, they turned to the Indian natives of the New World, virtually enslaving them for work in the mines or the fields. However, the natives did not work well enough to suit their European masters. Many failed to meet the physical demands of the grueling labor; even more died of disease. Conditions proved so difficult that extinction of the native stock loomed, and in some regions such as the Caribbean it actually occurred. Moreover, Roman Catholic missionaries sent to the New World tended to object to the enslavement of the Indians. These objections—coupled with the much more serious problem of the labor supply's depletion—caused a labor crisis for the Europeans that they solved by importing ever increasing numbers of black slaves from Africa.

Blacks may have sailed with Columbus, and others may have arrived in the New World early in the sixteenth century; however, the slave trade can be dated formally to 1513, when King Ferdinand of Spain approved the importation of black slaves into Spain's New World possessions. Initial shipments of slaves were sent to Cuba, Hispaniola, Puerto Rico, and Jamaica. Shortly thereafter, black slaves appeared in Brazil, a Portuguese colony. By the middle of the sixteenth century, perhaps as many as 100,000 African slaves had been transported to the Americas.

At first the Spanish and Portuguese controlled the slave trade. The former dominated the slave markets of the New World, while the latter controlled the source of the supply, the West African coast. In order to regularize the trade, the Spanish created the *asiento*, a system whereby Spanish authorities bestowed a royal grant to engage in slave trading on a few selected merchants or groups of merchants acting as a joint-stock company. Usually this system operated well, although occasionally a foreign vessel intruded into the comfortable world that the Spanish and Portuguese had built for themselves. The most famous of these interlopers was the English sea captain John Hawkins, who in 1562 sold his first cargo of African slaves to the Spanish colonists. By the end of the century, the Dutch had also joined in the trade.

Ambitious English and French traders did not really enter into the slave trade until their own New World colonies began to demand slave labor in the seventeenth century. The first slaves in what would become the United States landed at Jamestown, Virginia, in 1619. They were delivered by a Dutch merchantman.

During the seventeenth century, the slave trade expanded at a steady pace. However, toward the end of the century and throughout the eighteenth century it took off. The reason for its great expansion was a drastically increased demand for cheap labor (slaves) occasioned by an important shift in production. Beginning in the middle of the seventeenth century, planters in the New World started to cultivate labor-intensive crops. The cultivation was accomplished on a grand scale on large economic units called plantations. Plantation crops included cotton, indigo, coffee, ginger, and tobacco. However, sugar was by far the most important crop. Between 1713 and 1792, Britain's Caribbean islands shipped £162 million worth of goods to the mother country, almost all of it sugar or sugar products. The £162 million was more than 50 percent greater than the entire value of goods brought into Great Britain from India and China during the same period. Sugar was a phenomenal cash crop, but it required massive amounts of labor. More than 600,000 slaves were imported into the sugar island of Jamaica alone.

During the eighteenth century, merchants from many different countries practiced the slave trade. Great Britain dominated the trade, shipping perhaps 50 percent of the human cargo that originated in Africa. France was important too; perhaps as much as 25 percent of the slave trade belonged to France. Dutch, American, Danish, and Portuguese ships also participated. Spain still played an important role in the American market, but seldom engaged in shipping slaves from Africa.

The acquisition of slaves in Africa for the American market involved a large degree of cooperation between white traders and their African hosts. Typically, upon arriving in Africa the European slavers would make contact with the native leadership. European trading representatives who lived permanently at trading posts or factories on the African coast often arranged these meetings. Bargaining would then take place, and the African leaders would grant the Europeans the right to take slaves for shipment to the New World in exchange for European products. These chieftains also set the price for slaves and frequently placed a bounty or tax on each slave that went directly into the chief's pocket. To facilitate the quest for slaves, the leaders would provide the Europeans with native warriors and arrange liaison with native traders. Sometimes those sold as slaves to the Europeans were debtors or petty criminals, but most frequently they were prisoners of war. The designation "prisoner of war" was loosely applied; often slavers simply swooped down on unsuspecting villages, grabbed every man, woman, and child in sight, and hustled the whole lot off into slavery. In any event, the desire to capture prisoners of war to meet the European demand for slaves probably contributed to warfare among African tribes.

As for the Europeans, at first the slave trade was a monopolistic arrangement featuring government chartered companies that were granted the exclusive right to engage in slave trading. By the early eighteenth century, especially in Great Britain and France, independent merchants and companies successfully entered the field. Many European ports such as Bristol and Liverpool in Great Britain and Nantes in France grew wealthy and powerful thanks to their interests in the slave trade. So, too, did American cities such as Boston and Providence.

The slave trade was an integral part of what became known as the "triangular trade," a complex and sophisticated exchange of goods that involved Europe, Africa, and the New World. While there were many variations on a single theme, the most common form of triangular trade featured ships laden with European goods such as cloth, spirits, iron, brass, guns, and gunpowder landing at African ports. These European products would be exchanged for slaves. The slaves would then be transported to the New World, usually Brazil, the Caribbean islands, Latin America, or what would become the southern United States. There the human cargo would be exchanged for plantation products, usually sugar or sugar products such as molasses, that would be sent back to Europe for sale.

The leg of the triangular trade that brought slaves from Africa to the New World was called the middle passage, and it was brutal in the extreme. In order to maximize profits, slavers crammed as many bodies as they could into the holds of their boats. Africans were manacled and arranged head to toe with barely enough overhead room to sit upright in their place. They wallowed in their own filth among rats and vermin except when permitted on deck, where the crew exercised them under harsh conditions. Disease was rampant, and to save money the slavers cut rations to the bone. The average middle passage lasted from four to ten weeks. Although many Africans died en route, the significant profits that the slavers made provided economic justification for the ill treatment of the slaves.

Not surprisingly, verifiable figures about the slave trade are difficult to find. Nevertheless, most experts conclude that approximately 10 to 11 million Africans were brought to the New World. Of that number, about 40 percent ended up in Brazil and another 40 percent in the Caribbean. The remaining 20 percent ended up in British North America and Spanish America. Frequently the slave population dwarfed the European one.

For example, at the time of the French Revolution, the population of Saint Domingue (Haiti) consisted of 500,000 slaves and only 35,000 whites.

At the height of the eighteenth-century slave trade, slavers annually brought about 80,000 Africans to the New World. Those sold in the British Caribbean had a life expectancy of about seven years. Needless to say, the slaves had no legal rights, being regarded simply as pieces of chattel.

Toward the beginning of the nineteenth century, the transatlantic slave trade began to disappear. Descriptions of the horrors of the middle passage shocked and disgusted Europeans. In Great Britain, the Quakers took a stand against the slave trade as early as 1727. Slave rebellions in the New World also called attention to the slave trade. The Jamaican slaves rose in rebellion in 1760 and in the 1790s, and the famous British literary figure Samuel Johnson shocked his audience at an Oxford gathering when he raised his glass to toast "the next insurrection of the Negroes in the West Indies."

The trade in human flesh also offended many who embraced the ideals of the Enlightenment. For rational people, the sale of one human being by another seemed indefensible. Thomas Paine asked his fellow revolutionaries in North America how they could seek freedom from Great Britain yet continue to trade in human lives.

The work of British abolitionists Thomas Clarkson and William Wilberforce bore fruit in 1807 when Great Britain outlawed the slave trade, although five years earlier Denmark had been the first country to stop trading in slaves. Between 1808 and 1836, the United States, Holland, France, and Portugal followed suit. Most of the newly independent states of Latin America also banned the slave trade at this time. However, since slavery itself continued to exist, especially in the southern United States, Cuba, and Brazil, a clandestine transatlantic slave trade continued until after the close of the American Civil War (1865) and the abolition of slavery in Cuba (1886) and Brazil (1888).

------

## INTERPRETIVE ESSAY
### Kenneth Banks

The Atlantic slave trade was the largest and most gruesome forced migration of people in history. People from western Europe transported people from West Africa to labor in the mines and on the plantations of the Americas. In the process, the slave trade disrupted traditional societies in West Africa, created entirely new societies in the Americas, and greatly influenced European thought on natural rights and race. But even as the slave trade reached its height in the eighteenth century, widespread opposition to it grew apace, reaching the point where many in western Europe and the new United States associated it with evil and economic inefficiency. Why the slave trade became vilified at the height of its economic success is a riddle that continues to intrigue many people today.

Scholars have hotly contested the dimensions and impact of the slave trade. One of the most controversial aspects is determining the total number of Africans enslaved and transported across the Atlantic. Because records of the actual numbers of people captured and transported were rarely kept, the total will never be known for sure. A further complicating factor is that the Atlantic slave trade drew upon the same region of West Africa as the concurrent, smaller, but longer-lived slave trade to the Islamic nations of North Africa and the Middle East. Most scholars now believe that European ships delivered some 10 or 11 million Africans to the New World between 1450 and 1850. Of this number, nearly 5.5 million arrived in the eighteenth century alone, making it by far the most important period of the slave trade. This number far outstripped the half million free European immigrants who arrived during the same time. The trade reached its peak in the 1780s, when more than 80,000 slaves crossed the Atlantic every year.

Slave ships sailed from nearly every port in Europe and many in the Americas. Yet due to its complicated and capital-intensive nature, only the wealthiest nations and a handful of ports dominated the trade. Great Britain led the way, followed by France, although the French took the lead in the decade prior to the French Revolution in 1789. Together these two nations accounted for 75 percent of all the slaves transported during the century. Behind them came the Portuguese in Brazil, the Dutch, Spanish, Danish, and, sporadically, Swedes and various German traders. England's thirteen mainland colonies (the United States after 1783) also participated on a small scale. Every year, dozens of ships left the major ports of Liverpool, Bristol, London, Nantes, La Rochelle, Bordeaux, and Bahía and Rio de Janeiro in Portuguese Brazil, and made for the west coast of Africa.

European slavers carved out specific territories to conduct their trade. The French dominated the Senegambia region in the north, while the English and Portuguese shared the Guinea coast further south. The largest center of slave trading, from the Gold Coast to the Bight of Biafra, was monopolized by the English, although some Dutch and French slavers traded there as well. Further south, the Portuguese controlled the slave trade from south of the Zaire (Congo) River to modern-day Angola. Large monopolies such as the Royal Africa Company or the French Compagnie des Indes Orientales initially controlled the forts where slaves were held to await ships. However, by the 1720s they had been largely replaced by independent traders. In this way, the slave trade became one of the first important domains of European commerce to escape mercantilist controls, one of the first "free trades" to emerge.

Since Europeans tended to die quickly from tropical African diseases, they situated their forts (called "factories") on coastal islands or in river estuaries, or conducted trade directly on board their ships. Gaining a full cargo often took weeks, as ships tramped from fort to fort in search of slaves. Few Europeans ventured inland. This not only meant that African coastal chiefs dictated the terms of trade in most areas, but also that European knowledge of Africa was effectively limited to the coast. Europeans thus gained only a hazy understanding of West African societies and political developments.

Most slaves were captives taken in wars or in slave-raiding expeditions during periods of territorial expansion of inland African states. For example, as the Asante (Ashanti) Kingdom in the Gold Coast interior expanded after 1700, its rulers flooded the nearby coast with captives taken during war. Wars in the Bight of Biafra and Angola created similar gluts of slaves. Contrary to contemporary European beliefs, very few slaves were condemned criminals or sorcerers. However, it was common for famine-stricken people to sell themselves into slavery to survive during West Africa's frequent droughts. As warfare increased, the slave trade expanded, and African traders procured slaves from increasingly farther inland, often marching them over 500 miles to the coast from the Angolan hinterland.

The Atlantic slave trade affected the societies of West Africa in four major ways. First, millions of people, mostly young men and women in the prime of their lives, were either taken captive or forced to flee; in either case, marriage patterns and agricultural labor suffered. Loss and instability combined to alter substantially the demographics of entire regions for decades. According to demographer Patrick Manning, a severe decline in population likely occurred in all the slave-exporting regions at least once during the eighteenth century. Two of the hardest hit, the Bight of Benin and the Angolan hinterland, suffered declines of up to 20 percent. Second, the slave trade affected the nature of warfare.

Slaves in themselves became a valuable commodity and not merely an unfortunate by-product of war. Third, the European demand for slaves led to a dramatic restructuring of the very nature of slavery within Africa itself. For example, although men and women appeared to have been enslaved in equal numbers, males outnumbered females more than two to one upon arrival on the coast. The imbalance is explained by the rapid increase of female slavery among the victors and the coastal kingdoms encouraging their inland contacts to provide more males for the slave trade. At the same time, ethnic groups decimated by raids often lost many of their young men, thereby exacerbating the population decline. Fourth, it appears that the slave trade affected West Africa's overall economy, but to what extent is not entirely clear. Not surprisingly, African export trade grew at the same rate as British trade to the Americas. More than half the trade goods consisted of European or Indian cloth, with the remainder composed of metal tools, beads, weapons, and, by the end of the eighteenth century, hogsheads of tobacco and alcohol. Scholars such as Walter Rodney and Joseph Inikori have emphasized the destructive role of guns in spurring war, and that of alcohol in destabilizing village life. However, other scholars have noted that cloth exports did not undermine domestic production, and that the trade in guns and alcohol did not reach its peak until the mid-nineteenth century. The evidence available suggests that the slave trade had a marginal impact on the West African economy, although it had highly localized impacts in certain years.

Once slaves were assembled in *baccarroons*, or compounds, on the coast, the final stage began. European captains loaded their human cargo on board ship for the middle passage, or transatlantic voyage to the Americas, a gruesome ordeal that lasted from four to ten weeks. Shipboard mortality for slave and crew varied widely; on average, at least one in six slaves died on the voyage, and one in five of the crew. By the end of the century, mortality for slaves had declined to one in fifteen, a decrease attributable to higher slave costs and less time spent tramping rather than to humanitarian concerns. Most slaves were sold to work the diamond and gold mines of Brazil, or the sugar and coffee plantations there and in the West Indies. British traders transported relatively fewer slaves to the thirteen colonies of North America, which received about 500,000 in the eighteenth century. Although slaves labored as agricultural workers, servants, and even semiskilled artisans in all the mainland colonies, most were forced to grow tobacco in the Chesapeake Bay region or cultivate rice in the South Carolina lowlands.

While brutal conditions existed on all plantations, sugar planting was especially harsh and deadly. The days were long, the climate hot, and the work physically draining. Fields were notoriously riddled with disease-ridden rodents and poisonous snakes, and the milling equipment mangled or chopped off human limbs with shocking regularity. The relentless demand for year-round labor, coupled with periods of intense work during harvesting and milling, also hindered stable family life. High mortality and low fertility rates were the result. In short, slaves died by the thousands every year, and their numbers were not replaced by natural birth. The only way planters could ensure an adequate labor supply for the insatiable sugar market was to import new African slaves continually.

Market conditions and security concerns led to a constant forming and reforming of African peoples, languages, and cultural heritage. Planters mixed new arrivals as much as possible to discourage collaboration by people of the same ethnic or linguistic group. Only with difficulty did slaveholders force slaves to build neat rows of barracks rather than round thatched huts arranged according to kinship customs, a process still incomplete in the newly developing sugar lands of the late eighteenth century such as Cuba, Trinidad, and Guyana. African music, dance, stories, spiritual beliefs, cuisine, and medicinal knowledge not only informed African creole society (slaves born in the Americas), but were widely transmitted to European planter societies as well. In addition, scholars are only now beginning to appreciate the important contribution of African knowledge to cultivating colonial crops in locales such as French Louisiana and British South Carolina.

The slave trade also profoundly rearranged traditional trading patterns in the Americas, forming an early international economy based on free intercolonial trade and widespread smuggling. Official licenses to import slaves, such as the *asiento*, which allowed Great Britain to transport 4,800 slaves annually to Spanish America after 1713, were only marginally important. The unleashing of trading activity between the West Indies and the thirteen colonies proved to be far more important in the long term. American slave trading itself was relatively small in scope and was dominated by Boston and Newport, Rhode Island. Some twenty-five ships a year sailed to West Africa from these two ports on the eve of the American Revolution, carrying mainly rum. Of far greater consequence was the economic opportunity afforded by both legitimate trade and smuggling in the West Indies. Food, cloth, shoes, tools, building supplies, and horses were desperately needed on plantations. Anglo-American ships from New England and the mid-Atlantic colonies supplied them, legally to Jamaica and illegally to the French West Indies and Spain's American colonies. In addition, the small Dutch islands of St. Eustatius and Curaçao, as well as Danish St. Thomas, served as clandestine entrepôts of smuggled slaves for English, French, and Spanish masters alike, where slaves might be bought without paying high duties. The size of this clandestine trade is hard to determine, but an official record from 1765 indicates that over ninety American ships crowded into the harbors of French Martinique alone. Thus, the slave trade indirectly contributed greatly to the economic prosperity of the Americas.

The slave trade also added a dimension of insecurity to plantation societies. Unlike creole slaves, who had been brought up under slave regimes, newly arrived slaves retained knowledge of warfare tactics and vivid memories of their former lives. While it is difficult to make any precise correlation, it is striking that the major slave revolts in the West Indies occurred shortly after unusually high importations of new African slaves. In the case of the successful 1791 slave revolt in Saint Domingue (which became Haiti in 1804), several scholars have credited the large influx of recent Congolese arrivals with forming the backbone of the revolutionary army. Folk stories and spiritual beliefs, especially voodoo rites and ceremonies, were instrumental in fostering a sense of common cause among the otherwise disparate ethnic and linguistic groups. This first successful slave rebellion sent a shiver of fear down the spines of slaveholding societies from Maryland to Minas Gerais.

Few historians today believe that the slave trade fueled the Industrial Revolution in Great Britain. Yet it is now known that between 1750 and 1775, West Indian produce grown by slave labor was the fastest growing component of British commerce, comprising about one-third of export trade by 1770. Slave traders also increasingly assumed the debts of planters, and effectively became absentee plantation managers themselves, tying more Europeans ever more closely to the world of plantation slavery. By 1769 the West India Merchants and Planters Club established itself as a powerful voice in Great Britain's Parliament. In France, the slave trade enriched the commerce of the maritime cities, where slave-trading merchants built fabulous estates, invested in titles, and contributed toward new public buildings.

The increase in the slave trade is reflected in the total amount of trade with European captains. According to estimates by the economic historian David Eltis, this trade grew from an average of £450,000 a year in the late seventeenth century to nearly £4.4 million by 1790. Part of the growth is due to the rise of slave prices. However, the price rise seldom corresponded with either the availability of slaves or the demand for them. Instead, internal factors such as higher land tolls imposed by African kingdoms and the higher demand for slaves by increasingly cen-tralized African states determined their selling price on the coast. Longer forced marches through the different disease zones increased the death toll and, of course, increased the price of survivors. Thus the slave trade acted as a critical stimulus to western Europe's export economy.

Even as the Atlantic slave trade grew, many religious leaders and thinkers voiced serious misgivings over the role of slavery and the slave trade in a progressive society. Slavery did not officially exist in either Britain, France, or Holland; yet white colonists were free to come and go as they pleased with their black slaves. Quakers opposed the trade as early as 1727, issuing rebukes against those of its members who dealt in slaves or owned them. Quaker Anthony Benezet stirred the first ab-olitionists with his portrayal of the evils of the slave trade in his *Historical Account of Guinea* (1766). Of perhaps greater importance was the ever growing number of African slaves and free colored peoples in British and French port towns. Their demands for justice and the size of their communities acted as a potent reminder of the slave trade's reach into the very center of European society.

From the 1760s, Africans threatened with transportation back to the colonies sought aid from sympathetic English professionals and religious leaders. Two legal cases in particular galvanized popular opinion and helped build a large antislavery campaign in Great Britain. The first was the case of James Somerset, an African-American who protested against returning with his master to Virginia in 1772. His case was championed by antislavery activist Granville Sharp and was widely reported in the London papers. While the court pointedly did not free Somerset, the Lord Chief Justice ruled that he could not be forced to return with his owner. The precedent for ensuring freedom for the African community in Great Britain had been set. The second case shocked popular opinion. In 1783 an insurance case was heard concerning the ship *Zong*. While on the middle passage, its captain had tossed 131 sick slaves overboard to drown in order to collect insurance money. One of the leaders of Lon-don's free African community, Ouladah Equiano, alerted Sharp, and newspapers reported the case in detail. The case shocked a Great Britain already reeling from the loss of its American colonies, and forced many to question smug perceptions of Britain as the leader of European civi-lization.

By 1787 a coalition of British leaders, including nine prominent Quak-ers, formed the Society for the Abolition of the Slave Trade. Abolitionist leaders such as Thomas Clarkson, William Wilberforce, and the father and son team of James Stephen Sr. and Jr. began the exhaustive task of compiling information on the extent and horrors of the slave trade, and started to push for reform in Parliament. Their efforts were aided by the popular support provided by Baptist, Methodist, and later Anglican congregations in the newly industrializing heartland of England. Women from the newly emergent middle class organized and collected petitions, sponsored speakers, and wrote and distributed anti–slave-trade pamphlets. Opposed to them were the West India lobby and the powerful merchants of England's slaving ports. Rising concerns over the bloody events in revolutionary France and Saint Domingue diverted energy and support during a crucial parliamentary vote in 1792, but the anti–slave-trade forces eventually triumphed. The British Parliament banned the trade in 1807, to be effective the following year. In the United States, by 1780 the slave trade had been banned by several states, including Virginia. However, Article 9 of the new Constitution specifically allowed the slave trade to continue until 1808, at which time American participation in the slave trade officially ended.

Why did Great Britain take the lead in attempts to abolish the slave trade at the very height of its expansion and profitability, committing "econocide," as economic historian Seymour Drescher has suggested? Most informed people in western Europe and even many in the West Indies earnestly believed that with the demise of the slave trade, slavery would "wither on the vine." Therefore, abolitionists first directed their attention to ending the slave trade, not to ending slavery itself. Popular support for anti–slave-trade campaigns also drew upon several other factors. In England, Revivalism proved to be critical. To be reborn implied destroying sin by combatting it actively, and nothing appeared more degenerate and sinful than the holding of one human by another. Moreover, both West Indian slaves and the emerging middle and working classes in England's industrial towns were overwhelmingly Baptists and Methodists. The horrific conditions of the slave trade and slavery not only embarrassed the English Baptists and Methodists, but alarmed them over their own future. It was also easier to fight on behalf of unfortunate souls 5,000 miles across an ocean than to protest conditions at home and risk social upheaval. In this sense, the anti–slave-trade campaigns acted as a safety valve that allowed the expression of domestic political discontent without fundamentally changing conditions.

New perceptions of society and commerce were critical as well. Adam Smith, among others, called slavery "inefficient," and proclaimed that greater commercial prosperity and social stability would be guaranteed by the pursuit of economic self-interest and free wage labor. Moreover, Smith and other thinkers viewed the slave trade as a cruel commerce, and regarded slavery as a gate barring access to new fields of wealth. In this sense, they saw slave labor as antithetical to emerging ideas of civilization and "progress." Among Enlightenment thinkers such as Baron Montesquieu and Denis Diderot, publisher of the *Encyclopédie*, new concepts of universal human rights clashed with traditional notions of inequality based on birth. At the same time, increasingly vocal demands for economic and political liberties rendered the unfreedom of slavery an anachronism.

Inspired by English activity, abolitionists throughout Europe mobilized support, but with varying degrees of success. Denmark became the first nation to end its tiny slave trade, by order of its royal council in 1792. The council had passed the measure in anticipation of the British ending their trade, and it called only for the gradual end of the trade over a ten-year period. The sharp decline of Holland's slave trade was tied to the economic stagnation of its few American colonies in the late eighteenth century, and left the Dutch indifferent to ending the slave trade. British occupation of Dutch territories during the Napoleonic Wars effectively ended the slave trade there. However, slavery itself endured in the colonial possessions of both Holland and Denmark until the mid-nineteenth century. In the case of Spain and Portugal, their slave trade proved to be so profitable that it flourished well into the nineteenth century.

In France, antislavery and anticolonial forces drew together to support a small but influential abolitionist campaign. The popularity of the cause grew swiftly after the appearance of Abbé Raynal's *Philosophical and Political History of the Two Indies* in 1770. By the early 1780s, elite supporters of the French Enlightenment guided attempts to bring abolitionist concerns before Louis XVI. Inspired by the English antislavery campaign and the wide circulation of anti–slave-trade literature in France, a Société des Amis des Noirs similar to its English counterpart was founded in 1789. It boasted reforming thinkers such as Brissot, the Abbé de Sièyes, Condorcet, and later, Mirabeau. However, the slave trade and slavery received little attention from the revolutionary National Assembly that met after the taking of the Bastille in 1789. Although the Assembly officially ended the slave trade and slavery in 1794, both were reinstituted ten years later after Napoleon Bonaparte assumed full power. France ended its slave trade under British pressure in 1818, although the high profits still lured many illegal slave traders until effective suppression in 1831.

Today the only tangible remains of the slave trade are the manacles, stocks, and ship's papers locked in museums, and the moldering stone forts dotting the West African coast. But the legacy of the slave trade continues to reverberate on three continents today. African nations today cite the Atlantic slave trade as a major historical obstacle to economic development, and seek redress from western Europe and the United States. In the Americas, people of West African descent are slowly rediscovering and reclaiming the cultural roots severed long ago. Nevertheless, racial prejudice and economic inequality remain firmly implanted in many societies. The legacies of the Atlantic slave trade still continue to cast a heinous pall over the relations of nations and neighbors alike.

## SELECTED BIBLIOGRAPHY

Anstey, Roger. *The Atlantic Slave Trade and British Abolition, 1760–1810.* London: Macmillan, 1975. Landmark reevaluation of both Eric Williams' work and the role of British abolitionists.

Barker, Anthony. *The Africa Link: British Attitudes to the Negro in the Era of the Atlantic Slave Trade, 1550–1807.* Totowa, NJ: Frank Cass, 1978. Examines the often contradictory image of Africa and Africans in the English mind.

Coughtry, Jay. *The Notorious Triangle: Rhode Island and the African Slave Trade, 1700–1807.* Philadelphia: University of Pennsylvania Press, 1981. Important regional study of one of the most prominent Anglo-American slave-trading ports.

Curtin, Philip D. *The Atlantic Slave Trade: A Census.* Madison: University of Wisconsin Press, 1969. The seminal and still the most comprehensive quantitative analysis of the slave trade.

———. *The Rise and Fall of the Plantation Complex: Essays in Atlantic History.* Cambridge: Cambridge University Press, 1990. A short, useful overview of the plantation economy's impact on three continents.

Davis, David Brion. *Slavery and Human Progress.* Oxford: Oxford University Press, 1984. Detailed study showing how the British and Anglo-Americans transformed their perceptions of the slave trade during the eighteenth and nineteenth centuries.

Drescher, Seymour. *Econocide: British Slavery in the Era of Abolition.* Pittsburgh: University of Pittsburgh Press, 1977. The first work to demonstrate fully that the British ended their slave trade despite increasing profitability.

Eltis, David. *Economic Growth and the Ending of the Transatlantic Slave Trade.* Oxford: Oxford University Press, 1987. The best economic analysis of the peak years of the slave trade from 1780 to 1850.

Fick, Carolyn. *The Making of Haiti: The Saint-Domingue Revolution from Below.* Knoxville: University of Tennessee Press, 1990. Includes a controversial argument emphasizing the critical importance of African culture to the success of the revolution.

Inikori, Joseph E., ed. *Forced Migration: The Impact of the Export Slave Trade on African Societies.* New York: Africana, 1982. A collection of essays by noted

African historians emphasizing the damage the slave trade did to Africa.

Inikori, Joseph E., and Stanley Engerman, eds. *The Atlantic Slave Trade: Effects on Economies, Societies, and Peoples in Africa, the Americas and Europe*. Durham: University of North Carolina Press, 1992. A more expansive collection on similar issues presented by the first editor in 1982.

Klein, Herbert S. *The Middle Passage: Comparative Studies in the Atlantic Slave Trade*. Princeton, NJ: Princeton University Press, 1978. The best descriptive summary of the mechanics of the slave trade.

———. "The Volume of the Atlantic Slave Trade: A Synthesis." *Journal of African History* 23, 2 (1982): 473–501. Corrects and refines Curtin's earlier study of the overall slave trade.

Manning, Patrick. *Slavery and African Life: Occidental, Oriental and African Slave Trades*. Cambridge: Cambridge University Press, 1990. A brief study of the demographic impact of the trade on Africa.

Oldfield, J. R. *Popular Politics and British Anti-Slavery: The Mobilisation of Public Opinion Against the Slave Trade, 1787–1807*. Manchester: Manchester University Press, 1995. A thorough reevaluation of the abolitionists, portraying them as the first to master manipulation of mass media.

Palmer, Colin. *Human Cargoes: The British Slave Trade to Spanish America*. Urbana: University of Illinois Press, 1981. Despite its title, one of the best brief descriptions of slave trading and the middle passage.

Schwartz, Stuart B. *Sugar Plantations in the Formation of Brazilian Society, 1550–1835*. Cambridge: Cambridge University Press, 1985. Indispensable work on any aspect of the slave trade and slavery in Brazil.

Solow, Barbara L., ed. *Slavery and the Rise of the Atlantic System*. Cambridge: Cambridge University Press, 1991. Collection of essays on economics and politics by several of the most eminent historians of the Atlantic world.

Stein, Robert Louis. *The French Slave Trade in the Eighteenth Century*. Madison: University of Wisconsin Press, 1979. The best work in English on the second-largest European slave-trading country in the eighteenth century.

Williams, Eric. *Capitalism and Slavery*. Chapel Hill: University of North Carolina Press, 1944. The classic Marxian study of slavery and the slave trade. Although Williams' argument that slavery fueled the rise of British industrialization has been largely discredited, this remains one of the best works on the subject ever written, brimming with insight and outrage.

# The French Revolution, 1789–1799

## INTRODUCTION

For many, the French Revolution came as a surprise. Although France had been declining gradually for several decades, it remained the most important continental European state. It was strong, populous, wealthy, and influential. However, it was beset with internal difficulties, the most serious one being a maldistribution of wealth and power. Large segments of the French population rejected the status quo, although few if any Frenchmen advocated revolution.

Like most eighteenth-century countries, France was agrarian. Peasants comprised perhaps 80 percent of the population. Although French peasants were better off than their counterparts in other European countries, they chafed under a system that required them to pay the bulk of the taxes and that retained many of feudalism's vestiges.

Discontent among the French middle class, especially the merchants, matched that of the peasants. Resentful of regulations that hindered trade and commerce, France's middle class desired a market-driven free economy. It also embraced other Enlightenment ideas such as equality under the law and reform of the tax system. In short, the middle class hoped to achieve social prestige and political influence equal to its growing wealth.

The execution of the French king Louis XVI on January 21, 1793, foreshadowed the onset of the French Revolution's most radical phase, the Reign of Terror, which claimed thousands of lives. (Reproduced from the Collections of the Library of Congress)

The town dwellers—and there were not many of them except in Paris, which had a population of about 600,000—were restless as well. France's artisans, small shopkeepers, and day laborers were in a state of economic decline. During the 1780s, rising unemployment and skyrocketing prices had only served to intensify their misery.

The immediate cause of the Revolution was a fiscal crisis. France's budget was badly out of balance, and the country faced bankruptcy as expenditures far exceeded revenues. Service on the national debt, which had soared as France bankrolled the American Revolution, ate up 50 percent of the state's income. Furthermore, the tax burden was unevenly distributed; the nobility and the Roman Catholic Church were virtually exempt from taxation.

The French monarchy determined to resolve the crisis by taxing the nobility. Not surprisingly, the nobility resisted. Many nobles flatly rejected the monarchy's proposals; others, influenced by the Enlightenment and the American Revolution, would consent to taxation only if the king would share political power with them, an idea the monarchy rejected. The nobility relied upon the *parlements,* or traditional law courts, to thwart the monarch's will. The nobles were unintentionally aided by the king himself. Louis XVI was a weak and stupid ruler who regularly jettisoned reforming ministers and failed to confront his insubordinate nobility.

The stalemate between king and nobility was broken only when an increasingly desperate Louis XVI decided to call into session the Estates General, an ancient French assembly that had last met in 1614. Elections for the Estates General were held during the winter of 1788–1789, and when it assembled at Versailles it had a decidedly moderate character. In addition to representatives from the First Estate (the clergy) and the Second Estate (the nobility), there were representatives of the Third Estate (the rest of the French population). However, the representatives of the Third Estate were chiefly lawyers, and they sought reform, not revolution.

Almost immediately, the Estates General deadlocked over the question of whether to vote by estate (thereby giving those in favor of the status quo a two to one majority) or to vote by head (thereby giving those in favor of reform a majority). As usual, the king vacillated. As the controversy deepened, the Third Estate first proclaimed itself the National Assembly, and then in the Tennis Court Oath declared that it would not disband until France had a constitution. This was a revolutionary act, and the king prepared to summon troops to disperse the Estates General.

At this juncture, the common people weighed in. On July 14, 1789, riotous Parisians seized the Bastille, an ancient prison fortress, and effectively wrested control of the city from royal authority. Similar disturbances, known as the Great Fear, swept the countryside. Peasants attacked the nobility's châteaux, frequently destroying records that registered their obligations to the lord of the land.

As the situation spun out of control and the king dithered, on August 4 the Estates General declared the end of feudalism in France. Three weeks later it issued the Declaration of the Rights of Man and of the Citizen, which began with the stirring proclamation that "men are born free and equal in rights."

Faced with a growing crisis, the king finally roused himself. He quietly began to assemble loyal troops with the intention of disbanding the Estates General once and for all. However, once again the common people intervened. On October 4, a crowd consisting mainly of Parisian women marched to Versailles, rioted, and forced the royal household to accompany it back to Paris, where the king became its virtual prisoner. The Estates General, or rather National Assembly, also relocated from Versailles to Paris, where it gradually came under the capital's influence.

Nevertheless, from October 1789 until September 1791 the National Assembly steered a moderate course, reshaping France into a constitutional monarchy with guarantees of equality under the law. Although the king retained considerable power, the right to make laws passed to a legislative chamber elected on the basis of a limited suffrage. Civil rights were established, and new taxes on land and business income replaced the bewildering and unfair system that had frustrated so many Frenchmen. A laissez-faire approach to economics was adopted, which did not please the urban poor, and the Civil Constitution of the Clergy subordinated the powerful Roman Catholic Church to the state. Coming upon the confiscation of Church lands, the Civil Constitution outraged the papacy, which ordered French Catholics to oppose it, thereby dividing French society.

The National Assembly completed its work in October 1791 and gave way to the Legislative Assembly, the newly elected French parliament. Expected to last indefinitely, the Legislative Assembly disappeared in less than a year as the level of discontent in France rose dramatically. France became polarized, and the middle or moderate center was eclipsed.

Many Frenchmen, including the royal household, the nobility, the upper levels of the bureaucracy, the officer corps, and devout Roman Catholics, opposed the changes that had taken place. The king himself validated this opposition when he made a clumsy and unsuccessful attempt to flee France in June 1791. This incident, known as the Flight to Varennes, ended with the king's forced return to Paris. Louis XVI was now a discredited figure in the eyes of all but the most conservative Frenchmen.

Confronting the conservatives, a growing radical movement worked to extend the Revolution. Motivated in part by personal ambition, the radicals congregated in political clubs, especially the Jacobin Clubs that became synonymous with the most radical phase of the French Revolution. The radicals also enlisted the Parisian crowd, first to gain power and then to tighten their grip on it.

International considerations played a major role in changing the Revolution's direction. A steady stream of French aristocrats fled the country and took up residence at foreign capitals throughout Europe. These émigrés denounced the Revolution and tried to enlist the support of their hosts. However, even though Europe's royal courts loathed the Revolution, they shied away from any attempt to destroy it.

But the French political extremes welcomed the prospect of war. The conservatives saw war as a win-win situation. If France lost, then the Revolution would be defeated; if France won, then the king and the aristocratic army could claim victory and more easily move against the Revolution themselves. The radicals believed that war would demonstrate the unreliability of the conservatives and the ineffectiveness of the moderates, thus preparing the way for the radicals to take over. Moreover, the Jacobins, led by the Girondist faction, had concluded that only the spread of the Revolution to other countries could make it safe within France. They saw war as a way to rouse the rest of Europe to revolution. Consequently, it was France that declared war on Austria in April 1792.

The war went poorly for France; however, the fact that its opponents—Austria and its ally, Prussia—were actually rivals and deeply suspicious of each other saved France from utter disaster. Meanwhile, the Jacobins prepared to seize power. Throughout the summer of 1792 they worked to gain the trust of the Paris crowd, and in early August the mob erupted. It attacked the Tuileries, the royal residence, and forced the royal family to flee for their lives. Using the mob as its instrument of force, the Jacobins took over the capital and established a commune, or revolutionary municipal administration. The commune soon exercised supreme authority. It rejected the constitution, dismissed the Legislative Assembly, and called for elections to a National Convention to draw up a new and more radical constitution. At the same time, hysteria swept the capital, culminating in the September Massacres, when more than a thousand opponents of revolution were lynched. In this atmosphere, the elections to the National Assembly returned a strong radical majority backed by the might of the Parisian mob.

First meeting in September 1792, the National Convention declared France a republic. Shortly thereafter it tried Louis XVI for treason and executed the hapless monarch in January 1793. It also declared its intention to spread the Revolution beyond France, a step that alarmed the rest of Europe.

In April 1793 the Convention created the Committee of Public Safety to carry out the duties of government. Consisting of twelve men working in secret, the Committee of Public Safety instituted what is commonly known as the Reign of Terror. Officially designed to combat the "counterrevolution" in France, the Reign of Terror really served to rid the Jacobins of any real or potential rivals. And when Jacobin unity shattered, it was used by one radical faction to eliminate other radical factions. The Reign of Terror also claimed a number of social misfits such as prostitutes, although most of its victims were simple peasants and workers. Getting under way in summer 1793, the Reign of Terror claimed about 40,000 victims by the time it was dismantled in July 1794.

During this most radical phase of the Revolution, power passed to a handful of extreme revolutionaries, the most famous being Maximilien Robespierre, a provincial lawyer who was both incorruptible and a fanatic for "virtue." Other important leaders included Jean-Paul Marat, a firebrand journalist, and George Danton, who organized the defense of the regime and was later executed by his fellow radicals.

In addition to raining terror down on the French population, the Reign of Terror also transformed French society. Under the April 1793 Law of the Maximum, the revolutionaries imposed price controls, although paradoxically most of the leadership continued to uphold the doctrine of laissez-faire. A new calendar was introduced, with 1792 being designated as Year I and the names of the months changed to reflect the passing of the seasons. Of more lasting importance was the introduction of the metric system to replace the traditional (and chaotic) systems of weights and measures. Styles changed as well. Men abandoned the aristocrat's knee breeches in favor of the common man's trousers, and women dressed in styles reminiscent of republican Rome or democratic Athens. There was also a concerted attack on Christianity. The revolutionaries substituted "temples of reason" for churches, and Robespierre tried to bridge the gap between believer and nonbeliever by declaring that Frenchmen should worship a "Supreme Being."

Faced with an Austro-Prussian invading force now supported by Great Britain, Holland, Spain, and Portugal, the revolutionaries introduced the levée en masse, or conscription. Many other civilians were put to work on projects designed to protect France from its external enemies. By the spring of 1794, the army of revolutionary France counted 800,000 men and represented a nation in arms. This army's high morale and the divisions that plagued its opponents led to a series of French victories in summer 1794 that lifted the threat to the republic's existence.

Meanwhile, the Terror ground on, now condemning some of its most ardent supporters to the guillotine. This provoked a reaction, and on July 27, 1794, Robespierre, the living embodiment of the radical phase of the French Revolution, was executed.

What followed is known in history as the Thermidorian Reaction, named after the month in the new calendar (Thermidor) when Robespierre was overthrown. Many of those who replaced Robespierre and his friends were former Jacobins who now yearned for stability and a more moderate course. They repealed many of the National Convention's more radical measures and in 1795 introduced a new constitution for France. Through the imposition of property qualifications, this constitution guaranteed that those who sat in the legislature would be men of means and thus "responsible." Any thought of reviving the monarchy was quashed, and executive power was turned over to a five-man board of directors, thereby giving rise to the term "Directory," which describes this period in French history. However, the Directory proved transitory. Characterized by corruption, political paralysis, and a failure to end the war that had entangled France since 1792, the Directory fell victim to a coup d'état in November 1799 featuring the ambitious young military figure, Napoleon Bonaparte.

---

## INTERPRETIVE ESSAY
### Donald H. Barry

On July 14, 1789, during the first year of the decade-long French Revolution, thousands of Parisians rose in armed insurrection against the perceived threats by the king's government and its military units to destroy a popular reform movement. After arming themselves with crude weapons such as stones and knives, looting munitions depots of guns and powder, and seizing the municipal government in Paris, these revolutionaries captured the Bastille, an ancient fortress that had interned political prisoners for centuries and that now symbolized the tyranny and oppression of their society, to be known in the future as the Old Regime. This uprising in Paris soon spread throughout all of France, destroying many traditional institutions in provincial towns and rural villages. The uprising also ensured the survival of the national legislative body, called the National Assembly, which had been meeting under threatening conditions at the royal palace of Versailles eleven miles southwest of Paris. Bastille Day, as it has become known, achieved recognition as one of the most famous single days in history. To millions of people throughout the world, this event marked the beginning of modern democracy.

Opinions of Bastille Day, however, have differed drastically ever since. Charles James Fox, a prominent English politician of that era, proclaimed: "How much the greatest event it is that ever happened in the world! And how much the best!" Others would concur with the sharply contrasting assessment of French historian Hippolyte Taine in 1875, who described Bastille Day as "spontaneous anarchy" perpetrated by "ruffians," "the mob," "bandits," "men of the vilest class." To Taine, the entire Revolution was an unmitigated human catastrophe.

In truth, no other series of events in history has inspired such heated controversy and inflamed debate as the French Revolution. The main reason for this extreme disagreement is that the Revolution passed through several different phases while simultaneously featuring glorious triumphs of human creativity and achievement as well as horrifying orgies of murder and savagery; magnanimous acts of kindness as well as deliberate acts of brutality; impressive instances of thoughtfulness as well as disheartening examples of mindlessness; and great progress toward democracy, justice, and freedom as well as anticipation of modern dictatorship and totalitarianism. In so many ways, the ten years of the French Revolution embraced the virtues and evils of our modern world.

Most scholars regard the French Revolution as history's most significant revolutionary upheaval. This assessment is due in part to the fact that it occurred uniquely in the world's most advanced and influential nation. For example, in the eighteenth century France was the center of the intellectual movement known as the Enlightenment, in addition to being the leader in science and literature. French was *the* international language spoken by educated and professional people throughout the Western world. Somewhat equally with England, France was the wealthiest nation in Europe. It also possessed the largest population under a single government. Other peoples and countries viewed *la grande nation* as potentially the most powerful state in every classification. Consequently, France was considered the pacesetter in new trends and modern developments. Thus when France exploded in insurrection in 1789, all of Europe and the Americas followed events closely, and the popular masses beyond French borders dreamed of emulating its accomplishments. Truly, the French Revolution assumed a worldwide impact within three years of its inception.

Moreover, the French Revolution, more than any other series of events in history to that point, became a popular and democratic movement. This means that the vast majority of French people actively participated in many of its major developments and also benefitted from their consequences while creating a fairer and more equitable society for nearly all citizens.

In particular, the French Revolution went far beyond the American Revolution (1775–1783) in at least five areas. First, in the realm of popular participation the American Revolution had remained the work of a minority of people rather than the substantial majority that was involved in the French Revolution. Second, women participated extensively in the French events, and there were discussions about equal rights for females; this had not been the case in America. Third, the French Revolution at its zenith abolished slavery, an abominable institution that the American Revolution perpetuated. Fourth, one revolutionary government in France successfully inaugurated some aspects of modern socialism, meaning the utilization of national resources for the benefit of all in society; nothing of the kind occurred in America. And fifth, during the French Revolution (and for the first time in history) a strong central government mobilized its population and marshalled its national resources in order to surmount an unprecedented crisis, thereby anticipating governmental action during World War I (1914–1918) and World War II (1939–1945); the leaders of the American Revolution never considered the idea. In summary, these factors contribute mightily to an understanding of the awesome and unparalleled importance to the world of the French Revolution.

An appreciation of the enormous international impact of the French Revolution must begin with an analysis of the famous slogan popularized during its first year: "liberty, equality, fraternity." The words "liberty" and "equality" meant "freedom" and "democracy." Those in favor of freedom and democracy supported certain concepts: elimination of special privileges for exclusive groups or individuals; extension of greater civil liberties such as the freedoms of speech, press, assembly, ballot, and religion; introduction of written constitutions to document the rights of citizens as well as the definite powers of government; establishment of elected national representative assemblies to help rule nations in addition to enacting laws; and abolition of the form of government known as absolute monarchy in which royalty wielded unlimited authority, and its replacement either with constitutional monarchy limited in power by constitutions and elected legislatures, or with democratic republics where all rulers were elected by popular majorities.

Regarding the concepts of liberty and equality, the Revolution would clearly demonstrate a dilemma that our modern world painfully struggles with today. It is sometimes impossible to accomplish simultaneously a preservation of personal freedom and a pursuit of equality; one of them must occasionally be sacrificed to achieve the other. There is an eternal tension between the two, because efforts to attain the elusive objective of a level playing field for all must inevitably produce governmental regulations and prohibitions that restrict and diminish the individual's area of dominion. Thus during the first two years of the Revolution (1789–1791) the attempts both to expand freedoms and to extend greater opportunities for more people made impressive advances, probably with liberty prevailing over equality. The Reign of Terror reversed that earlier trend, with shared sacrifice and social solidarity predominating over individual wishes. And finally, the last five years of the Revolution witnessed curtailment of both, after which a long struggle would ensue to regain them.

Yet, in spite of restrictions on the practice of liberty and equality, the two words became sacred all over the world. Even their future opponents would have to utilize the two terms in order to justify their denial. No ruler of France after 1789 could ever survive without acknowledging that ultimate sovereignty rested with "the people."

Furthermore, the French Revolution unleashed an outburst of optimism that the world had never previously experienced, even in comparison to the various movements of religious zealotry. The compelling reason for these heightened expectations is that the Revolution held out very real prospects for a better world in this life, whereas religion could only promise an unsubstantiated paradise in another life after death. The Revolution certainly brought many major disappointments, but its accomplishments clearly outweighed its failures. Above all, the French Revolution inaugurated the movement toward modern democracy that has presided over more progress and happiness for mankind in the past two centuries than was achieved by the previous six thousand years of authoritarian rule by kings, queens, emperors, empresses, despots, tyrants, and priests.

The word "fraternity" was more vague and came to mean different things to different people. Most frequently, however, it has been translated as "nationalism." Before the Revolution, Frenchmen identified themselves mainly as members of a certain class or occupational group with sharply defined status, and as subjects of a king and royal government that was normally contemptuous of the masses; now the French people saw themselves primarily as citizens possessing certain equal rights, access to justice, and influence over government. This enhanced status, based on the principle of fairness, quickly stimulated a profound sense of pride as well as patriotic feelings of community, solidarity, and brotherhood that had rarely existed in history. In particular, this modern nationalism encouraged millions of Frenchmen to endure enormous sacrifice for the fatherland. Even though deep social cleavages (rural vs. urban interests, farm workers vs. farm owners, unskilled city laborers and lower middle class vs. well-to-do bourgeoisie) seriously divided society during some stages of the Revolution, nationalism eventually revived, intensified, and spread throughout the world.

Later, beyond the Revolutionary Era, "nationalism" developed into movements that supported specific objectives: independence from foreign domination for subjected peoples; unification of divided states whose populations shared a common identity, such as the Germans and Italians; cultural and political autonomy, signifying self-determination or semi-independence for certain ethnic groups ruled by a different yet dominant power; and respect for cultural and linguistic diversity. Revolutionary France became the first modern state to demonstrate the potential consequences of nationalism. It could be a beneficial force when promoting cooperation, collective effort, social cohesiveness, ethnic pride, and cultural creativity. On the other hand, it could be a harmful force when leading to intolerance, prejudice, ignorance, and conflict with ethnically different people. In summary, freedom, democracy, and nationalism—the forces that shaped the modern world—originated in the experiences of the French Revolution more than in any other series of events.

In the realm of politics, furthermore, the terminology employed by the modern world to describe political views is rooted in the French Revolution. The expressions "left wing" (describing either the "radical" wish for extreme and rapid democratic change, or the "liberal" support for steady and substantial democratic progress) and "right wing" (describing either the "conservative" view of opposing most democratic efforts in favor of preserving traditional society, or the "reactionary" position of resisting all democratic reforms for the perpetuation of wealth, privilege, and the status quo) began in 1791 in the Legislative Assembly with the practice of the more democratic delegates sitting on the left side of the hall, as observed from the speaker's podium, and their opponents sitting on the right side. Meanwhile, the "moderates" seated in the mid-

dle between these opposing factions favored a balance between democratic change and oligarchic nonchange.

An economic study of the Revolutionary Era is also very instructive
for an understanding of the modern world. By the late eighteenth century, a form of commercial capitalism had existed in western Europe for
at least five centuries. Since approximately 1500, states had pursued cap-
italistic policies known as mercantilism. Mercantilism called for a strong
central government to manage the overall economy through controls
such as tariffs, regulations, subsidies, exemptions, and monopolies. The
primary purpose of mercantilism was to achieve wealth and power for
the nation by attaining economic self-sufficiency. However, mercantilism
also subordinated the interests of individuals to those of the state. Consequently, although mercantilism had increased the national wealth of
France and raised general living standards somewhat, its benefits had
remained largely in the hands of the upper classes, leaving the masses
in or near poverty.

Vestiges of feudalism, some aspects of which could be traced back
more than one thousand years, also shaped the Old Regime economy.
Under feudalism, peasant farmers owed special taxes and labor services
to noble lords in rural areas. In urban areas laborers sometimes owed
similar obligations to more skilled craftsmen or tradesmen. Feudalism
also extended exclusive privileges to powerful local organizations of
merchants and businessmen. The traditional feudal structure tended to
inhibit trade and investment and to retard the development of a truly
integrated national economy.

The Enlightenment thinkers of the eighteenth century embraced the
ideas of free-enterprise capitalism (or in French *laissez-faire*, meaning
"leave alone") that stressed little or no governmental interference in economic matters, abolition of regulations, and much freedom for "market
forces" of supply and demand to determine wages and prices. In a reversal of mercantilism, free enterprise placed the interests of the individual above those of the state. These views appealed especially to the
educated few, professionals, and well-to-do businessmen who believed
that such practices would be more rational and lead to greater profits.

The policies of free enterprise triumphed during the first four years of
the Revolution (July 1789–June 1793). Mercantilism and feudalism were
swept away, and men of wealth and training (upper bourgeoisie) guided
the national government. For many, economic progress and expansion
followed. Nevertheless, two problems emerged to compel a new direction. The first concerned major foreign and civil wars that required a
powerful central government to marshal the nation's economic resources

and to manage and control production. The second problem related to the persistent suffering of the masses. Capitalism has always placed more power to dictate wages and prices in the hands of property owners than in the hands of workers. Moreover, in a free-market economy businessmen easily manipulated "market forces" of supply and demand for personal gain. This caused the masses to suspect conspiracies in the exploitation of shortages and inflation, and to demand governmental action.

As a result of these two problems, the central government during the Reign of Terror (June 1793–July 1794) adopted regulatory and even socialistic measures that succeeded in stabilizing the economy and winning the wars. The aftermath of the Terror (July 1794–November 1799), however, brought mainly a return to free enterprise. These last five years of the Revolution, called the Directory, were characterized by lower-class misery, corruption, default on governmental debts, and much uncertainty. The Directory survived economically on the plunder stolen by French armies from other countries.

The Revolution reached its most dramatic, radical, and significant phase during the Reign of Terror. The Terror was essentially a wartime emergency government that resorted to extreme measures to surmount awesome problems: the threat of foreign invasion, with nearly every nation in Europe at war with France; civil war inside the country, with royalist or dissident rebellions in several provinces; economic instability caused by chronic inflation and scarcity of vital commodities; the disruption of society instigated by traitors and counterrevolutionaries; and a power struggle among the leading politicians for control of the national government in Paris.

The Terror's response to these threats was unprecedented in history. The government ordered a total mobilization of all French society. History's first conscription law drafted into the army all unmarried men between the ages of eighteen and twenty-five; married men labored to produce war materials and to transport supplies; some women made uniforms and tents while others served in hospitals; children ran errands and performed simple tasks; and older citizens encouraged the younger ones.

For dealing with domestic opposition and rebellion, the national government established a supreme political police known as the Committee of General Security, which hunted down and arrested suspected traitors. Thereafter, a special Revolutionary Tribunal in Paris judged whether or not to condemn them as "enemies of the people." Conviction almost invariably led to execution by the guillotine, a device invented in 1792 for beheading its victims by means of a heavy convex blade that slid down a vertical frame. It was this utilization of the guillotine that primarily gave the Reign of Terror its "terrifying" aura by terminating over 20,000 lives in little more than a year.

In the realm of economics, rationing was employed against scarcities, while requisitioning of food and other supplies forced farmers and businessmen to sell necessities to the national government at dictated prices unrelated to market value. Meanwhile, forced loans were extracted from wealthy citizens. Most important, perhaps, wage and price controls stabilized the currency somewhat, thereby partially easing the fears of lower-class consumers.

In many ways, the most extensive and fascinating reforms affected social and cultural matters. Slavery in the French colonies was abolished. Creation of the metric system (based on the decimal system of numbers) introduced such a superior standard for weights and measures that the international scientific community would adopt it. Strict censorship of the press, speech, and assembly became vital to prevent the undermining of public confidence in the "great cause." Furthermore, the desire to glorify the Republic and the Revolution while eliminating vestiges of the monarchy and the Old Regime inspired the national government to promote changes in clothing styles, popular forms of address (from "Sir" or "Mrs." to "Citizen"), names for places and people, music themes, architectural features, theater productions, and all popular amusements. Even the calendar underwent major modifications, as the names of the months received new designations, the years were assigned Roman numerals (September 1792 being designated as the start of year I), and the weeks were lengthened from seven days to ten. In addition, the Convention converted several royal palaces into public museums (most notably, the Tuileries Palace emerged as the renowned Louvre Museum of today), archives, and libraries. There was even an official campaign to discourage the practice of traditional Catholic Christianity in favor of the mere recognition of an impersonal, remote, scientifically perceived "Supreme Being." Never before in history had a movement so profoundly changed popular culture and all of society.

To accomplish these far-reaching goals, the National Convention in Paris assumed temporary dictatorial authority as a highly centralized, all-powerful national government. Standing alone was the Committee of Public Safety, a twelve-man executive cabinet that actually ruled France. This executive cabinet, although supposedly selected from and responsible for its acts to the Convention, actually exercised almost total and independent authority over the entire nation.

To guarantee that its policies were being implemented, the Committee of Public Safety dispatched specially empowered "representatives-on-mission" from Paris to the provinces and armies for the purpose of reviewing the actions of officials and generals. Failure to satisfy these deputies could precipitate the "swift, severe, and inflexible justice" of the guillotine. Ironically, the Revolution, which began as the most liberating movement in history, had now degenerated into the most pervasive and coercive dictatorship yet known.

Although frequently criticized for its excesses, the Terror had significant positive results. All things considered, it achieved great success in surmounting the crises confronting France and saving the nation. By the end of 1793, foreign armies had been expelled from French territories and Republican armies had seized the offensive and carried the Revolution to other countries. Meanwhile, all internal rebellions were defeated or contained, and the economy was stabilized and organized for huge improvements in productivity. In the process, a surge of patriotic pride, passionate idealism, and selfless community spirit galvanized French society.

Indeed, the dramatic success of the Terror led to the final power struggle among the more radical revolutionaries in the spring and summer of 1794. Maximilien Robespierre, the dominant figure on the Committee of Public Safety, purged moderates who desired an end to the Terror and radicals who wished to promote more socialist and egalitarian policies until his own ambitions and excesses precipitated his downfall and execution on July 27, 1794 (9 Thermidor according to the revolutionary calendar). The ensuing Thermidorian Reaction dismantled some of the measures and institutions of the Terror, while returning the First Republic to a moderate or even conservative course.

During the Revolution's last five years, the first theorist to espouse communism as later developed by Karl Marx and Vladimir Lenin appeared. He was François-Noel Babeuf, who called himself Gracchus in honor of the ancient Roman Republic's reforming brothers; his plot to topple the government was called the Conspiracy of the Equals. Babeuf's most influential idea called for the seizure of power in a coup d'état by a small, secretive, tightly knit, and well-organized band of dedicated revolutionaries, who would then impose a dictatorship on society until the uneducated popular masses could develop widespread appreciation of and support for their policies. Babeuf and his followers hoped to abolish private property and to distribute the necessities of life equally to all. Furthermore, the Babouvists devised innovative tactics: secret and separate cells of members, code-named agents, infiltration of enemy organizations, and subversion of military and civilian authorities. Their plans, however, were betrayed; Babeuf and his comrades were arrested in May 1796, and he was executed a year later. Yet his goals and methods would live on in the careers of future revolutionaries and the organizations they created.

Finally, the French Revolution raised a major issue for our modern world; namely, how do individuals or societies resist tyranny and defend moral principles when confronted with superior military force? In response to this question, the French during their great Revolution employed five different means of action that the world would later utilize. The first, the most famous and spectacular, is armed popular insurrection or a mass uprising as illustrated by Bastille Day. However, the instances of this course of action being successful or even attempted over the past two centuries have been rare.

The second means of action is guerrilla warfare, a term meaning "little war" in Spanish. This involves the use of unconventional and irregular hit-and-run methods of fighting by weaker and smaller groups against stronger and larger forces. A striking example of its effectiveness occurred soon after the Revolutionary period when the French armies of Napoleon failed to subdue the Spanish during the Peninsular (Iberian) War of 1808–1814. However, the first instance of guerrilla war happened in March 1793 in the backward western central region of France called the Vendée. A peasant rebellion against the national government resorted to fighting tactics featuring ambushes, torture, and ferocious atrocities fired by religious zeal. This uprising was not completely quelled until Napoleon's reign. Later, guerrilla warfare would appear in the Boer War, World War II, and the Vietnam War, among others.

The third means of action is terrorism, or a campaign of random and unpredictable assassinations, bombings, destruction of property, and executions in an effort to harass, intimidate, or eliminate enemies. Obviously, terrorism can be used by individuals or groups outside or even inside government. The French Revolution contained a multitude of terrorist incidents. Scholars today still debate the potential effectiveness of terrorism; most have concluded that it can result in some short-term gains but minimal long-term success.

The fourth means of action is the violent seizure of power by a small, well-trained, and dedicated group of revolutionaries overthrowing the established government in a coup d'état. Their intention is to rule dictatorially, but their wish is to gain widespread popular support quickly to bolster their regime. The primary example during the Revolution was Babeuf's failed conspiracy. Since then, the modern world has experienced countless attempts yet few successes. The Bolshevik Revolution of 1917 in Russia, however, would greatly shape the twentieth century.

The fifth means of action eventually became known as passive resistance or civil disobedience. This response is particularly fascinating because, unlike the previous four means of action, it rejects violence. A nonviolent refusal to support a regime or to cooperate with established authority has taken different forms at different times: boycotts, strikes, ostracism or shunning those people dealing with the designated enemy, and quiet disloyalty and nonsupport of the government in its campaign against opponents.

The most famous written expression of these ideas was by an American, the New England author and eccentric Henry David Thoreau in his celebrated essay of 1849, *Resistance to Civil Government*, or, as it is more commonly known, *Civil Disobedience*. Later the Irish used these methods against British imperial rule, Mohandas Gandhi applied them effectively in India, Martin Luther King, Jr. employed them in the American civil rights movement of the 1960s, and recently the peoples of Russia and eastern Europe utilized them in contributing to the collapse of communism. Interestingly, the methods of passive resistance, civil disobedience, and nonsupport have arguably proven to be the most effective in the struggle against oppression.

In the French Revolution, the very unpopular, corrupt, and undemocratic Directory government fell easy victim to an overthrow by the lionized, charismatic, and brilliant young general Napoleon Bonaparte. The French people overwhelmingly acquiesced in the event; there was no sorrow manifested toward the departure of the Directory, or to the end of the Revolution, for that matter.

## SELECTED BIBLIOGRAPHY

Brinton, Crane. *A Decade of Revolution, 1789–1799*. New York: Harper and Row, 1963. One of the classic interpretative works by a great American historian.
Cobb, Richard. *The People's Armies*. New York: Oxford University Press, 1987. An impressive analysis of Parisian lower-class paramilitary groups.
———. *The Police and the People: French Popular Protest*. Oxford: Oxford University Press, 1970. A superb study of individual experiences and diverse developments, providing the reader with an appreciation of the complexities and nuances of the era.
Cobban, Alfred. *Aspects of the French Revolution*. New York: W. W. Norton, 1968. A thoughtful series of essays challenging the pattern of systematic deductions by other historians, especially Marxists.
Darnton, Robert. *The Kiss of Lamourette: Reflections in Cultural History*. New York:

W. W. Norton, 1990. Chapter 1 contains an excellent summary of the Revolution's significance.

Doyle, William. *The Oxford History of the French Revolution*. New York: Oxford University Press, 1989. One of the most balanced general histories on the subject.

Gottschalk, Louis R. *Jean-Paul Marat: A Study in Radicalism*. Chicago: University of Chicago Press, 1967. A good brief biography of probably the most intriguing and influential of the professional revolutionaries.

Hampson, Norman. *A Social History of the French Revolution*. Toronto: University of Toronto Press, 1966. A good synthesis of the Revolution's development as it related to social and economic realities.

Kennedy, Emmet. *A Cultural History of the French Revolution*. New York: Random House, 1989. Probably the finest book in English on the Revolution's effects on cultural institutions and artistic activities.

Landes, Joan. *Women and the Public Sphere in the Age of the French Revolution*. Ithaca, NY: Cornell University Press, 1988. Perhaps the best work on the role and impact of women during this epoch.

Loomis, Stanley. *Paris in the Terror*. New York: Avon Books, 1973. An entertaining account of life in Paris during the Terror, focusing on human rather than political aspects.

McManners, John. *The French Revolution and the Church*. New York: Harper and Row, 1970. A solid study of the very important subject of religion and institutional Christianity as they related to the Revolution.

Palmer, Robert R. *The Age of the Democratic Revolution: A Political History of Europe and America, 1760–1800*. 2 vols. New York: Random House, 1962. A renowned comparative study of the entire era as well as the relationship of the French Revolution to other revolutions.

———. *Twelve Who Ruled: The Year of the Terror in the French Revolution*. New York: Random House, 1941. The best volume on the personalities and policies of the Committee of Public Safety.

Popkin, Jeremy. *Revolutionary News: The Press in France, 1789–1799*. Durham, NC: Duke University Press, 1990. A fascinating rendition of the impact of journalists and journalism on events.

Rudé, George. *The Crowd in the French Revolution*. New York: Oxford University Press, 1959. An interesting description of the composition and motivations of the participants during the insurrectionary uprisings.

Schama, Simon. *Citizens: A Chronicle of the French Revolution*. New York: Alfred A. Knopf, 1989. Brilliantly written yet extremely conservative in interpretation.

Soboul, Albert. *The French Revolution: 1787–1799*. Translated by Alan Forrest and Colin Jones. New York: Random House, 1975. The best Marxist treatment of the Revolution, strong in socioeconomic generalities but weak in cultural, human, and political matters.

Sutherland, Donald M. G. *France 1789–1815: Revolution and Counter-Revolution*. New York: Oxford University Press, 1986. Arguably the best general work on the Revolution as well as the Napoleonic era.

Talmon, J. L. *The Origins of Totalitarian Democracy*. New York: W. W. Norton, 1970. Scholarly work on the theories, pursuit, and practice of the subject.

Tocqueville, Alexis de. *The Old Regime and the French Revolution*. Translated by Stuart Gilbert. Garden City, NY: Doubleday, 1955. A classic interpretive analysis first published in 1856 by the celebrated commentator on France and America.

# Appendix A

# Glossary

*Age of Imperialism*. Reaching a climax in the late nineteenth century, the Age of Imperialism is that time in history when the Europeans managed to bring virtually the entire globe under their control.

*Aurangzeb (1618–1707)*. Aurangzeb was the last of the effective Mogul rulers in India. With his death, the Mogul Empire collapsed and the way was open for British and then French penetration of the subcontinent.

*Balance of Power*. One of the dominant concepts of international relations, the balance of power holds that preventing the dangerous growth of power in one nation or combination of nations is desirable. An effective distribution of power among nations often can be accomplished through alliance and counteralliance.

*Baroque*. Baroque is a kind of artistic style that was very popular from the middle of the sixteenth century to the middle of the eighteenth century. It featured many flourishes and much elaborate ornamentation.

*Borodino, Battle of (1812)*. This very bloody battle occurred on September 7, 1812, at the village of Borodino, located to the west of Moscow. Napoleon's invading forces triumphed, but the beaten Russian army retreated intact and ultimately defeated the French emperor.

*Bourbons*. The Bourbons were the ruling house of France from 1589 until 1793, and from 1814 until 1830.

*Burke, Edmund (1729–1797).* An English author and politician, Burke first gained notice for his support of the American Revolution, portraying the rebellious colonists as defenders of traditional English rights. His greatest fame came from his *Reflections on the Revolution in France* (1790), a work that condemned the French Revolution and set down the principles of modern conservatism.

*Charles I (1600–1649).* As king of England, Charles was a staunch supporter of divine-right monarchy. His unwillingness to compromise this principle brought him into conflict with Parliament and provoked a civil war, at the end of which parliamentary forces executed the defeated Charles.

*Charles V (1500–1558).* Head of the Habsburg family, Charles V was the most powerful man in Europe. Simultaneously, he was king of Spain and Holy Roman Emperor. He wished to bring all of Europe under his control, not only for political reasons but also to eradicate Protestantism and to reestablish Roman Catholicism as the only form of Christianity in western and central Europe.

*Cincinnatus (c. 5th cent. B.C.).* Cincinnatus was an early Roman hero. According to the story, Cincinnatus, a simple Roman farmer, answered the call of duty when foreign forces threatened the Romans. He left his farm, led the Romans to military victory, and, instead of exploiting his popularity for self-gain, returned to his farm. He came to symbolize early Roman simplicity, selflessness, and virtue.

*Clive, Robert (1725–1774).* Clive was an employee of the East India Company who rose to great prominence in India. Clive was chiefly responsible for expelling French influence from the subcontinent and bringing much of India under British control.

*Congress of Vienna (1814–1815).* Meeting in the Austrian capital at the conclusion of the Napoleonic Wars, the Congress of Vienna redrew the map of Europe and defined European political orthodoxy.

*Enclosure.* Enclosure is the act of hedging or fencing fields and commons. The end result of enclosure was consolidated and more easily manageable farm holdings. Advanced agricultural techniques could now be applied more frequently and effectively.

*Enlightened Despotism.* Evolving from the medieval and early modern concept of monarchy, enlightened despotism tended to downplay the idea of divine right and instead justified itself in terms of reason and secular usefulness. With enlightened despotism, the state came to be seen as an abstract but eternal entity of which the monarch was merely the first servant. Enlightened despots employed reason and logic to promote reforms designed to strengthen their state and—not coincidentally—themselves as well.

*Glorious Revolution (1688).* The Glorious Revolution marks the overthrow of James II, the last Stuart to rule England. James and his family went into exile in Louis XIV's France, while in England the revolution settled the lengthy struggle between Parliament and a divine-right monarchy in favor of the former. William and Mary now took the throne of England.

*Goebbels, Joseph (1897–1945).* Goebbels was Adolf Hitler's Reich Minister for Public Enlightenment and Propaganda. As World War II drew to a close, Goebbels remained at Hitler's side and encouraged the Nazi dictator to resist surrender.

*Gracchus Brothers (Tiberius, 163–133 B.C.; Gaius, 153–121 B.C.).* At the time of the Roman Republic, the aristocratic Gracchus brothers were advocates of sweeping reform measures that favored the disadvantaged. They were also personally ambitious. Their concern for the downtrodden angered the Roman ruling class, and the brothers were subsequently murdered.

*Great Power.* Great Power is a synonym for any important and powerful state. Eighteenth-century Great Powers included both Great Britain and France.

*Habsburgs.* The Habsburgs were the ruling house of Austria from 1267 until 1918. They also served as Holy Roman Emperors from 1438 to 1806.

*Hegel, Georg Wilhelm Friedrich (1770–1831).* A German philosopher, Hegel proposed that history moves according to the triad of thesis, antithesis, synthesis. According to Hegel, the status quo is the thesis. The antithesis will arise to challenge the thesis, or status quo, and out of this struggle the synthesis, a combination of thesis and antithesis, will emerge. In time, the synthesis will become the new thesis, and the process will repeat itself.

*Hundred Years' War (1339–1453).* A seemingly interminable series of wars fought on French soil between the English and the French, the Hundred Years' War resulted in the ruin of England and its expulsion from France except for the port of Calais.

*Jacobite.* Jacobite is a term used to describe those who, in the eighteenth century, would return the House of Stuart to the throne of Great Britain.

*James II (1633–1701).* James II was king of England at the time of the Glorious Revolution (1688). A strong supporter of divine-right monarchy, James was deposed by parliamentary forces that favored a constitutional monarchy. He and his family fled to France, where they resided at the court of Louis XIV.

*Kremlin.* Kremlin is a Russian word meaning fortress. The Moscow Kremlin was the seat of the Russian government from the fourteenth century to the eighteenth century. In the twentieth century, the Soviets also located their government there.

*Levée en masse.* Instituted during the French Revolution's Reign of Terror, the levée en masse was a form of conscription. All able-bodied Frenchmen were to defend the country and its revolution.

*Magna Carta (1215).* Resulting from the ongoing medieval conflict between the monarch on one hand and the nobility, church officials, and townsmen on the other hand, Magna Carta required the English king to respect the historical rights and privileges of his opponents. King John I signed Magna Carta under duress, but later Englishmen cited it as legal grounds for resisting royal authority.

*Malthus, Thomas (1766–1834).* An English economist, Thomas Malthus endorsed the concept of laissez-faire, or free-market economics. In particular, he argued that mankind reproduces so relentlessly that the supply of food will frequently fall short of demand. The result will be a "natural" thinning of the population by war, disease, or famine to achieve greater equilibrium between supply and demand. Malthus argued that nothing such as relief for the poor should be done to interfere with this process.

*Manifest Destiny.* A very popular concept in the United States during the nineteenth century, Manifest Destiny called for the United States to bring the entire North American continent under its control.

*Marx, Karl (1818–1883).* A German publicist, historian, philosopher, and sociologist, Karl Marx is generally regarded as the father of modern socialism. The most cogent synopsis of his ideas is found in his *Communist Manifesto* (1848).

*Mercantilism.* Mercantilism was a popular economic theory during the sixteenth, seventeenth, and eighteenth centuries. It was designed to create a self-sufficient economy for a nation, and it featured a quest for colonies to increase government revenues, a determination to establish a favorable balance of trade, and intrusive governmental regulation of economic life, often at the expense of the individual.

*Metaphysics.* Metaphysics is defined as the branch of philosophy that seeks to explain reality or the nature of being. It also seeks to explain the origin and structure of the world.

*Middle Passage.* The middle passage is another name for that part of the slave trade that featured the sailing of a vessel loaded with slaves from West Africa to America. Conditions for the slaves were unspeakably horrible, and many died en route to the New World.

*Mogul Empire.* In the sixteenth century, a powerful Moslem warrior conquered the bulk of the Indian subcontinent and established a dynasty that lasted until 1707. The Mogul Empire resisted European penetration, especially into the interior of India. With the death of Aurangzeb, the last strong Mogul emperor, a scramble for power in India ensued, which Great Britain ultimately won.

*Nietzsche, Friedrich (1844–1900).* Nietzsche was a nineteenth-century German philosopher whose world view became popular after his death and greatly influenced the thinking of many twentieth-century figures. Nietzsche identified courage, action, and will as model virtues. He glorified the "supreme" individual, who by sheer force of personality would lead and dominate the masses.

*Nine Years' War (1688–1697).* Also known as the War of the League of Augsburg, the Nine Years' War was one of several wars fought by Louis XIV during the latter part of the seventeenth century and the first few years of the eighteenth century. During this war, the Dutch and the English were France's chief foes. The war ended in a virtual draw.

*Northwest Ordinance (1787).* Under pressure from American settlers moving westward, the government of the American Confederation passed the Northwest Ordinance to regulate the settlement of lands north of the Ohio River. The Northwest Ordinance provided that these lands would be divided and become states rather than colonies once fairly loose requirements were met.

*Old Style.* A form of the calendar traceable to Julius Caesar, Old Style, or O. S., was superseded by the Gregorian calendar, or New Style (N. S.), in 1582. In the eighteenth century, several countries including Great Britain and Russia continued to use Old Style. During that century, the Julian calendar was eleven days behind the Gregorian calendar.

*Paine, Thomas (1737–1809).* An English radical author, Paine supported both the American Revolution and the French Revolution. His *Common Sense* (1776) provided a popular rationale for the American insurgents, and *The Rights of Man* (1791–1792) rebuked those who defended the Old Regime and advanced the radical idea that government should serve the people.

*Peace of Westphalia (1648).* The Peace of Westphalia marked the end of the Thirty Years' War. It signaled the failure of the Habsburg bid for supremacy in Europe and divided the German-speaking lands into more than three hundred states, each of which was virtually sovereign.

*Puritans.* The Puritans were radical English Protestants who followed the teachings of John Calvin. Unhappy with the worldliness of early seventeenth-century England, some Puritans immigrated to the New

World in order to establish a "purer" society. Puritans landed in Plymouth in 1620 and founded the Massachusetts Bay Colony in 1629.

*Raynal, Guillaume (1713–1796).* A priest turned social critic, the Abbé Raynal in his influential *L'Histoire Philosophique et Politique des Établissements et du Commerce des Européens dans les Deux Indes* (1770) attacked the slave trade. His book provided a rallying point for the growing number of late eighteenth-century Europeans opposed to the slave trade.

*Reign of Terror (1793–1794).* At the height of the French Revolution, the most radical revolutionaries gained control of the state and introduced the Reign of Terror, which sought to crush all signs of opposition to the revolutionary government. During this period, thousands of people were executed.

*Ricardo, David (1772–1823).* An English economist, Ricardo advocated a laissez-faire approach to economics. His "iron law of wages" proclaimed that because the supply of labor—a function of the poor's relentless procreation—will usually exceed the demand for labor, the most that any worker could hope for was subsistence wages. Ricardo warned against any governmental intervention in this "natural" process.

*Smith, Adam (1723–1790).* Adam Smith was a Scottish professor who embraced the ideas of the Enlightenment. In 1776 he wrote an influential book on economics, *The Wealth of Nations*, that promoted the concept of laissez-faire, or the elimination of restrictions, especially governmental ones, on commerce and industry.

*Stalin, Joseph (1879–1953).* Joseph Stalin was the dictator of the Soviet Union from 1928 until 1953. He often expressed admiration for Peter the Great and practiced a form of Russian nationalism behind a facade of Marxism.

*Streltsy.* The *streltsy* were irregular units of militiamen stationed in Moscow. During the late seventeenth century, the *streltsy* played an important role in Russian political life until crushed by Peter the Great in the wake of a failed rebellion.

*Toynbee, Arnold (1852–1883).* Toynbee, a British historian, argued in *Lectures on the Industrial Revolution of the Eighteenth Century in England* that the wealth of the middle class derived from the Industrial Revolution was, in fact, attributable to the labor of the working class.

*Tudor.* The Tudors were the ruling family of England from 1485 until 1603. Famous Tudors included Henry VIII and Elizabeth I.

# Appendix B

# Timeline

| | |
|---|---|
| 1700–1721 | Great Northern War |
| 1700 | Charles II of Spain dies |
| | Asante Empire in the ascendancy |
| 1701–1714 | War of the Spanish Succession |
| 1701 | Frederick I takes title "King in Prussia" |
| 1702 | William III of England dies |
| 1703 | Founding of St. Petersburg |
| 1704 | Battle of Blenheim |
| 1707 | Union of England and Scotland |
| 1709 | Battle of Poltava |
| | Battle of Malplaquet |
| 1713 | Treaty of Utrecht |
| 1714 | Treaty of Rastadt |
| 1715 | Louis XIV of France dies |
| 1718 | Charles XII of Sweden killed |
| 1721 | Treaty of Nystadt |
| 1722 | Table of Ranks (Russia) created |
| 1725 | Peter the Great of Russia dies |

| | |
|---|---|
| 1726 | Jonathan Swift publishes *Gulliver's Travels* |
| 1727 | Isaac Newton dies |
| 1733–1738 | War of the Polish Succession |
| 1733 | Kay's flying shuttle |
| 1739 | War of Jenkins' Ear |
| 1740–1748 | War of the Austrian Succession |
| 1741 | United sultanate of Oman and Zanzibar established |
| 1748 | Montesquieu publishes *On the Spirit of the Laws* |
| | Treaty of Aix-la-Chapelle |
| 1750 | J. S. Bach dies |
| 1751 | Publication of the *Encyclopédie* begins |
| 1756–1763 | Seven Years' War; known in America as French and Indian War |
| 1757 | Battle of Plassey |
| 1759 | Voltaire publishes *Candide* |
| | Great Britain captures Quebec |
| | Battle of Kunersdorf |
| 1760 | End of Maratha Confederacy in India |
| 1762 | Rousseau publishes *The Social Contract* |
| | China's population reaches 200 million |
| 1763 | Peace of Paris |
| | Peace of Hubertusburg |
| 1764 | Hargreaves' spinning jenny |
| 1765 | Stamp Act |
| 1767 | Arkwright's water frame |
| 1769–1774 | Russo-Turkish War |
| 1769 | Watt's steam engine |
| 1770 | Boston Massacre |
| 1772 | First Partition of Poland |
| 1773 | Boston Tea Party |
| 1774 | Joseph Priestley discovers oxygen |
| 1775 | Battle of Bunker Hill |
| 1776–1783 | American War of Independence |
| 1776 | American Declaration of Independence |
| | Adam Smith publishes *Wealth of Nations* |

Edward Gibbon publishes *The Decline and Fall of the Roman Empire*

Thomas Paine publishes *Common Sense*

1777 Battle of Saratoga

1779 Crompton's spinning mule

1780 Maria Theresa of Austria dies

1781 Cornwallis surrenders to Washington at Yorktown

Immanuel Kant publishes *The Critique of Pure Reason*

1783 Cort's rolling mill

Treaty of Paris

1784 Cartwright's power loom

1786 Frederick the Great of Prussia dies

1787 United States Constitution

1789–1799 French Revolution

1789 Gathering of the Estates General

Storming of the Bastille

George Washington becomes president of the United States

French Declaration of the Rights of Man

1790 Edmund Burke publishes *Reflections on the Revolution in France*

Benjamin Franklin dies

1791 W. A. Mozart dies

Slave uprising in Haiti

United States Bill of Rights

1792–1815 Wars of the French Revolution and Napoleon

1792 France becomes a republic

Mary Wollstonecraft publishes *Vindication of the Rights of Woman*

1793–1794 Reign of Terror

1793 Louis XVI executed

Second Partition of Poland

Whitney's cotton gin

British Board of Agriculture created

1794 Robespierre executed

1795 Third Partition of Poland

Great Britain secures control of the Cape Colony

| 1796 | Catherine the Great of Russia dies |
|------|-------------------------------------|
|      | Edward Jenner develops smallpox vaccine |
| 1797 | Treaty of Campo Formio |
| 1799 | Napoleon Bonaparte comes to power |

# Ruling Houses and Dynasties

## AUSTRIA

### House of Habsburg

| | |
|---|---|
| Leopold I | 1658–1705 |
| Joseph I | 1705–1711 |
| Charles VI | 1711–1740 |
| Maria Theresa | 1740–1780 |
| Joseph II | 1780–1790 |
| Leopold II | 1790–1792 |
| Francis II | 1792–1835 |

## BRITISH ISLES

At the start of the eighteenth century, the monarch ruled as king of both England and Ireland. Since 1603, the same family had also ruled as king of Scotland, a separate country. However, in 1707 the Act of Union officially joined England and Scotland. The monarch became king of Great Britain and, separately, remained king of Ireland.

### House of Stuart

| William III | 1689–1702 |
| and Mary II | 1689–1694 |
| Anne | 1702–1714 |

### House of Hanover

| George I | 1714–1727 |
| George II | 1727–1760 |

In 1801, the kingdom of Great Britain, which had been formed in 1707, was expanded to become the United Kingdom of Great Britain and Ireland.

| George III | 1760–1820 |

## FRANCE

### House of Bourbon

| Louis XIV | 1643–1715 |
| Louis XV | 1715–1774 |
| Louis XVI | 1774–1792 |

### The First Republic

| Convention | 1792–1795 |
| Directory | 1795–1799 |
| Consulate | 1799–1804 |

## PRUSSIA

In 1618 the elector of Brandenburg added the Duchy of Prussia to his holdings and began to call himself the duke of Prussia.

### House of Hohenzollern

| Frederick III | 1688–1713 |

As the price for entering the War of the Spanish Succession in 1701, the elector demanded and received from the Habsburg emperor the title of king. Henceforth the Hohenzollern electors would be known as kings of Prussia.

| Frederick I | 1701–1713 |
| Frederick William I | 1713–1740 |

| Frederick II | 1740–1786 |
| "the Great" | |
| Frederick William II | 1786–1797 |
| Frederick William III | 1797–1840 |

## HOLY ROMAN EMPIRE

### House of Habsburg

| Leopold I | 1658–1705 |
| Joseph I | 1705–1711 |
| Charles VI | 1711–1740 |

### House of Wittelsbach

| Charles VII | 1742–1745 |

### House of Lorraine

| Francis I | 1745–1765 |

### House of Habsburg-Lorraine

| Joseph II | 1765–1790 |
| Leopold II | 1790–1792 |
| Francis II | 1792–1806 |

## RUSSIA

### House of Romanov

| Peter I | 1689–1725 |
| "the Great" | |
| Catherine I | 1725–1727 |
| Peter II | 1727–1730 |
| Anna | 1730–1740 |
| Ivan VI | 1740–1741 |
| Elizabeth | 1741–1762 |
| Peter III | 1762 |
| Catherine II | 1762–1796 |
| "the Great" | |
| Paul | 1796–1801 |

## SPAIN

### House of Habsburg

| | |
|---|---|
| Charles II | 1665–1700 |

### House of Bourbon

| | |
|---|---|
| Philip V | 1700–1746 |
| Ferdinand VI | 1746–1759 |
| Charles III | 1759–1788 |
| Charles IV | 1788–1808 |

## CHINA

| | |
|---|---|
| Qing Dynasty | 1644–1912 |

## JAPAN

| | |
|---|---|
| Tokugawa Period | 1603–1867 |

## AFRICA

| | |
|---|---|
| Osei Tutu,<br>   King of Asante | 1670–1717 |
| Agaja,<br>   King of Dahomey | 1708–1740 |

## INDIA

| | |
|---|---|
| Aurangzeb | 1658–1707 |

# Index

# About the Editors and Contributors

KENNETH BANKS is assistant professor of history at the University of North Carolina–Asheville. He received his Ph.D. from Queen's University, Canada, and has contributed to the *Historical Dictionary of the British Empire*. He is currently researching shipping and communications in the eighteenth-century French empire.

DONALD H. BARRY is professor of history at Tallahassee Community College. He received his Ph.D. from Florida State University. He is the author of *European History: An Outline and Synthesis* (1995), and has contributed to *Statesmen Who Changed the World* (1993).

ROBERT D. CORNWALL is currently teaching at Manhattan Christian College. He received his Ph.D. from Fuller Theological Seminary. He is the author of *Visible and Apostolic: The Constitution of the Church in High Church Anglican and Non-juror Thought, 1688–1745* (1993) and has contributed articles to *Enlightenment and Dissent* and the *Anglican Theological Review*.

JOHN E. FINDLING is professor of history at Indiana University Southeast. He received his Ph.D. from the University of Texas and is the author of *Dictionary of American Diplomatic History* (1980; 1989), *Close Neighbors, Distant Friends: United States–Central American Relations* (1987), and *Chi-*

*cago's Great World's Fairs* (1995). With Kimberly D. Pelle, he co-edited *Historical Dictionary of World's Fairs and Expositions, 1851–1988* (1990) and *Historical Dictionary of the Modern Olympic Movement* (1996), and with Frank W. Thackeray, he co-edited *Statesmen Who Changed the World* (1993) and the other volumes in the Events That Changed the World and Events That Changed America series.

RICK KENNEDY is professor of history at Point Loma Nazarene College. He received his Ph.D. from the University of California at Santa Barbara. He is the editor of *Aristotelian and Cartesian Logic at Harvard* (1995).

DAVID MITCH is professor of economics at the University of Maryland Baltimore County. He received his Ph.D. from the University of Chicago. He is the author of *The Rise of Popular Literacy in Nineteenth-Century England* (1992) and contributed to *The British Industrial Revolution* (1993). In 1995 he was a Fulbright lecturer at the London School of Economics.

LINDA E. MITCHELL is associate professor of history at Alfred University. She received her Ph.D. from Indiana University. She is the editor of *Women in Medieval European Culture* (forthcoming) and has contributed to *Historical Reflections*. She is currently completing a book on widows in medieval England.

THOMAS PRASCH is assistant professor of history at Washburn University. He received his Ph.D. from Indiana University. He is a contributing editor to the *American Historical Review* and has published on such subjects as the role of women in imperialism, Victorian responses to Islam, and Victorian photography.

TAYLOR STULTS is professor of history at Muskingum College. He received his Ph.D. from the University of Missouri. With the late Melvin C. Wren, he is the author of *The Course of Russian History* (1994). He has contributed articles to *Statesmen Who Changed the World* (1993) and *The Twentieth Century, Great Events* (1996).

FRANZ A. J. SZABO is professor of history at Carleton University. He received his Ph.D. from the University of Alberta. He is the author of *Kaunitz and Enlightened Absolutism, 1753–1780* (1994), which won prizes from both the American Association for the Advancement of Slavic Studies and the Austrian Cultural Institute. He is also executive director of the Austrian Canadian Council Foundation.

FRANK W. THACKERAY is professor of history at Indiana University Southeast. He received his Ph.D. from Temple University. He is the author of *Antecedents of Revolution: Tsar Alexander I and the Polish Congress Kingdom* (1980). He has contributed articles to *The Polish Review* and *East Central Europe,* and written chapters for *Eastern Europe and the West* (1992) and *Imperial Power and Development* (1990). With John E. Findling, he is editor of *Statesmen Who Changed the World* (1993), and the other volumes in the Events That Changed the World and Events That Changed America series. Professor Thackeray is a former Fulbright scholar to Poland.

ANDREW P. TROUT is professor of history emeritus at Indiana University Southeast. He received his Ph.D. from the University of Notre Dame. He is the author of *City on the Seine: Paris in the Time of Richelieu and Louis XIV* (1996) and *Jean-Baptiste Colbert* (1978). Professor Trout has written numerous articles on seventeenth-century France and the economic policies of Alexander Hamilton.

**The Greenwood Press "Events That Changed the World" Series**

Events That Changed the World in the Twentieth Century
*Frank W. Thackeray and John E. Findling, editors*

Events That Changed the World in the Nineteenth Century
*Frank W. Thackeray and John E. Findling, editors*

HILLSBOROUGH COMMUNITY COLLEGE

3 7777 40007 4233

LINCC

For Reference

Not to be taken from this room

Dale Mabry